FROM GRIDIRON TO GRASSLAND:
THE RISE AND FALL OF
BRITAIN'S RAILWAY
MARSHALLING YARDS

by MICHAEL RHODES

FROM GRIDIRON TO GRASSLAND: THE RISE AND FALL OF BRITAIN'S RAILWAY MARSHALLING YARDS

by Michael Rhodes

Published by Platform 5 Publishing Ltd, 52 Broadfield Road, Sheffield, S8 0XJ. England.

Printed in England by The Lavenham Press, Lavenham, Suffolk.
ISBN: 978 1 909431 25 6

Front cover:- Taken at sunset at the end of November 1984 from the A19 flyover, the hump in the Tees "down" yard is still in operation, although it will close within months. (**M. Rhodes**)

Front inset (left):- Class 20 Nos. 20176 & 20070 wind out of the "up" sorting sidings at Toton with the afternoon mixed freight to March Whitemoor on 3 June 1981. (**M. Rhodes**)

Front inset (right):- Class 76 No. 76051 leaves the west end of Tinsley sorting sidings on 23 September 1980 with the 8T30 trip working to Deepcar. (**M. Rhodes**)

Back cover:- In August 1993, Class 60 No 60079 arrives in the "up" reception yard passing the 115 levered Stapleford and Sandiacre Signal Box. Just peeping through the bridge in the background is Class 60 No. 60082 with a Peak Forest to Washwood Heath stone train. Half a dozen Class 20s, surplus to requirement are stored in the old engineers' sidings above the signal box. (**M. Rhodes**)

CONTENTS

From Gridiron to Grassland:
The Rise and Fall of Britain's Railway Marshalling Yards

Introduction

Three decades ago as a young surgeon, I started writing articles about freight traffic for Murray Brown at Rail Enthusiast. Teaching anatomy on a basic salary and with a young family, money was tight and the extra income from the articles was most welcome. During 1985 I produced pieces about Bescot and Tinsley yards which seemed to be well received and I realised that very little had been written about this facet of the railway industry. Curiosity turned to serious research and in 1988 "The Illustrated History of British Marshalling Yards" was published by OPC/Haynes. To the surprise of both publisher and author the book sold so well it was reprinted. It remains one of the few books to document the mechanised marshalling yards of Great Britain.

Fast forward nearly 30 years and I put together a summary of Britain's marshalling yards for The Railway Magazine and realised just how much had changed since my original research. Documents in Kew and other archives, which had previously been embargoed, had become available. In addition many other authors had produced excellent articles about some of the yards which had been neglected in my original book and to them I am very grateful. I have included all of their work in the reference sections at the end of each chapter, as well as document names and references for official material. Of course the biggest change since the original reference book has been the complete abolition of wagonload freight traffic and the closure of nearly all Britain's major marshalling yards. Most really have returned to some form of grassland.

Putting together 500 images, over 50 plans and 80,000 words has been quite a daunting task but I have had tremendous help from many fellow authors and enthusiasts, not to mention the production team at Platform 5 Publishing who took a chance on my idea to revisit the subject of marshalling yards for a second time. Of course scanning and digital cameras have transformed the way books are produced and no longer are hundreds of hours in the darkroom needed to produce prints for a book. Transparencies can be scanned at home and no longer suffer the ignominy of being stuck to a drum scanner and destroyed forever. Because of this I have included as much colour material as possible in the book.

Many photographers have contributed generously to enhance my own pictures and collection. Each is acknowledged alongside the pictures they have contributed to the book. Several people have also helped with information and documents, chief amongst these being Alex Fisher from Great Rocks Junction. His relentless searches at Kew and his willingness to trade a visit to Kew for images of Wath which I had taken 35 years ago, helped lay the foundation for much of the new material presented in the book. Similar contributions over and above the call of duty were made by James Skoyles (Hull), Malcolm James (Rogerstone) and Ivan Stewart (Mottram and Ripple Lane). My overseas visits have been greatly aided by the generosity of the former CEO of Norfolk Southern Railroad, Wick Moorman, who both fixed up visits to his properties and also put me in touch with other railroads in North America.

Of course at the core of all the chapters of this book has been the kindness and hospitality of railway men and women, both at home and abroad. Hundreds have welcomed me on visits, both official and impromptu. The puzzled look of the yard master at Köln Gremberg Yard when I turned up in my suit, fresh from a medical conference, will live long in the memory. I was invited to a barbeque on one visit to Strang Yard in Texas and was even offered membership of the local Freemason Lodge in Cincinnati!

The opportunity to travel overseas in the last three decades has also been helpful in understanding the developments in marshalling yard technology and construction in Europe, North America and to some extent China. Whilst the last automated hump yard in the UK at Scunthorpe closed in 1990, new yards are still opening in Europe and the USA. Moorman Yard in Bellevue, Ohio re-opened at the end of 2014 following an extensive rebuild which gave it an amazing 80 sorting sidings. In Germany a state-of-the-art hump yard is nearing completion in Halle and in China new yards open nearly every year. These "Grand Central Termini" of the freight railway continue to flourish and evolve around the globe. Sadly the UK story is one of invention, proliferation and innovation, followed by rationalisation, closure and return to nature. This story is documented in the next 284 pages, from the Edge Hill Gridiron, to the closure and disappearance of almost all of the UK's marshalling yards.

Finally, my thanks go to my long suffering wife Irene who knows when I say we have to make a slight detour whilst driving in the UK or abroad, that there is likely to be a railway involved somewhere!

Michael Rhodes
Attleborough, Norfolk, 2016

CHAPTER 1

MARSHALLING YARDS

An Introduction

Introduction

A marshalling yard is simply a collection of railway tracks used to sort freight wagons. Tracks for freight traffic have existed since the dawn of the railways, but purpose-built facilities, designed for the traffic levels of the day didn't appear until after 1870. It was in 1873 at the Edge Hill Gridiron that gravity was first used to assist in sorting wagons and over the next three decades the basic layout of the modern hump marshalling yard evolved. This book looks back over the development of the marshalling yard, drawing heavily on original source material dating back to the 1890s. It then traces the automation and expansion of marshalling yards in Britain up to and through the 1955 Modernisation Plan. Thereafter the decline of yards in Britain, culminating in

the closure of the last automated hump yard in 1990, is chronicled. This is not the end of the story however; yard construction and improvement continues in Europe, the USA and China (where new hump yards spring up every year!) and we'll take a closer look at that in the final chapter of the book.

The 19th Century: Early Developments

The arrival in 1825 of the railways as we know them, was for the carriage of freight traffic. Yet it was over 50 years before the first custom-made freight yard appeared. Reference to early texts finds that freight yards "grew like Topsy", and were regularly in need of expansion as freight traffic grew. This led to many yards evolving

*Above:- There were dozens of non-mechanised hump yards all over the UK (these are described in Chapter 4). Inspired by the example of American yards at the turn of the century, gravity was used at most of the more important freight yards in the UK. A typical smaller manual hump yard is seen here at Bathgate. North British Railway Reid 0-6-2 tank No. 69156, which spent its entire working life allocated to Bathgate shed until withdrawal in February 1962, is seen here propelling loaded 16-ton mineral wagons over the hump. (**Ben Brooksbank, Wiki Commons**)*

Above:- Competing to be one of the first yards in the world to utilise gravity for shunting, were the sidings built in Shildon to handle coal from the Durham pits, bound for Teeside. The yards here had reception sidings which happened to be higher than the sorting sidings and so wagons were pushed down the hill from east to west into 20 sorting sidings. There was, however, no purpose built hump. In the early 1980s the remains of the yard were used to hold wagons destined for repair in Shildon Wagon Works. Class 08 No. 08200 is seen shunting the old sorting sidings in October 1983. The reception sidings were beyond the steel girder bridge in the background; these closed very early in the 1930s when the freight railway to Teeside was de-electrified and tonnages of Durham coal dropped significantly. (**M. Rhodes**)

Above:- The yard at Dresden Friedrichstadt was completed in May 1894 and operated on a continuously falling grade with a particularly steep fall from the reception sidings to the classification tracks. Initially brakemen were employed to wind the brakes down on wagons as they were shunted onto the slope into the sorting sidings, but in 1928 the yard was modernised and converted to rope-operated hump (similar to that which survived into the 1990s at Chemnitz Hilbersdorf). As the Second World War drew to a close, the yard was almost completely destroyed by Allied bombing and it took several years to rebuild it in the then German Democratic Republic. The retarder equipment was supplied by the USSR and primary rail brakes were supplemented by entry retarders to each track, fashioned as screws lying alongside the running rail. It was one of the busiest yards on the Reichsbahn handling 5000 wagons every day through its 34 sorting sidings. By the time of this view, taken from the hump control tower in 1992, throughput had fallen to 1600 wagons a day as a result of a drastic fall in wagonload traffic after the reunification of Germany in 1989. The hump ceased operation in 2009 and by 2015 the sorting sidings were used to store surplus wagons, with freight trains marshalled in the 20 reception sidings to the east of the old hump yard. (**M. Rhodes**)

Left:- *Whilst this book deals mainly with mechanised hump yards, modernisation of British Railways included investment in both non-mechanised hump yards and flat yards (see Chapter 4). One of the biggest such projects was the provision of sidings at Hither Green for continental traffic. Here, in 1968, Class 71 No. E5002 departs with a train of ferry vans, destined for the Dover train ferry. There was optimism that traffic to and from Europe would increase greatly in the 1960s, something that never materialised. Even with the construction of the Channel Tunnel, rail freight traffic to and from Europe is nothing more than a trickle when compared to road haulage. (J.H. Cooper-Smith)*

Right:- *The first hump yard built in Germany was at Mulheim Speldorf and it opened in 1876. As good fortune would have it I ended up in the signal box at Speldorf in 1997 whilst visiting a friend in the area. At the time I had no idea of the significance of the overgrown sidings here, which had been one of the first hump yards in the world, if not the first. The land is now covered in housing. (M. Rhodes)*

in piecemeal fashion and becoming an operational nightmare. One of the first railway companies to grasp the nettle of burgeoning freight traffic was the Midland Railway, who after 30 years of increasing coal traffic built the first yard at Toton in 1871[1]. This yard used horses to shunt its many sidings and it was not until 1900 that a hump was introduced and steam engines used to push the wagons over it. The operation of the new hump yard was all manual, with shunters changing the points and running alongside the wagons to slow them down by pushing on the brake with their shunters' pole.

In 1873 the London & North Western Railway started work on the Edge Hill Gridiron (described in detail in Chapter 4), famous as the first gravity-assisted yard in the world. This was not a hump yard as we know them, but took advantage of the lie of the land at Edge Hill to allow gravity-assisted shunting on a continuously falling grade[2]. Two other 19th Century developments were

crucial in shaping what we think of as a marshalling yard. In 1863 at St. Etienne, the French first designed a yard with sequential arrival, sorting and departure tracks, all on a continuously falling grade. Then in 1876 the first purpose-built hump yard was opened in Germany at Mulheim Speldorf. It is perhaps this design which is most often associated with the phrase "marshalling yard". It should be noted that a sort of one-sided hump was used as far back as 1869 at Shildon Yard by the North Eastern Railway, but the hump at Speldorf was of the more conventional design where wagons were pushed up a grade, then fell under gravity on the other side. Hump technology developed in the last decade of the 19th Century, particularly in Germany. In the 1890s a new hump yard was built in Dresden at Friedrichstadt[3], along the banks of the River Danube where the hump earthworks were elevated 17.73 metres above the floodplain. The yard still functions today, although the hump closed in 2009.

Above & left:- The first yard to have two hump systems side by side was opened at Oberhausen Osterfeld Süd in 1891. The westbound hump is seen during a visit in 1985 at which time the four group retarders were supplemented by the use of Hemmschuh in the sorting sidings. Class 290 No. 290036 draws out a string of wagons for re-humping and is captured from the control tower. In 2015, the yard remains one of 20 mechanised hump yards still operational in Germany, still busy with large tonnages of wagonload traffic from local industries, but less important than it used to be as it is not part of the core national network made up of nine yards. The main yards for the Ruhr area are Köln Gremberg and Hagen Vorhalle. (Both M. Rhodes)

In 1891, another first was the construction of the yards at Oberhausen Osterfeld Süd. Here two parallel hump systems were built for east and westbound traffic. These yards were also some of the first to use mechanical retarders or rail brakes. These rail brakes, developed by Dr Frölich in the 1920s, were the first mechanical rail brakes used in a marshalling yard and went on to become popular all over Europe. The examples installed in March Whitemoor, back in 1929, were still working when the "up" hump yard closed in 1980! Of course prior to the invention of rail brakes, free rolling wagons had to be slowed down manually. In the UK and USA this was done by a shunter, who would run along beside the wagon and use his shunters' pole to apply the brakes. A different approach was used in Germany where "Hemmschuh" were developed. These metal wedges were placed under the leading wheel of a wagon as it rolled down the hump and friction with the rail slowed the wagon. Placed by

a shunter, the "Schuh" would fall off the track into a collection scoop at a predetermined distance.

The other country where freight yards developed in the late 19th Century was the USA. The standard yard design in the late 1880s was called a "poling" yard. This meant a yard where a locomotive would draw back on a track adjacent to a track with wagons in. The front of the locomotive had a pole attached, which engaged with a socket at the rear of the wagon to be pushed. The locomotive set off, ramming the wagons forward. Accidents were frequent and wear and tear on locomotives was high. As yards became larger and busier, a falling gradient was often used to reduce the force needed to push the wagons forward. Droege notes in his seminal 1906 work[4] that "The author had charge of a large coal yard where 1,428 loads passed through in 10 hours 20 minutes, an average of 138 cars an hour".

OVERSEAS INFLUENCES ON BRITISH YARD DESIGN AND EQUIPMENT

USA

There was considerable interaction between railway engineers in Europe and the USA. Visits were not uncommon, particularly between the UK and USA. The first "summit" or hump yard in the USA was built at Honey Pot, on the Sunbury Division of the Pennsylvania Railroad in 1890. In 1899 this yard handled 176 cars in one hour and three minutes, almost three cars per minute. The performance so impressed railway builders and engineers that the rush for hump yards started in the USA. In the first 5 years of the 20th Century, over a dozen hump yards were built. These included the massive Clearing yards in Chicago, which remain busy today, the Dewitt yards in Syracuse (now largely derelict) and a hidden gem in the swamps of New Jersey; Oak Island Yard. This last yard was built in the first couple of years of the 20th Century by the Lehigh Valley Railroad and was the site of a visit by "officers of The North Eastern Railway of England" in 1903. A demonstration was organised during which 153 cars were classified in 42 minutes! The gentlemen were no doubt impressed because it was not long thereafter that the first purpose-built hump yard was opened in the UK at Wath-upon-Dearne in 1907 (see Chapter 4).

Germany

It was exchanges between the UK and Germany, between the World Wars, that led to the construction of the UK's first mechanised hump yard at March Whitemoor. A visit by engineers from the LNER in 1925, to the newly opened Hamm Yards[5], formed the basis for close co-operation; the German Frölich retarder, built by Thyssen, was used in Britain's first mechanised hump yard opened in 1928.

Faced with increasing goods traffic in the 1920s, the Deutsche Reichsbahn embarked on a widespread modernisation plan for its marshalling yards. Two yards were modernised in the Essen Division and were the subject of intensive study to assess the impact of modernisation. The west-east yard at Hamm was opened in October 1925 and the smaller yard at Duisburg Hochfeld Süd in March 1928. In the 1930 report which describes the savings and improved efficiency of these two yards, the authors credit Hamm and Duisburg as the inspiration behind new yards in Bremen, Basel Muttenz, Whitemoor England and Milano. Scribbled on the cover

Above:- Taken from the window of a British Airways Boeing 777 coming in to land at Newark airport, the hump and 30 classification tracks of Oak Island Yard can be clearly seen. The yard is much as it was at the turn of the 20th Century when built by the Lehigh Valley Railroad, albeit with automated retarders and longer arrival tracks than when first opened. It is the only hump yard in the vicinity and is relatively small by American standards. This is because most wagonload freight is sorted before it arrives on the East Coast at large yards like Selkirk in Albany, New York, or Willard and Bellevue yards in Ohio. (**M. Rhodes**)

Left:- Taken for an official report by the Essen division of the Deutsche Reichsbahn, this picture shows the hump at Duisburg Hochfeld Süd. The three large retarders to hold trains at the exit of the arrival tracks are clearly seen, as are the two smaller Thyssen retarders at the entrance to the sorting sidings. (**M. Rhodes collection**)

of the archived report are the notes of the LNER engineers who visited Germany in the 1920s and 1930s. They make fascinating reading:

1. What is the cost of the new hump yards – 350,000 Reichsmarks

2. Points should be as close to the hump as possible

3. Engine fitted with speedometer – 1.5 metres per second

4. Instructions given to engineman by radio

5. Every wagon or wagons must be braked

6. One metre height of hump per 5 metres of railbrake.

7. 12,000 Reichsmarks per 5 metres of brake.

The two yards at Hamm and Duisburg were quite different in that Hamm had what is now regarded as a more conventional layout, with reception sidings leading to a hump and then a balloon of 32 sorting sidings. In Duisburg the reception sidings were several metres higher than the sorting sidings and there was no hump, but rather a falling grade from the reception sidings down a 3.25 metre drop (as compared to 3.08 metres drop for the Hamm hump). This meant that wagons had to be held in the reception sidings by positioning a lengthy 15 metre retarder at the exit of each of the three reception sidings, which was opened to release the wagons once shunting began. Two further retarders were then placed at the entrance to the 22 sorting sidings, as compared to four retarders in the Hamm Yard. Wagon speeds were noted to be up to 8 metres per second using this size of hump which speeded up sorting, but also made it impossible to obtain wagon control using the traditional hand held "skids" or Hemmschuh. Hence the development of the Thyssen manufactured, Frölich patented, mechanical retarder.

The operating instructions for the retarder operator hark back to a different age when we are told - "Just as a man weighs a stone when about to throw it, so should the brake operator be able to test the running quality of a truck by means of a sensitively controlled retarder". Much is made of the skills needed to be a successful brakeman, whose job responsibility was clear - "He is responsible for the safe shunting of the wagon and its contents into the sorting siding". If things went wrong then the brakeman had an electric horn. A blast on this alerted the shunters in the yard that additional braking using a hand-held skid was required. The instruction manual remarks wryly that - "Good

brakesmen make less use of the electric horn than do less efficient operators".

With increased speed of shunting and a more rapid throughput of wagons, it became impossible to change the points quickly enough by hand. It was therefore decided to automate the first eight sets of points in Hamm, as these were responsible for 80% of changes during the humping of a 50 wagon train. Fast point-operating gears which threw the point over in 0.6 seconds were duly installed. Activity in the yard was controlled from the Brake Control Tower which housed a switch operator and a brake operator, working closely together. As already mentioned, an electric horn was provided to alert shunters as to runaway wagons and there was also a loudspeaker to communicate with the yard master at the hump crest. A radio transmitter, capable of sending Morse Code-type signals, was used to communicate with the shunting locomotive.

What then was the impact of all this mechanisation? Two measures were used to assess this; the first was repeated trials comparing the speed with which a standard 50 wagon train could be sorted. The second was the throughput and cost per wagon shunted in the new yards, as compared to neighbouring non-mechanised hump yards.

Above:- Duisburg Wedau southbound hump yard was used as a comparison to the new yards at Hamm and Duisburg Hochfeld Süd. It was a non-automated hump with Hemmschuh used to slow wagons. The same method was still in use in 1985 when I visited and continued to work well, even with much heavier modern wagons. This aspect of hump marshalling never really caught on in the UK and it is only ever mentioned as being used in Nuneaton where the Hemmschuh were called "slippers". (**M. Rhodes**)

Right:- The hump at Berlin Wustermark Yard hasn't seen any shunting for a couple of decades, but the "Schuh catcher" is still in place half-way down the hump. These scoops were placed strategically throughout major yards to knock the Schuh off the rails and collect half a dozen or so up before the shunter had to pick them all up and take them back to the hump summit. (**M. Rhodes**)

Above:- Despite all the modernisation of German yards in the last couple of decades, the humble Hemmschuh is still widely used in 2016, especially in smaller yards like Ingolstadt. The 20-track mechanised hump yard here has two primary retarders, but control of wagons in the sorting sidings still relies on Hemmschuh, which can be seen lined up alongside each sorting siding. (M. Rhodes)

Time taken to shunt 50 wagons (minutes)

	Hamm mechanised yard - 1 hump loco	Hamm mechanised yard - 2 hump locos	Hamm non-mechanised yard	Duisberg Wedau southbound non-mechanised yard
Work at hump	12.2 minutes	7.8 minutes	19.5 minutes	21.7 minutes
Work in the "valley" (preparing train for departure)	15.3 minutes	10.8 minutes	24.7 minutes	32.2 minutes

The increase in efficiency of a mechanised yard was therefore somewhere between 90 and 100% when compared to a good non-mechanised yard. In typical Germanic fashion, the authors of the studies on Hamm and Duisburg standardised the time needed to shunt a train as follows: 4 minutes for the locomotive to travel round behind the train, 2 minutes to push the train to the hump, 9 wagons per minute for shunting and finally 3 minutes for closing up the train in the sorting sidings, for correcting false shunts, moving damaged wagons and taking water. Further it was stated "The inspection offices continually supervise the keeping of these standard times". Working to these targets the capacity of the mechanised hump yard at Hamm was 3900 wagons per 24 hours with a single hump locomotive, increasing to 5800 wagons if two hump locomotives were deployed. In Duisburg Hochfeld Süd it had taken 65 minutes of locomotive time to shunt a standard 50 wagon train

before mechanisation. This was reduced to just 8 minutes after modernisation. The yard had formerly been able to classify 1800 wagons in 24 hours when working under "extreme pressure", but after modernisation, capacity increased to 2720 wagons per 24 hours. As for costs, these fell at Duisburg from 23.4 Reichsmarks for a standard 50 wagon train to 5.85 Reichsmarks after mechanisation. The drop in marshalling costs at Hamm was less dramatic, but a 50 wagon train in the mechanised yard was costed at 9.8 Reichsmarks, as compared to 14.2 Reichsmarks in the parallel non-mechanised yard and 20 Reichsmarks at Duisburg Wedau.

Not surprisingly given these results it was German yard design which most influenced British yard building between 1928 and 1955. By the time of the 1955 Modernisation Plan, there were five mechanised hump yards in the UK, two at Whitemoor, two at

Eastern of France Railway Company

L.N.E.R. Engineers' Visit

of the

Blainville Shunting Yard

(Eastern of France Railways)

on June 16 th. 1930.

Left:- The Official visit by LNER engineers was recorded in an elaborately put together illustrated report. (**M. Rhodes collection**)

Above & Left:- These two views show the automatic shoe retarders installed in Blainville and also in the major yards at Bordeaux and Vaires, near Paris. The upper image is looking towards the sorting sidings, with the hump behind the photographer. The shoe is clearly seen attached to metres of springs in the tube adjacent to the running rail. The shoe is engaged on the running rail, ready to retard an approaching wagon. In the second image, the retarder is shown disengaged from the track, as the wagon has passed over it. The levers to place and remove the retarding shoe are clearly seen in the foreground. (**Both M. Rhodes collection**)

Toton and one in Hull (see Chapter 5). All these yards employed German rail brakes of the Frölich design and were modelled closely on the yards at Hamm.

France

Less well recognised, but of considerable importance, was the influence of French Railways. We know that engineers from the LNER visited Blainville in 1930[6]. After visiting and writing a comprehensive report, engineers recommended that the spring-loaded retarders employed in Blainville should be installed in a small group of sidings in the UK to test their braking capabilities on British wagons. It seems the trial never took place, but the influence of French mechanisation

and working practices were significant. Similar designs of retarder were considered much later in the 1950s by the BR Railway Technical Centre in Derby and are described in Chapter 3.

Blainville Yard was a major marshalling point on the Strasbourg to Paris main line. With 16 receiving tracks, 47 classification tracks, 11 of which were used as departure tracks and a capacity to handle over 3200 wagons in 24 hours, the yard was a major installation. Several technological developments had been introduced by the time of the 1930 visit by the LNER. Most striking was the new "R" retarder at the entrance to the classification tracks. The design, which never caught

Right:- By the time of my visit in 1995, the automatic shoe brakes had long gone in Blainville. They had been replaced by more conventional rail brakes, as can be seen in the distance in this view from the hump crest. By 2014 it seems that just three of the five rail brakes remained, controlling access to the 24 sorting sidings on the right of this view.

*Above:- In the second view of Blainville in 1995, French "Crocodile" No. BB12083 stands in the departure sidings with an afternoon trip freight to Woippy, the largest and busiest French marshalling yard. Woippy is one of just three French hump yards predicted to survive beyond 2016, the other two being at Villeneuve St. Georges in Paris and Sybelin in Lyons. (**Both M. Rhodes**)*

on outside France, involved the automatic placement of a "shoe" in front of the wagon. The shoe was attached to a steel plate, which in turn was connected to a tube containing 12 to 18 steel springs, each 18 inches in length and made from 3/8ths steel rod, wound into a 3 inch diameter spring. The wagon would strike the shoe and be slowed by the compression of the springs. Once

the springs reached maximum compression a switch was activated by the shoe, breaking an electrical circuit and causing the shoe to be removed from the running rail, thereby letting the wagon roll slowly forward. Seventy six of these devices were installed at Blainville at a cost of £160 each. The impact on working practices at the yard was considerable, with the number of wagon

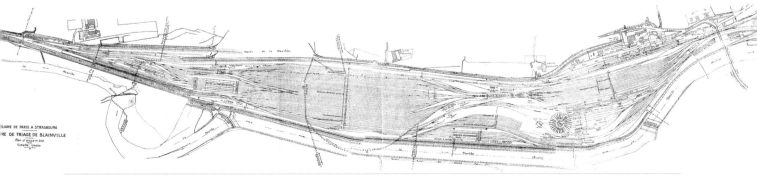

*Above:- The official plan of Blainville attached to the report of the 1930 visit by LNER engineers. (**M. Rhodes collection**)*

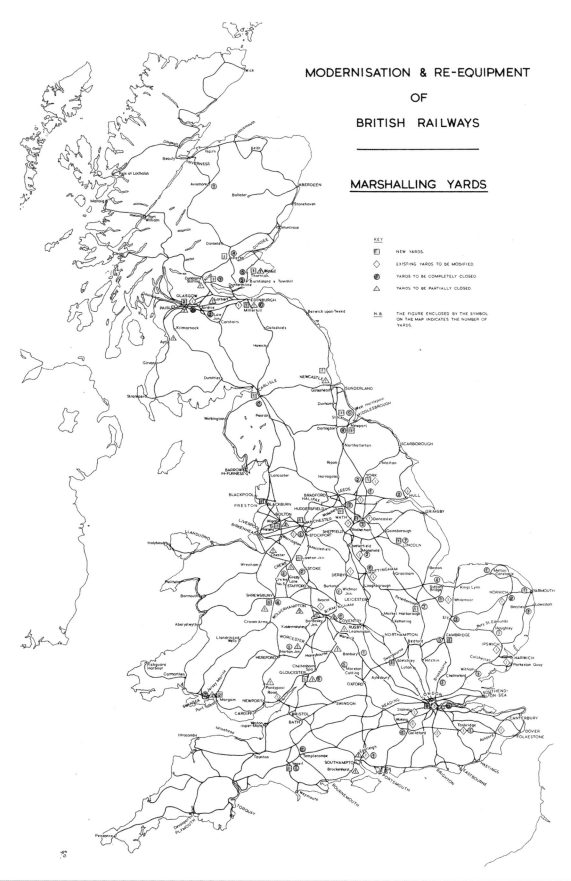

Above:- When planning the new yards to be built in Britain, this shows the first thoughts of the modernisation committee. Note the new yards to be built at Shrewsbury, Gloucester and Yeovil, as well as the modified yards planned for Tonbridge, Ashford and Redhill. Much changed by the 1963 Beeching Report and even more by the 1967 National Yard Survey. (**M. Rhodes collection**)

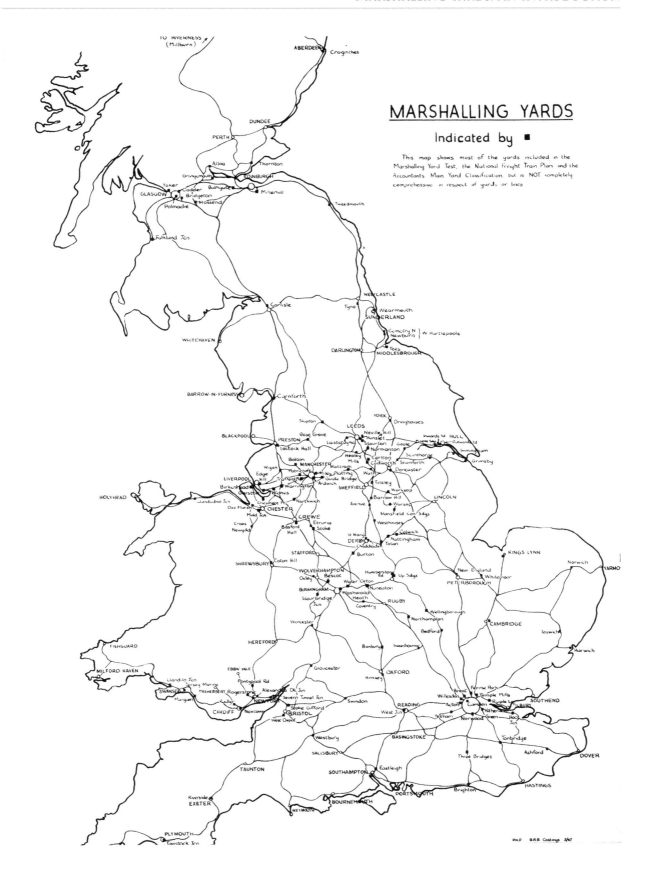

MARSHALLING YARDS

Indicated by ■

This map shows most of the yards included in the Marshalling Yard Test, the National Freight Train Plan and the Accountants Main Yard Classification but is NOT completely comprehensive in respect of yards or lines

Above:- By the time the 1966/67 yard survey was executed, there were far fewer yards in Britain. This map shows the yards that the BRB elected to survey. (**M. Rhodes collection**)

chasers reduced from 15 per shift to just 4. There was also a reduction in the number of serious and indeed fatal injuries which had numbered 3 or 4 every year.

During the visit in June 1930, 2900 wagons were shunted in 16 hours by one hump engine and it was noted that a train of 61 wagons was shunted in six and a half minutes. Although the number of wagon chasers was significantly less, the number of staff at Blainville was much higher than in UK yards of this era. The yard master was based at the hump crest and in addition to the four chasers per shift, there were a further 15 "hand shoes men", eight working at the entrance to the sorting sidings and seven finally braking wagons and coupling up completed trains. Add to this a shunter at the hump to signal cuts to the switchmen, one uncoupler and chalker in the reception yard, two switchmen in a cabin at the foot of the hump, and one brakesman operating the semi-automatic "shoe" brakes in the main leads to each balloon of the sorting sidings and a total of 25 men per shift was hardly a big saving when compared to non-automated yards in the UK. The working conditions were however noted carefully by the visiting team from the LNER. The French worked an eight hour shift without a meal break. The shunting locomotive was single-manned and only five minutes was allowed to run round each train. Not only that but it was noted that Sundays did not attract enhanced payment, although the French had 64 days annual leave, 12 of which had to be granted consecutively!

Another innovation which has been developed and modified, especially in Germany, was the use of road mules to propel wagons which stop short of the other wagons in the sidings. The yard at Blainville had two road tractors which ran on "rubber" wheels along wooden boards, or suitably flattened pathways, between the sorting sidings. With a 24 horse power motor and measuring just 96 cm across, these small road tractors greatly reduced the work created by short shunts, as well as keeping wagon damage to a minimum.

Modernisation 1955 to 1990

A detailed account of the modernisation of Britain's yards is to be found in Chapter 2 whilst descriptions of the yards built as a result of the modernisation programme are in Chapters 6 and 7. The drive to centralise the marshalling of wagons, along with the desire to implement "total wagon control" led to Britain's most sophisticated yards built at Tinsley, Bescot and finally Scunthorpe West. These used the Dowty retarder system which has gone on to find favour in Europe, the USA and even China.

It is often suggested that the 1955 Modernisation Plan was ill-conceived when it came to freight carriage by the railways, but this seems unduly harsh. It is also

of course the result of using that most convenient of historical tools, the "retrospectoscope". The pace of change during the first decade of the modernisation programme was as rapid as it was unexpected. The road network improved beyond recognition and the lives of working men and women improved dramatically. A railway network which had often been the only means of access to towns and villages in the early 1900s, now had to compete with metalled roads to every corner of the country, cheap motor cars increasingly owned by every family and larger and more efficient lorries which could deliver goods to the doorstep, night and day.

As these changes took place, the plans for new yards in the UK were scaled back and the last three major yards were opened in 1965, 1966 and finally in 1970. By the time that Scunthorpe West Yard opened in 1970, Ripple Lane, one of the early modernisation yards had already closed, such was the pace of change.

As freight was increasingly handled in block loads and the railway struggled to compete for wagonload traffic, the hump yards, built just a couple of decades earlier, began to close. One by one, humps were taken out of action and yards shunted from the departure end. By 1985, all but the hump at Scunthorpe had been abandoned with the remnants of wagonload traffic handled by the air-braked Speedlink network. This too ceased to operate in 1991 and it was perhaps no coincidence that the last operational hump yard in Scunthorpe closed shortly before this in 1990. Since then the vast tracts of land occupied by these once busy freight centres have more often than not returned to woodland. This is not however the end of the story for the marshalling yard.

A Worldwide Perspective

In Chapter 8 of this book, we look at the role that the mechanised hump yard plays around the globe. Far from extinction, this form of freight classification is alive and well and continues to provide a crucial means of sorting wagonloads of freight at major centres in the USA and Europe, as well as in China, the world's fastest growing economy. It is often asked why this remains the case when wagonload freight has all but vanished from our rail network for the last 25 years. Of course distances between major centres are small in the UK with cities of 500,000 often no more than 50-100 miles apart. This compares to much larger distances on mainland Europe and larger still in the USA and China. This is however not the only factor that mitigates against wagonload rail traffic and the marshalling yards so crucial to handling it. Government policy, in particular in respect of road regulation and rail subsidy, varies across Europe, with the UK most unhelpful to rail freight. Subsidy and regulation are of course much less relevant in the USA and China; in these countries the sheer volume of long distance wagonload freight means

*Right:- The great hope for retention of wagonload traffic were the new yards of the 1955 Modernisation Plan. Each new yard was a massive infrastructure project and made headline news. The official booklets produced each time a yard opened are testimony to the importance British Rail attached to these developments. (**M. Rhodes**)*

that large mechanised hump yards are the only practical solution for the booming rail freight traffic in those countries. With the new 80 classification track Moorman Yard opening at the end of 2014 in Bellevue Ohio, the marshalling yard is alive and well in 2016.

REFERENCES

1   British Railways London Midland Region, Modernisation
      Up Marshalling Yard at Toton, The Railway Gazette,
      Nov-Dec, 1951.

2   Droege JA, Yards & Terminals and Their Operation,
      The Railroad Gazette, New York, 1906; 136.

3   Rangierbahnhof. Wiki Series, Memphis USA. 2011.

4   Droege JA, Yards & Terminals and Their Operation,
      The Railroad Gazette, New York, 1906; 99.

5   German State Railways, Essen Division. The Mechanised Gravity
      Marshalling Yards at Hamm and Duisburg Hochfeld Süd. 1930. Kew Archive Z LIB 29.

6   LNER Engineers Visit of the Blainville Shunting Yard on June 16th 1930. BRB Archives, LNE 4/66.

Right:- Many docks in the UK were provided with extensive yards, several with over a hundred sidings. These acted less as marshalling yards and more as storage for the vast tonnages of coal that used to be exported from the UK. The ports at Swansea, Barry, Cardiff, Newport and indeed Immingham all had yards with over 100 tracks back in the 1960s. The yards at Immingham have been subsumed by several coal import terminals, whilst those in Barry, Swansea and Newport have all but disappeared. The remains of the once vast sidings in Cardiff Docks serve the local steel plant which recycles scrap

*metal into steel rods and steel bars. Back in 1988 Class 08 No. 08836 pulls a string of wagons with steel bars and steel rods from Scunthorpe out of the yard and will deliver them to Tremorfa Works, to the left of this view. Adjacent is Class 08 No. 08848 with empty Redland brick wagons which have delivered their cargo to the private siding seen in the background on the right of this view. In 1988, Cardiff Tidal still had nearly 40 tracks and was very busy as it had just taken over much of the work formerly undertaken by Severn Tunnel Junction marshalling yard. Today the yard is much smaller and less busy with just a couple of trains a day at most, as compared to the 30 or 40 that used the yard when this image was taken. (**M. Rhodes**)*

CHAPTER 2

THE 1955 BRITISH RAILWAYS MODERNISATION PLAN
1955–1968

INTRODUCTION

It is great to have 20/20 hindsight! Looking back at the 1955 Modernisation Plan[1] we can see now the way in which the different plans for freight traffic might interact. The main aim of the plan was "to improve transit times, reliability and punctuality" for freight traffic. The two key changes set out were the reduction in yard numbers and second, the provision of new motive power and continuous braking on trains. Initially it was planned that £75 million would be made available to introduce vacuum braking throughout the wagon fleet and £80 million to build or rebuild 55 new yards, with closure of 150 smaller yards. As for the wagon fleet, it numbered 1,141,500 in 1955! The plan was to reduce this to 752,000 by 1974 and concentrate on high capacity wagons, which in 1955 were regarded as 24.5-ton hoppers. Investment in wagon building was to be £177 million.

As the plan progressed it became clear that the original objectives were not going to meet the demands of the modern railway. In 1959 a re-appraisal of the plan was published[2]. For the first time there is mention of rationalisation of the rail network. The reader should bear in mind this is a good four years before the Beeching Report. There is also a recognition that things were changing in society. There were concerns about wage costs and also with other matters in the country such as coal production and the growth of road transport. Back in 1957, Britain mined an astonishing 224 million tons of coal per annum (as compared to less than 20 today). Road transport was having a big impact on the carriage of general goods and much of the 1959 report is spent describing how goods depots round the country were to be modernised and centralised - a fascinating concern when we now have no general goods carried by rail, except of course for container traffic. These problems notwithstanding, the 1959 report detailed good progress on the construction and planning of new marshalling yards which will be detailed below.

The first flush of enthusiasm for new hump marshalling yards, so clearly evident in the 1955 British Railways Modernisation Plan, was waning by the 1959 review of progress and had evaporated by the time the Beeching Report[3] was issued in 1963. There had been ambitious schemes for new hump yards in Gloucester and Shrewsbury that never came to fruition due to a fall in freight traffic, and the same was true for schemes at Tonbridge, Ashford and Eastleigh on the Southern Region. Other schemes were partially fulfilled, such as at Swanbourne, near Bletchley, although that was so very soon to become a patch of waste land.

Four major yards opened in 1963 – Carlisle Kingmoor and a trio on the North Eastern Region at Tyne, Tees and Healey Mills.

Carlisle had long been a bottleneck for cross-border freight with several routes converging, each with their own freight yard. In the 1950s, the city had 10 major freight yards and trip working between them kept several dozen engines busy throughout the day. Not surprisingly, BR's 1959 London Midland Region freight train plan proposed an all-new yard three miles north of the city at Kingmoor.

A similar situation pertained in the North East with much duplication of traffic due to multiple yards. In 1960, there were four separate departures from Tyneside to York Dringhouses Yard and these could be combined into a single freight once Tyne Yard opened in 1963.

On Teeside, there were nine million tonnes of rail freight in and out of the industrial area in 1959 and delays in the yards at Newport (near Thornaby) were extensive. Newport's yards were therefore rebuilt to create Tees Yard with its two hump configuration.

At Healey Mills, near Wakefield, the need for a yard to handle east-west freight flows was pressing, especially with the numerous Yorkshire mines and export traffic to Hull, Immingham and Goole.

The Beeching Report was a very significant undertaking and made detailed study and analysis of railway freight traffic. Beeching was remarkably far-sighted about rail freight[4] and made two crucial recommendations which, if they had been followed, might have led to more freight on the rails today. First he identified the problem of marshalling coal from 600 rail-connected collieries and advised cutting out the marshalling yard by operating directly from pithead to power station. That became the merry-go-round (MGR) network and continues to this day, albeit with imported coal. Second, he envisaged more container traffic and, whilst his initial plans were not fully implemented, the modern day rise of containers and intermodal may yet prove Beeching right.

There was no mention at all of marshalling yards in his report however, signalling the end of BR's plans for new yards. After 1963, only the yards on which work had started were completed and, after 1966, there were to be no new ones until Wembley in 1993[5].

Above:- Back in 1966, the majority of coal traffic was still handled in 16-ton, unbraked mineral wagons. This view of Class 40 No. D355 at Hall Royd Junction, shows a rake of empties returning from Lancashire power stations to the Yorkshire coalfields. Train 7N71 was one of several daily trip freights from Rose Grove Down Grid to Healey Mills. In addition empties ran daily from Bamber Bridge (2), Lostock Hall, Aintree (2), Blackpool, Wyre Dock (2), & Blackburn to Healey Mills, Bamber Bridge to Carlton sidings, Manvers Main and Laisterdyke, White Birk Power Station to Laisterdyke, not to mention numerous conditional extra services. Flows along this line alone accounted for as many as 24 trains per day in and out of Healey Mills Yard. **(Vernon Murphy - M. Rhodes collection)**

1955 - MODERNISATION OF BRITISH RAILWAYS REPORT

A survey undertaken prior to the production of the 1955 report found that the vast majority of yards in the UK were flat-shunted and "small and inconveniently sited". It was noted that passage of freight wagons into the sidings in such facilities was often slow and that the use of gravity, and where possible the addition of mechanical retarders and power operated points, would speed the passage of the wagons into the sidings and be more efficient - a conclusion which is fascinating when compared to the actual cost findings of Britain's yards when they were analysed in 1966 (see later). The cost of the new yards was set at £80 million; a significant proportion of the freight budget.

Every other innovation for freight in 1955 would ironically work to reduce the need for the very 55 new or refurbished yards which the plan was to spend £80 million on! Centralised goods depots were planned to reduce trip working within large cities at a cost of £50 million. The wagon fleet was to be modernised with the abolition of unfitted wagons. Amazingly this was not completed until 1991, when the unfitted hoppers used between Blyth North and Lynemouth were replaced with air-braked stock! The introduction of continuous vacuum braking on freight trains would allow increased speeds (from 20-25 mph to 45-50 mph), but also alongside wagon redesign came increased block working avoiding marshalling yards altogether. The introduction of vacuum brakes also had other spin-offs. When unfitted wagons ran, there had to be catch points to "catch runaways" whenever the gradient was 1 in 260 or more. Vacuum braking freight would allow the abolition of thousands of such points on the main lines of Britain. Not just that but there were over 1000 locations where the brake force of the locomotive alone was insufficient to proceed safely down a steep gradient and at these places the guard had to descend from the train, which was stopped in a loop or sometimes on the main line, and pin down the manual brakes. Once at the bottom of the incline, the train had to stop again to allow the brakes to be released. Labour intensive and extremely time consuming! Another bonus of vacuum braking, which was to cost £75 million, was the ability to reduce the number of locomotives allocated to freight traffic by 2000 because of the anticipated reduction in transit times and better wagon turn around.

The wagon fleet itself numbered over 1,100,000, in itself a factor in the clogging up of many sidings and yards. Particularly in the coal industry, mineral wagons were used not just to transport coal, but jokingly as storage bunkers, with thousands of wagons sitting in yards and sidings awaiting orders and providing free mobile storage for the NCB, all on the British Railways tab! The British Transport Commission made an undertaking in the report that by 1974, 50% of

coal would travel in 24.5-ton vacuum-fitted hoppers. In the event the introduction of the 32.5-ton HAA air-braked merry-go-round hopper, as envisaged by Beeching, superseded this recommendation and by the mid 1970s much power station coal had moved over to MGR working. It wasn't just the various collieries that had a habit of using freight wagons as mobile storage and the report states a little plaintively, "a substantial contribution (to improving wagon transit time) will have to be sought through the co-operation of traders..."

In 1955 the wagon stock was as follows:-

Open (merchandise) -	309,700
Covered (merchandise) -	148,000
Mineral	606,900
Special	2,300
Cattle	12,600
Steel-carrying	47,100
Brake Vans	14,900
Total	**1,141,500**

It was planned that by 1974 a reduction to 752,000 vehicles might be possible. Remarkable when one considers that in 2015 the number of freight wagons on the British railway network is less than 100,000.

The final decision pertaining to marshalling yards was to allocate £80 million to build 55 new yards and close 150 smaller, mainly flat-shunted yards. As well as capital expenditure it was noted that at least £10 million would be needed for research and development. Much of this formerly embargoed research work has now come to light (see section below on research). Office and personnel costs for the whole plan came to another £25 million. The total spend on the plan was £1,200 million, spread over 15 years, making an outlay of £80 million per annum. This was 5% of the GDP in 1953 and shows how seriously the modernisation of the railways was taken. It was noted that up until the 1955 Modernisation Plan, the railways had not really benefitted from any of the post-war spending used to modernise other areas of the country's infrastructure. It was envisaged that once the plan was approved by parliament it would be introduced at the "fastest possible pace" and with "no departure from its original outlines". Tide and time proved this latter assertion to be badly mistaken.

Below:- The "common carrier" obligation of the railways, which meant it offered goods services between all 1000 of its goods depots, is well illustrated in this 1962 view at Evesham. Class 03 No. D2123 is busy shunting 11-ton vanfits, laden with agricultural produce and sundries. A Standard Class 4 No. 75055 (allocated to Bletchley at the time of this shot) waits at the signal with what is almost certainly an inter-regional fitted freight, carrying as it does, general goods and containers in vacuum-fitted wagons. (A.A. Vickers - M. Rhodes collection)

1957 - MARSHALLING YARDS PANEL PROGRESS REPORT [6]

Each section of the 1955 Modernisation Plan had a sub-committee which was responsible for overseeing progress. The Marshalling Yards Panel made its first report on progress between January 1955 and 30th November 1957. Like many other documents, the report was embargoed until the late 1990s and therefore not available at the time of publication of "The Illustrated History of British Marshalling Yards"[7] in 1988. The opening remarks make interesting reading because, although the inflationary pressures of the day lead the panel to conclude that the budget for the planned yards should be £90 million, they have managed to reduce the cost to £75 million. This was obviously the result of downscaling the original plans, but no specifics are given as to exactly which yards are no longer needed. The panel note that each region is responsible for their own projects, but they (the panel) will co-ordinate the national structure of the freight network. In doing so the outer ring route around London (using the Cambridge to Oxford line as an arterial route for freight) was a key project, as was eliminating duplicate pre-grouping facilities in the larger rail centres. Re-evaluation of the initial plan led to the decision to build 27 new yards, modernise 26 existing yards, completely close 158 yards and partially close another 37. A summary of the key projects is listed in the table overleaf.

Yard	Progress
EASTERN REGION	
Ripple Lane	Work proceeding
Peterborough	An outline scheme under consideration *(later abandoned in the 1960s)*
Colwick	A modified scheme is being examined *(a 50 track hump yard was under consideration, but was never built and the yard closed completely in 1970)*
Doncaster	Preliminary investigation is still in hand
Ferme Park Up	An outline scheme is being examined in detail
Ferme Park Down	A scheme was to be shortly prepared but didn't envisage major works
Mansfield	The scheme was deferred pending review of proposed extension of electrification *(this suggests that it was possible the Woodhead scheme was to be extended along GC lines as far as Mansfield Coal Concentration Sidings)*
Lincoln	Scheme to eliminate 7 yards and concentrate marshalling on a new layout at Pyewipe Junction and the present East Yard
LONDON MIDLAND REGION	
Manchester North	A new yard was planned at Moston but had to be abandoned; new site being explored
Manchester South	The lack of suitable ground led to the suggestion of a new hump yard to the west of Cheadle
Swanbourne	Approved 25th July 1957; authority to spend £350,000 on preliminary work
Carlisle	Development of new humps yard approved by British Transport Commission 27th June 1957
St.Helens, Fleet Lane	Analysis of traffic revealed inadequacy of current site - a new location is being sought
Chatterley	Suggested location for a new hump yard in the Stoke area - development being examined
Bescot	Physical limitations of the site have slowed progress on development and a new traffic flow study is instigated
Chaddesden	Original plans for complete modernisation have been shelved in favour of limited development
Adswood & Edgeley	Detailed plans for a new yard in Stockport have been drawn up after traffic flow surveys
Preston	A comprehensive new marshalling yard scheme is being considered to replace all local yards
NORTH EASTERN REGION	
West Riding	East-west traffic to be diverted away from Leeds to travel via Normanton and be marshalled at Healey Mills which may be modernised *(in the event it was with the new hump yard opened in 1963)*
Newport (Yorkshire)	New "up" and "down" hump yards approved by the Commission and Parliamentary powers awaited for land purchase etc. Research commissioned for retarders capable of handling heavy steel wagons
West Hartlepool	Consideration of a new double-ended flat yard with knuckles on the shunting necks - at early stages
Hull	Eastrington Loops approved in the BTC 1957/58 Bill
York	York "up" marshalling yard remodelling approved by BTC 18th July 1957
	Dringhouses "up" yard had a longer shunting neck and extra sorting sidings approved on 16th May 1957 by the BTC
Tyneside	Enquiries regarding a solution in this area were still at an early stage
SCOTTISH REGION	
Cadder	A site for the new hump yard to the north of Glasgow had been selected and detailed drawings undertaken
Mossend	Chief Engineer to approve final site for a new yard, the design of which has been finalised
Elderslie	The development of this scheme is in abeyance
Perth	Earthworks completed and track laying in the new hump yard to start soon
Slateford	Slow progress with stage 1 *(of five stages)* completed by September 1958
Millerhill	Earthworks of new hump yard completed and track laying underway
SOUTHERN REGION	
Eastleigh	Parliamentary powers to be sought in 1958/59 BTC Bill to allow construction of new hump yard here
Yeovil Junction	New yard scheme here still under consideration
Hither Green	Original plans for a new yard here abandoned in favour of minor work on the "down" sidings
Feltham	Proposed new goods terminal to be built adjacent to the "down" marshalling yard
Woking	Drawings for a new yard here completed and land available

Tonbridge	Scheme for a new hump yard approved in principle and final drawings due in the near future
Redhill	Scheme for new yard approved and meetings underway to finalise plans
Ashford	Approval in principle for a new yard from the BTC on 22nd May 1957
WESTERN REGION	
Gloucester	Opposition to a new hump yard at Elm Bridge led to a new site between Quedgeley and Standish being selected
Margam	BTC authorised a new hump yard with 12 reception and 48 sorting sidings on 27th June 1957
Severn Tunnel Junction	Expansion approved by BTC 21st November 1957
Shrewsbury	Questions raised about the viability of the proposed new hump yard which is put on hold whilst traffic surveys are repeated
Swansea (Jersey Marine)	Planning for a new hump yard being undertaken

As well as individual yard plans, a pivotal part of the 1957 update was the idea of a Cambridge to Tonbridge "outer circle" line around London. The Cambridge to Oxford line offered connections to all routes north on the GE, GN, Midland, LNW, GC and GW routes. This allowed all traffic to avoid congestion in London by travelling south from Oxford, via Didcot, Reading, Guildford, Redhill and Tonbridge. So crucial was this plan that new hump yards were planned at Swanbourne, west of Bletchley, a burrowing junction at Reading and a new hump yard in Tonbridge. It is ironic to reflect that Beeching closed the Cambridge to Oxford through route less than a decade later, only for Network Rail to identify it as a key cross-country corridor in the 21st century.

Above:- The yards at Peterborough New England were extensive as this 1923 view shows. As late as 1967, when Peterborough was designated as a primary yard in the National Freight Train Plan, there was the possibility of a new hump yard being built here. As passenger train speeds increased and all un-fitted freight was re-routed away from the ECML in 1970, via the Joint Line from Doncaster to March, the yards at Peterborough fell into disuse. (**M. Rhodes collection**)

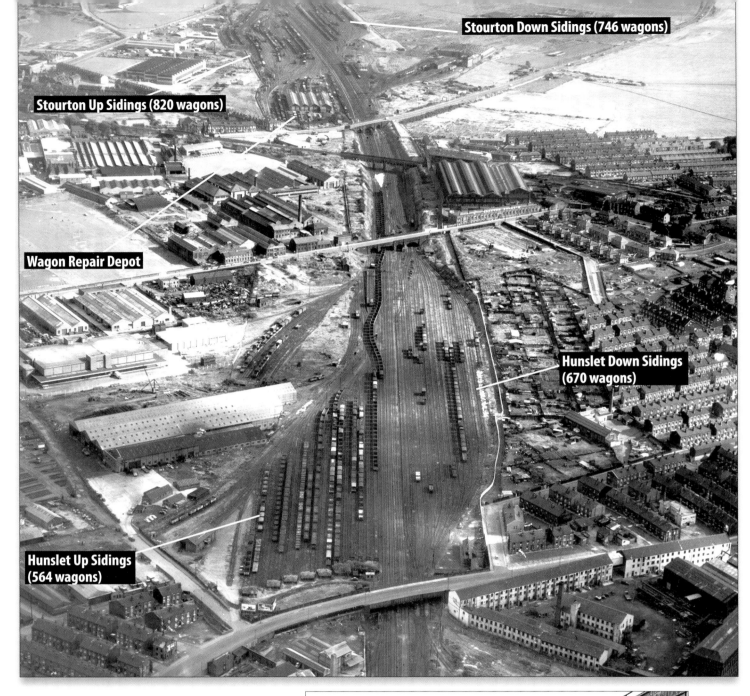

Stourton Down Sidings (746 wagons)

Stourton Up Sidings (820 wagons)

Wagon Repair Depot

Hunslet Down Sidings (670 wagons)

Hunslet Up Sidings (564 wagons)

Above:- The North Eastern Region planned four new hump yards at Tyne, Tees, Healey Mills and Stourton. The last of these was never constructed. In this BR ER picture taken in 1962 the sidings at Stourton are in the distance. Labels have been added to help identify which sidings are which. As can be seen there was plenty of land for a new hump yard at Stourton. **(BR ER - M. Rhodes collection)**

Right:- In the original 1955 Modernisation Plan a new yard was envisaged for Lincoln. It was to be situated west of the town at Pyewipe Junction. Again, falling traffic led to cancellation of these plans and Lincoln remained unchanged well into the 1980s when this view was taken. On 4 October 1986, Class 37 Nos. 37221 & 202 ease out of the yard with 6H52, the West Burton to Peterborough flyash train. Class 31 No. 31107 has just arrived with 9G09, the daily trip freight from Doncaster, whilst Class 08 No. 08102 shunts engineers' wagons. **(M. Rhodes)**

1959 - British Transport Commission Modernisation Plan - Update [8]

Changes in both British industry and the railways of Britain in the previous 5 years framed the 1959 review of the 1955 Modernisation Plan. In 1957, 167 million tons of coal were carried by rail (61% of all freight by tonnage), with UK production a staggering 224 million tons. With the switch to North Sea Gas not even on the horizon, it was predicted that by 1963 domestic consumption of coal would remain between 200 and 210 million tons per annum and thus rail haulage would be of a similar magnitude to the 1957 figure. In 1957 the UK produced 21.7 million tons of steel per annum and expansion was planned to an annual output of 28 million tons by 1963. Cheap steel from the Far East was again not even on the horizon and traditional steel producing nations in Western Europe and the USA could only foresee expansion. To support this burgeoning business, the railways carried 65 million tons of minerals and finished steel each year.

In 1957 there were a staggering 42 million tons of general merchandise carried by rail; everything from fuel oil to sugar, tobacco, raw wool, cement and chemicals. Parcels traffic was expected to expand dramatically because of the new craze for "mail order shopping" and it was envisaged that new vans would be needed to handle this growing business.

On the railway side, the drive was for higher speeds and larger capacity wagons, as well as new goods depots and yards. The overall conclusion of the report's authors was that the events of the previous five years had led to only minor modifications in the original plan. If anything the imperative was to speed up implementation. By 1958, 250,000 wagons, or a quarter of the fleet, had been vacuum-braked; amongst wagons designed to carry general merchandise the percentage modernised was 60%. A new "Export Express Service" had dispatched 40,000 wagons in two years to British ports with general merchandise for export. In addition 20 large goods depots in the main cities were rebuilt and the first two marshalling yards of the modernisation programme, at Thornton and Temple Mills, were opened. Thirty smaller marshalling yards had been closed and between 1955 and 1958 traffic had been withdrawn from 80 branch lines.

Between 1954 and 1958, 300 miles of the network had been closed leaving 18,850 route miles of railway. With Beeching not even on the horizon, it was still envisaged that between 1959 and 1963 there would be a 10% reduction in route mileage. During the same time frame, 400 passenger and goods stations were closed, leaving 7,600. The rate of closure was to increase, with a further 1,000 closing by 1963. The wagon fleet, which had stood at 1.1 million in 1954, was down to 1 million by the 1959 review and further reduction to 750,000 was planned by 1963. It was planned that by 1963 all wagons used for the carriage of merchandise would be vacuum-braked and new containers would be introduced. The new "Condor" container service from London to Glasgow was seen as the way forward for many smaller items carried on general merchandise trains and new goods depots, connected by express container services, were envisaged.

Looking at bulk haulage, a new development saw the introduction of power-braked hopper wagons to carry iron ore from the Glasgow docks to Ravenscraig Steelworks. The discharge of a 1000 ton load took less than an hour which was regarded as revolutionary when compared to low capacity ore wagons and a wagon tippler. Between 1955 and 1958 there was a massive wagon building programme for coal traffic. One hundred and thirty thousand 16-ton metal bodied mineral wagons were introduced and 17,000 20 and 21-ton vehicles. This was vaunted as a big achievement as they replaced many wooden bodied vehicles, still in use on the national network. Eight thousand higher capacity wagons were also built, these were the 24-ton hoppers which in many ways heralded the way for the tremendously successful 32.5-ton HAA merry-go-round coal hopper, which was the mainstay of coal carriage during the 1970s and 1980s.

Marshalling yards were still at the centre of the plan and the target was to reduce these to 300 by 1963. Key projects in addition to the two new yards at Thornton and Temple Mills were listed by region. On the Eastern Region the scheme at Ripple Lane was nearing completion and plans were well advanced for a new yard at Tinsley. The third big scheme was at Peterborough where new "up" and "down" yards were planned. In the event this modernisation was abandoned in the late 1960s, as freight traffic was diverted away from the Midland and East Coast main lines and routed to East London via the Joint Line and March Whitemoor. The main scheme on the London Midland Region was the new yards at Carlisle Kingmoor, whilst lesser schemes planned modernisation at Crewe Basford Hall and Bescot. In the North East five new hump yards were planned at Hartlepool, Tyne, Stourton, Healey Mills and Tees ("up" and "down"). In the end only three were built with traffic levels failing to justify the yards at Hartlepool and Stourton. In Scotland schemes at Alloa, Perth and Millerhill were well underway, whilst on the Southern Region there were advanced plans for two new hump yards at Ashford and Tonbridge. Neither of the Southern schemes progressed because of the collapse in general merchandise traffic, caused by competition from road transport. This type of traffic was disproportionately important on the Southern Region where coal, steel and other heavy industry was not a major part of the landscape. One final yard which almost made it was at Swanbourne. Designated as a major marshalling site for traffic avoiding London, the yard began to be developed on a green field site, west of Bletchley. At least a dozen sidings were built and in 1982 when I visited, the remains of the yard could still be seen. However the large hump yard planned was never built and cross-country freight traffic all but vanished from the line when the route to Cambridge closed under the Beeching review.

PROGRESS FROM 1960 TO 1963 - "CONTINUED OPTIMISM" [9]

Between 1960 and 1963 it was business as usual for those implementing the original 1955 modernisation and re-equipment programme. Gradually new yards were designed and approved, as two progress reports from 1961 and late 1962 confirm. The dilemmas of how to design the best possible automated hump yard were debated within the British Railways Board, with the ideal design pinned at 50 sorting sidings. The reason for this was the excessive curvature and distances if larger fans of sidings were built. This conclusion is reflected in UK yards; only Tinsley, with the Dowty retarder system had a higher classification bowl with 53 sidings. Otherwise 48 was generally the maximum as reflected in Kingmoor "up" Yard and in Tyne Yard.

It was however in 1963, as the Beeching Report was nearing completion, that senior staff within British Railways began to ask whether speeding up the construction of yards and goods depots to try and retain goods traffic was wise. An alternative view, later confirmed by the Beeching Report, was that traffic was haemorrhaging so fast to the roads that no more major yards should be built until a clearer prediction on what traffic would be left in the 1970s and 1980s was available. Thus from 1963, no new schemes for marshalling yards were started and between 1963 and 1966 work concentrated on completing the schemes already underway.

1961 - BR MODERNISATION PROGRESS REPORT [10]

The headline used to describe the aims for freight traffic in this update on the 1955 Modernisation Plan was "fast reliable transits". Much of the 1961 review of the 1955 plan concentrates on the construction of modern goods depots to handle sundries traffic. In the year before the publication of the report, new goods depots had been opened at Hull, Stockton, Liverpool Huskisson, Liverpool Edge Hill, Liverpool Spekeland Road, Ardwick, Warrington, Chester, Peterborough and Lincoln. A specially ventilated goods depot had been constructed at Hither Green for perishable produce from the continent and new "robots" introduced in the Wolverhampton Goods Depot. The emphasis on new goods depots and their automation reflected the view that goods of all types would remain on rail and therefore massive investment to improve the efficiency of handling small consignments was needed.

As for the new marshalling yards, three pages of the report contain a eulogy for the new yard at Margam which had recently opened. The 178-acre site, with 33 miles of track, could handle 4500 wagons in 24 hours and was still held up as the way of the future for freight traffic marshalling. The review notes that Ripple Lane hump yard had also recently opened and that yards were under construction at Carlisle, Thornaby (Newport on Tees) and Tyne (Lamesley). Two further schemes in Scotland, at Perth and Millerhill, were almost completed. Interestingly the review continues to make note of plans for new mechanised yards at Gloucester, Shrewsbury and Stourton, near Leeds.

1962 - BRITISH RAILWAY PROGRESS [11]

The 1962 progress report was much the same as that produced in 1961 in that it trumpeted several new and automated goods depots which had been completed in the previous year. Most notably was a new sundries depot in Stoke-on-Trent which covered 17.5 acres and was equipped with mechanical handling and conveyor belts. The new depot allowed the closure of nine smaller depots in the area. Other depots listed as under construction included Derby St. Marys, Leeds Wellington Street, Gateshead (TCFD), Glasgow Sighthill, Watford and Leicester. One of the first of dozens of new coal concentration depots was opened at Enfield Chase.

Just as in the 1961 report, there was a eulogy for the new Carlisle Kingmoor Yard with 70 miles of track

Above:- Class 08 No. 08427 shunts Mansfield Concentration "down" yard on 25 June 1980. The "up" yard can be seen in the distance, just above and to the right of the Class 08. Amazingly when the 1966 yard survey was undertaken, the "down" sidings here shunted 4687 wagons in the week, whilst the "up" yard handled 4216. The 1957 review of yard building progress noted that the scheme to build a hump yard here was on hold, because serious consideration was being given to extending the GC electrification over the Woodhead Route to Wath Yard as far as Mansfield and this would obviously impact on any new plans for a hump yard. In the end nothing changed at Mansfield. The "up" and "down" sidings were increasingly used to stable sets of "merry-go-round" HAA hoppers in the early 1980s. After the miners' strike and subsequent pit closures, the yard was eventually totally closed in 1986. (**M. Rhodes**)

Above:- Swanbourne was to have been the pivotal yard for the North London Orbital Route. This view of Class 25 No. 25249, taken on the daily Aylesbury to Northampton freight in February 1983, gives a rare glimpse of where the yard was built. Within a couple more years all traces of the yard had disappeared under birch trees. (**M. Rhodes**)

and the capacity to sort 5200 wagons in 24 hours, the equivalent of 250 trains. Mention was made of the yard's ability to sort a train of 50 wagons within 7 minutes. The completed scheme at Ripple Lane was mentioned with its fully automated primary and secondary retarders and also the newly installed electronic static switches for all the points to the sorting sidings. Much was made of the future projects. The yards at Perth and Tees were already partially open and the £9 million scheme at Tinsley well underway. Work was also noted to be well underway at Millerhill, Tyne, Healey Mills and Stourton yards. This

is interesting in that the yard at Stourton was never mechanised, as indeed was the case at Ashford in Kent which is noted to be in the throes of modernisation in the report. The new hump at Basford Hall "down" Yard had been completed and some remodelling had been started at Bescot. The mood of the report is remarkably upbeat, with mention also made of the new mini tape recorders introduced at Temple Mills and Whitemoor to help staff record the wagon order for express freights from these yards. It seems the mood was that technology could solve all the woes of the 1960s freight railway and traffic would never be a problem.

Above:- *This 1963 view of Worcester shows the sheer scale of goods traffic, for which the new marshalling yards were designed. The combined sidings at Worcester still handled 3525 wagons in a week during the 1966 marshalling yard survey, mostly general goods as can be seen here. The new "container" concept is evidenced towards the top of the picture, whilst Class 45 No. D142 passes with 4N18, the 1455 Bristol to Dringhouses express goods train. This was one of the long-distance Class 4 freights introduced to speed up the transit of general goods and reduce marshalling over long journeys. Again a move designed to retain general goods traffic, which had all but vanished within a decade of this view. (A.A. Vickers - M. Rhodes collection)*

*Above:- One of the larger centralised goods depots built to try and retain general goods and sundries traffic was in Gateshead. The Tyneside Central Freight Depot (TCFD) is seen here, largely derelict in August 1990. The extensive railway yard and warehousing is largely disused, but the adjacent yard is now (1990), the main Speedlink collection point for Tyneside. Class 47 No. 47003 leaves with 6N74, the daily TCFD to Tees Yard Speedlink service. Speedlink too ended just months later, bringing the curtain down on wagonload traffic in the UK. (**M. Rhodes**)*

1963 - BEECHING REPORT [12] [13]

Ironically, the document which was to have the most profound effect on Britain's marshalling yards did not even mention them at all. The Reshaping of British Railways, known better as the Beeching Report studied freight traffic in great depth and made several far reaching recommendations, none directly regarding marshalling yards. By way of introduction, Beeching noted that the railways had historically "saddled themselves" with much non-profitable traffic. During the 19th Century, roads to many towns were poor and the horse and cart was a slow and difficult means of taking general goods traffic from one town to another. Thus the railways became the "common carrier" for goods, as the steel rails reached every corner of the country. It was not until the 20th Century that the internal combustion engine led to road development, but even then in the first decades of the 20th Century, goods traffic often had to use the horse and cart for much of its journey. The railways had a monopoly on goods traffic which led to complex and "random" movement

of small capacity wagons around an immensely complex network. So much so that in 1961, when the surveys which informed the Beeching report were undertaken, the average time between loadings of wagon was 11.9 days. The average transit took nearly 2 days and this for an average journey of just 67 miles. Such statistics might have been acceptable in the era before reliable road transport, but by 1961 as Britain's first motorway was being built, road carriers could easily deliver goods over this sort of distance in a day and reload their vehicles for another journey by the next day. Railways, with their traditional monopoly of goods traffic were in trouble.

Traffic carried in 1961 was made up mainly of coal (145.7 million tons), followed by minerals (54.3 million tons), general merchandise (34.3 million tons) and sundries (3.8 million tons). In 1961 there were 600 rail connected collieries, producing 197.5 million tons of coal. The table overleaf shows where the coal was destined and how much of it was carried by rail.

Above:- One of the first suggestions in the Beeching Report was to increase the amount of block workings, direct from siding to siding, thus avoiding marshalling yards. Just such a train is seen here at High Wycombe in the mid-1960s. Class 31 Nos. D5512 & D5502 head south with the daily Thame to Acton empty oil tanks. This was later to run direct to Ripple Lane and then to Thames Haven refinery, cutting out marshalling at both Acton and Ripple Lane Yard. Later the train was directed to Hoo Junction for the Grain refineries, but again without remarshalling en-route. Just such direct siding to siding working for bulk products, like fuel oil, led to the early closure of Ripple Lane in 1969. (**V. Murphy - M. Rhodes collection**)

Above:- A second crucial recommendation of Dr. Beeching, was the introduction of "merry-go-round" (MGR) working for power station coal traffic. This view, taken in 1980, covers two aspects of the impact of this policy. Class 47 No. 47303 passes West Hartlepool yards with an Easington Colliery to Drax Power Station MGR service. The yards here were to have been rebuilt and enlarged in the original Modernisation Plans, but direct MGR working from the Durham pits to Yorkshire removed the need for any yard at all here. The land is now derelict. (**M. Rhodes**)

Coal production and rail carriage in 1961

Destination	Tonnage delivered (millions)	Tonnage delivered by rail (millions)
Electricity generation	55.4	30.7
Gas production	22.5	11.0
Iron & steel works	31.2	18.0
Other industry e.g. cement	26.3	22.3
Household consumption	28.9	27.6
All other	27.5	22.9
Inter colliery/washery traffic	13.2	13.2

Right:- Perhaps the most insightful suggestion of Beeching was the introduction of widespread containerisation for general merchandise. Here in 1964 an Aberdeen "Liner" service crosses the Forth Bridge behind "new out of the box" Class 47 No. D1100. (A.A. Vickers - M. Rhodes collection)

Beeching noted that both for coal and mineral traffic, rail had the majority share of the traffic and the chance of increasing the amount of traffic on rail was small. He therefore concentrated on how the operation could be streamlined. The first issue was the National Coal Board's tendency to use BR wagons as mobile storage bunkers. So bad was this practice that in 1961, 22 million wagon days were wasted by wagons standing idle and acting as coal storage bunkers. Working with the NCB, this practice was gradually reduced. Second, the transport of single wagons to coal depots at wayside stations was costing 19 shillings per ton in transport costs, as compared to 10.6 shillings per ton when a block train could be used. To combat these two problems Beeching proposed setting up coal concentration depots for household coal, thus streamlining the operation greatly. Neither of these changes greatly impacted on the massive marshalling yards built to handle coal, like Toton, Healey Mills and Margam, but the drive for direct services from colliery to power station did. In 1961 the majority of coal was carried in 16-ton mineral wagons. Beeching saw the need for direct services on dedicated routes to avoid the marshalling yards and feed the burgeoning coal-fired power stations. At first this was done using 21-ton and 24-ton vacuum-braked hoppers, but by the late 1960s the HAA 32.5-ton air-braked merry-go-round hopper was being introduced and this single development probably led to the biggest fall in the number of wagons which needed marshalling in Britain's yards.

The one area where Beeching could see rail expanding its market share was general merchandise. During the week beginning 23 April 1961, a national traffic survey was undertaken and this revealed that 1,695,000 tons of goods went by rail that week. Seventy one percent of general merchandise was conveyed in block trains from siding to siding, or siding to dockside. This was profitable for the railway. In contrast, traffic which had to be handled in a goods station and transferred at one or both ends of

its journey to road transport, made big losses for the railway. Beeching was bullish in his solution to this dilemma. Build or modernise 100 sundries depots, closing the smaller wayside goods stations. This would mean a reduction from 950 goods depots, but increase the efficiency of handling general goods. The second suggestion was to introduce a dedicated network of "Liner" trains between these goods depots, with the specific aim of eliminating marshalling and speeding transit times. Beeching noted that such a plan would also have the advantage of eliminating "pilfering" and reducing paperwork. Again the drive was to eliminate marshalling of wagons and this development also contributed to significant falls in traffic at Britain's yards. More significant however was the rise of the road haulier and the almost complete collapse of railways as a way of carrying general goods. Ironically, had Beeching's plans for a national "Liner Network" been fully implemented with investment in new container wagons and terminals, there might still be some general merchandise on the railways in the 21st Century.

Beeching at no stage saw marshalling yards as anything but a nuisance! His suggestions that block trains should be introduced, especially for coal, were the nail in the coffin for Britain's yards. As early as 1969, new hump yards began to close (Ripple Lane) and by 1985 only one functioning hump yard was left (Scunthorpe West). The other big ideas of the Beeching Report like coal concentration depots and central goods depots, were overtaken by the introduction of North Sea Gas and the rise of road haulage. The suggestion that containerisation and "Liner" trains might benefit general goods handling was ahead of it's time, but perhaps the massive increase in container traffic from the ports of Liverpool, Southampton and most notably Felixstowe are justification of his ideas.

1967 - BRITISH RAILWAY BOARD - A STUDY OF MARSHALLING YARD COSTS CAPACITY AND UTILISATION [14]

In contrast to the various reports about the modernisation of freight yards, this detailed study is very different. It is clear that over-capacity in Britain's marshalling yards was becoming a problem in the mid-1960s. In addition the cost of handling wagons was becoming a serious issue. In 1966 the cost per wagon marshalled was seven shillings or 35 pence. Average utilisation of yards across the network was just 55%. So it was that for one week in October 1966, 200 distinct yards were studied in detail. Of these 99 were on the London Midland Region, 32 on the Eastern Region, 20 on the Western Region, 19 on the North Eastern Region, 18 on the Scottish and 12 on the Southern regions. The tables below show the throughput in each of the yards during the week ending Sunday 9th October 1966. The yards were of three types. The majority (148) were flat-shunted, with 32 gravity or hump yards without any mechanisation and just 20 mechanised hump yards. Published in 1967, the report was sealed in Kew record office until 1998.

The first task of the researchers back in 1966 was to devise equations to predict the amount of marshalling an average wagon carrying general merchandise would need, depending on the length of its journey. This was also done for mineral wagons which displayed different characteristics. Two logarithmic curves were devised which were very similar to the graphs devised by the SNCF in the early 1960s, albeit with longer distances in France. Having done this background research, attention was turned to the comprehensive one-week survey of 200 yards - chosen mainly because most of them were to be part of the core freight network that was being devised as part of the National Freight Train Plan[15]. With freight marshalling costing £18 million per annum at 1966 prices and traffic levels falling, the 1966 survey was undertaken to see what might be done to rationalise yards and reduce unit costs for shunting wagons.

The National Freight Train Plan (NFTP) was introduced on the Eastern, Southern and Western regions on 18th April 1966, with national coverage by the end of 1967. The aim of the plan was to concentrate sundries and wagonload traffic on key marshalling yards. Specifically the plan zoned the whole of BR with primary marshalling yards as the focal point of each zone. On the Eastern Region the primary yards were Peterborough New England, Whitemoor, Norwich, Ipswich, Parkeston Quay, King's Cross and Ripple Lane. Each goods terminal or smaller yard within a zone was to send all its traffic to the primary yard and services were then introduced connecting the primary yards around the country. An example of this was the introduction of daily services from Temple Mills to Millerhill and Carlisle Kingmoor, conveying traffic from its zone, as well as traffic from Ripple Lane. Similar services were set up from Temple Mills to Bristol and Severn Tunnel Junction, avoiding the traditional remarshalling in Acton Yard. Another aim of the plan was to rationalise traditional pre-1923 routes which had been developed to keep traffic on the route of a single company and redraw the freight routes on purely geographic grounds. By doing this traffic from the Southern Region to the Western Region was all sent via either Reading or Salisbury instead of the previous arrangement where eight different routes had been used. The NFTP had a major impact as yards not designated as primary yards were immediately downsized and quite quickly closed. The authors of the plan had hoped to increase reliability for wagonload traffic and win more of this business to rail. Sadly as we now know, the rise of the motorway and road haulage all but wiped such traffic from the railway within less than a decade.

Yard Throughput by Region

Region	Number of yards	Total wagons handled	Average number of wagons per yard	Utilisation percentage
Eastern	32	195,211	6,100	63%
London Midland	99	410,161	4,140	63%
North Eastern	19	108,058	5,690	45%
Scottish	18	83,653	4,650	47%
Southern	12	45,989	3,830	40%
Western	20	124,843	6,240	45%
Total	200	967,915	4,840	55%

The first analysis looked at yard performance by region and the most striking observation was the significant over-capacity on North Eastern, Scottish, Southern and Western Regions. In contrast, usage figures were higher at 63% on the London Midland and Eastern Regions, probably because of the still buoyant mineral traffic, which made up the majority of traffic in the yards on these two regions. With general merchandise being the most significant goods traffic on the Southern Region (where there were virtually no mines except in the Kent coalfield), over-capacity was at its most serious. The first immediate conclusion of the report was that "the

main potential for substantial reduction in the total cost of marshalling must lie in the selective closure of yards". The next question was to look at the unit costs of yards based firstly on their design and then secondly on their throughput. The next two tables show the results of these studies.

Yard Performance by Type of Yard

Type of yard	Number of yards	Proportion of yards	Number of wagons	Average throughput per yard	Utilisation percentage	Average cost per wagon (converted to decimal currency)
Flat	148	74%	530,219	3,580	56%	28p
Ordinary hump and gravity	32	16%	198,841	6,210	54%	33p
Mechanised hump	20	10%	238,855	11,940	53%	38p
Total	200	100%	967,915	4,840	55%	32p

Whilst all three types of yard have similar utilisation factors, it is striking how much more expensive shunting wagons through a mechanised hump yard is. Even though the mechanised yards required fewer employees, the high cost is a reflection of the installation and maintenance of the complex machinery required for wagon control. That said, the use of such yards was still being justified in 1966 because of more rapid wagon turn round and also concentration of traffic leading to a reduction in the number of times a wagon had to be marshalled on any given journey. It was also felt that damage to both wagons and their cargoes was less in the mechanised hump yards.

A second way of analysing costs was to break the yards down by their throughput. This however proved problematic because the yards with the highest throughput were all mechanised hump yards, which as we see from the table above, are inherently more expensive. Thus any benefit on costs from high throughput would be counter balanced by the higher cost of the mechanised yard - two variables acting in opposite directions and therefore likely to cancel each other out. The researchers therefore decided to look at throughput in the 148 flat-shunted yards to see if there was a relationship between the throughput and costs.

Yard Performance by Throughput (148 Flat-Shunted Yards)

Yard throughput (wagons/week)	Number of yards	Proportion of yards	Total wagons	Proportion of wagons	Cost per wagon
1-1000	11	7%	6,323	1%	52p
1001-2000	26	18%	41,362	8%	35p
2001-3000	31	21%	77,139	15%	30p
3001-4000	27	18%	93,696	18%	28p
4001-5000	22	15%	97,561	18%	28p
5001-6000	13	9%	72,354	14%	29p
6001-7000	11	7%	70,639	13%	26p
>7001	7	5%	71,145	13%	24p
Total	148	100%	530,219	100%	28p

The findings showed that costs dropped with increasing throughput, as one might expect. The aim of all this work was to see what size and type of yard was the most efficient at marshalling wagons and then to devise a plan to concentrate traffic on efficient yards. An added factor was of course the National Freight Train Plan of 1967, which placed geographical constraints on where wagons could be marshalled. Throughout the

system, in all types of yards, there was 34-35% "slack" or spare capacity and another aim of the research work was to see how low shunting costs would become if yards were more fully utilised. Five percent of the yards studied were operating at or above 90% of their capacity, but at the other end of the scale 5% of yards were using less than 25% of their capacity. The average over all 200 yards was 65% of capacity being used.

The permutations to improve efficiency were many, but no firm conclusion was drawn by the researchers. It was calculated that the yards studied could easily handle an additional 500,000 wagons per week without the need for more staff or additional locomotives. This in itself would reduce the cost of shunting each wagon from 35 pence to 23 pence. If the yards were used to their absolute maximum capacity, including the employment of extra staff and deployment of extra shunting locomotives, then the cost would fall further to just 21 pence per wagon shunted. Of course this assumes that the extra traffic of 500,000 wagons per week was out there for the railways to attract. Sadly, wagonload traffic was already in decline and the researchers suggested that closures should be made to concentrate as much traffic as possible on larger and more efficient yards, using as much of their capacity as possible to keep costs down. This report was the first time in British Railways' history when the talk was of rationalisation and not modernisation, closing yards rather than planning shiny new mechanised hump yards.

Perhaps because of this, the report was sealed in the Kew record office until 1998.

The throughput for all 200 yards, as well as unit costs per wagon shunted, are listed in the six tables below. The tables make fascinating reading. The busiest yard in the UK by far was Toton, handling 41,245 wagons in a week. Several other yards handled over 20,000 wagons in the week. Whitemoor at 30,324 was the next busiest complex followed by the various yards in Crewe with a throughput of 25,318. Two other Eastern yards at Scunthorpe and Temple Mills were the only other places to handle over 20,000 wagons in the week, with a throughput of 21,641 and 21,585 wagons respectively. As expected, many of the major hump yards around the country handled between 10,000 and 20,000 wagons in the week. Perhaps more surprising are the figures for the yards around Barrow Hill, which handled 17,173 wagons or perhaps the two hump yards at Washwood Heath which saw a throughput of 18,384 wagons between them.

LIST OF MARSHALLING YARDS INCLUDED IN THE STUDY OF MARSHALLING YARD COSTS 1967

		Wagon Throughput during test week	Resultant Unit Cost for test week £				Wagon Throughput during test week	Resultant Unit Cost for test week £
					20.	Laisterdyke	1,352	0.268
Table 1 - Southern Region					21.	Normanton	6,030	0.285
1.	Three Bridges	3,989	0.205		22.	Carlton North & South Sidings	9,784	0.201
2.	Norwood Up	2,393	0.494		23.	Cudworth H. & B.	4,799	0.174
3.	Norwood Down	2,076	0.513		24.	Hull Empty Mineral	3,614	0.222
4.	Eastleigh	7,367	0.273		25.	Hull Loaded Mineral	3,433	0.314
5.	Feltham	11,000	0.332		26.	Hull Inward Yard	6,331	0.440
6.	Ashford Down	1,998	0.324		27.	Tees Up	9,079	0.448
7.	Ashford Up	1,737	0.337		28.	Tees Down	9,451	0.385
8.	Hoo Junction	4,814	0.276		29.	Hartlepool Cemetery North	479	0.280
9.	Hither Green Sidings Down	5,437	0.263		30.	Hartlepool Newburn	1,458	0.462
10.	Hither Green Sidings Up	1,754	0.436		31.	Healey Mills	16,500	0.434
11.	Hither Green Sidings Continental	510	1.331		**Table 3 - Scottish Region**			
12.	Tonbridge West	2,914	0.297		32.	Bridgeton	4,071	0.240
Table 2 - North Eastern Region					33.	Cadder Down	5,303	0.249
13.	Tyne	14,350	0.436		34.	Cadder Up	4,994	0.241
14.	Wearmouth	1,391	0.284		35.	Falkland Jcn. Up/ Down/West	5,670	0.215
15.	Tyneside Central Freight Depot	2,810	0.237		36.	Grangemouth/ Dundas/ Fouldubs/ Gridiron	4,388	0.328
16.	Stourton Up	3,245	0.332					
17.	Neville Hill	2,911	0.281					
18.	Dringhouses	6,466	0.304					
19.	Hunslet Down	4,575	0.326					

		Wagon Throughput during test week	Resultant Unit Cost for test week £
37.	Mossend Down/ Goods/Mineral/ West	6,280	0.264
38.	Mossend Up/ Goods/Mineral	4,433	0.299
39.	Polmadie Top/ Bottom End	3,771	0.308
40.	Yoker Up/Down	2,405	0.253
41. *	Aberdeen Guild Street	2,873	0.134
42.	Aberdeen Craiginches Down	2,884	0.172
43.	Aberdeen Craiginches Up	2,248	0.187
44.	Alloa	6,173	0.154
45.	Bathgate	2,088	0.207
46.	Millerhill Down	8,829	0.347
47.	Millerhill Up	7,486	0.396
48.	Thornton Hump/ East End	7,590	0.413
49.	Inverness	2,167	0.334

Table 4 - Western Region

		Wagon Throughput during test week	Resultant Unit Cost for test week £
50.	Acton	9,930	0.238
51.	Reading West Jcn.	5,824	0.200
52.	Hinksey (Oxford)	3,341	0.416
53.	Swindon, Cocklebury (Up) Goods Yard (Down)	4,056	0.285
54.	Stoke Gifford, A, B.	6,645	0.248
55.	Bristol West Depot	6,529	0.235
56.	Westbury	3,316	0.225
57.	Exeter Riverside	5,841	0.270
58.	Tavistock Jcn.	5,212	0.321
59.	Gloucester New Yard and Barnwood	4,186	0.400
60.	Worcester London Yard, Hereford & North Sidings	3,525	0.345
61.	Severn Tunnel Jcn.	12,498	0.350
62.	Pontypool Road	4,341	0.282
63.	Alex Dock Jcn.	4,624	0.319
64.	Rogerstone	8,079	0.254
65.	Cardiff Pengam/ Newtown	6,608	0.556
66.	Radyr	6,513	0.283
67.	Margam Hump, Knuckle & Upside	15,445	0.400

		Wagon Throughput during test week	Resultant Unit Cost for test week £
68.	Jersey Marine	2,222	0.202
69.	Llandilo Jcn.	6,108	0.272

Table 5 - Eastern Region

		Wagon Throughput during test week	Resultant Unit Cost for test week £
70.	Temple Mills Main	18,571	0.332
71.	Temple Mills West	2,078	0.316
72.	Temple Mills East	936	1.019
73.	Ripple Lane Hump/East	8,265	0.401
74.	Parkeston	4,107	0.602
75.	New England Freight Yards - Up (coal)/Down	5,423	0.350
76. *	King's Cross Freight Yards	3,788	0.859
77.	Doncaster Bank	5,239	0.295
78.	Doncaster Belmont	2,901	0.358
79.	Scunthorpe	21,641	0.226
80.	Worksop Down	2,965	0.194
81.	Worksop Up (Gravitation)	5,527	0.166
82.	Grimsby East Marsh	2,289	0.294
83.	Grimsby West Marsh	2,804	0.138
84.	Cambridge	1,991	0.182
85.	Kings Lynn	1,849	0.204
86.	Ipswich	4,044	0.253
87.	Tinsley. Express Freight Sidings and Secondary Yard	17,810	0.484
88.	Wath 'B' (Up)	8,297	0.217
89.	Wath 'A' (Down)	8,876	0.190
90.	Warsop Jcn.	4,374	0.209
91. *	Rotherham Road	2,109	0.262
92.	Mansfield Concentration Sidings Up	4,216	0.082
93.	Mansfield Concentration Sidings Down	4,687	0.189
94.	Barrow Hill Summit Sidings	2,437	0.207
95.	Barrow Hill Seymour Junction	3,286	0.105
96.	Barrow Hill Old Yard	2,115	0.128

		Wagon Throughput during test week	Resultant Unit Cost for test week £
97.	Barrow Hill Up (Hump)	4,593	0.140
98.	Barrow Hill Down	4,742	0.119
99.	Whitemoor Up	13,966	0.240
100.	Whitemoor Down	9,715	0.243
101.	Whitemoor Norwood	6,643	0.123
102.	Norwich Thorpe	542	0.362
103.	Norwich Crown Point	2,385	0.265

Table 6 - London Midland Region

104.	Carlisle Down	8,108	0.548
105.	Carlisle Up	8,572	0.552
106.	Carnforth incl. Furness, Midland and L.N.W.	2,036	0.944
107.	Preston Northern Union	1,511	0.420
108.	Preston Ribble Sidings	2,920	0.250
109.	Preston Farington, Fast and Slow	1,909	0.456
110.	Rose Grove	3,762	0.242
111.	Burton East	3,045	0.169
112.	Burton West	6,065	0.148
113.	Colwick Down	4,427	0.412
114.	Colwick Up	6,928	0.312
115.	Chaddesden	8,444	0.468
116.	Derby St. Mary's	3,284	0.207
117.	Humberstone Road, Leicester	3,276	0.268
118.	Leicester Up and Down	5,603	0.289
119.	Nottingham, North, West & East	7,741	0.217
120.	Toton Down	18,270	0.304
121.	Toton Up	22,975	0.234
122.	Wellingborough Down	4,780	0.192
123.	Wellingborough Up	5,276	0.368
124.	Hasland Avenue Sidings incl. Exchange	7,956	0.137
125. *	Coalville Mantle Lane	3,133	0.247

		Wagon Throughput during test week	Resultant Unit Cost for test week £
126.	Blackwell. East Junction Sidings	4,511	0.128
127. *	Tibshelf Sidings	2,884	0.206
128.	Camden	3,791	0.463
129.	Brent Up.	375	0.469
130.	Brent South Sidings	2,309	0.242
131.	Brent Empty Wagon Sidings	7,672	0.219
132.	Brent Mid. Loaded Wagon Sidings	4,281	0.285
133.	Northampton Down Sidings	5,571	0.154
134.	Northampton Up Sidings	3,444	0.150
135.	Willesden Brent	5,881	0.312
136.	Willesden Sudbury Sidings	7,942	0.264
137.	Willesden F. Sidings	1,200	0.240
138.	Willesden S.W. Sidings	376	0.593
139.	Willesden Acton Lane Sidings	1,712	0.133
140.	Willesden High Level Sidings	857	0.520
141.	Bedford Top Yard	789	0.162
142.	Bedford Bottom Yard	1,082	0.109
143.	Bedford South Yard	274	0.544
144.	Edge Hill, Gridiron Park	8,050	0.792
145.	Ellesmere Port. East End, West End.	4,650	0.505
146.	Garston Speke Sidings, Low Level Up	5,510	0.501
147.	Northwich Down and East Sidings	7,010	0.391
148.	Warrington Arpley Junction	415	0.677
149.	Warrington Extension, N.E. Arpley Old Side	3,710	0.677
150.	Warrington Froghall	1,837	0.519
151.	Warrington S.E. Yard	1,840	0.298

		Wagon Throughput during test week	Resultant Unit Cost for test week £
152.	Warrington Walton Old Jcn.	1,075	0.691
153.	Wigan, incl. Bamfurlong, Ince, Moss and Springs Branch	5,929	0.590
154. *	Glazebrook	3,950	0.329
155.	Widnes West Deviation	2,980	0.403
156.	Banbury Hump Yard, North End	3,774	0.458
157.	Banbury Jcn. Down O.I.C. Sidings	3,112	0.188
158.	Bescot Downside, Down Local Sorting Sidings	8,062	0.461
159.	Bescot Upside, Up Local Sidings	6,485	0.400
160.	Coventry	1,845	0.472
161. *	Hednesford, Up and Down	2,477	0.440
162. *	Oldbury and Langley Green	1,341	0.265
163.	Stourbridge Jcn. Down	1,720	0.352
164.	Stourbridge Jcn. Up Sidings	2,391	0.319
165.	Washwood Heath Upside	7,720	0.277
166.	Washwood Heath Downside	10,664	0.351
167.	Water Orton	3,392	0.495
168.	Crewe Basford Hall Down Sorting Sidings	9,385	0.297
169.	Crewe Basford Hall Up	6,225	0.209
170.	Crewe Gresty Green	2,612	0.310
171.	Crewe Gresty Lane Downside	5,310	0.210
172.	Crewe Gresty Lane Upside	1,786	0.191
173.	Mold Jcn. East End Yard	1,997	0.341
174.	Mold Jcn. Slate Yard	979	0.596
175.	Mold Jcn. West End Yard	3,243	0.253
176.	Nuneaton Upside	3,736	0.236

		Wagon Throughput during test week	Resultant Unit Cost for test week £
177.	Nuneaton Downside	3,152	0.176
178.	Coton Hill Up and Down	3,496	0.402
179.	Stoke-on-Trent Cockshute	2,567	0.263
180.	Stoke-on-Trent North End	4,767	0.168
181.	Etruria Grange	3,250	0.106
182.	Etruria Up	3,407	0.198
183.	Llandudno Jcn. Old, New, Quay Yards	1,065	0.236
184.	Croes Newydd Up and Down	1,517	0.355
185.	Croes Newydd South Fork, Up and Down	1,560	0.440
186.	Ardwick Top Level (No.3.)	727	0.469
187. *	Ashburys	2,117	0.522
188.	Bolton, Burnden and Rose Hill	1,655	0.575
189.	Mottram	7,974	0.294
190. *	Godley Jcn.	1,542	0.500
191.	Guide Bridge Park/Avenue Liverpool Sidings	5,371	0.320
192. *	Ashton Moss North and South	2,385	0.279
193. *	Dewsnap	5,701	0.348
194. *	Moston	3,564	0.300
195.	Miles Platting Brewery	3,996	0.233
196.	Trafford Park East/West	3,278	0.358
197. *	Gowhole Up/Down	4,263	0.367
198.	Patricroft Up/Down/North	3,982	0.254
199.	Patricroft (Stott Lane, Weaste only)	2,128	0.241
200. *	Royton Jcn. Up/Down	1,155	0.457
201. *	Stockport Adswood	3,032	0.288
202. *	Stockport Heaton Norris Jubilee Sidings	2,326	0.338

Yards marked * are NOT shown on the BRB map of yards that it elected to survey, reproduced on page 17.

Mechanised Hump Yards	Non-Mechanised Hump and Gravitation Yards	
Tyne	Feltham	Barrow Hill Up (Hump)
Dringhouses	Normanton	Rose Grove
Hull Inward	Cadder Down	Colwick Down
Tees Up	Cadder Up	Colwick Up
Tees Down	Alloa	Chaddesden
Healey Mills	Bathgate	Wellingborough Up
Millerhill Down	Severn Tunnel Junction	Willesden Sudbury Sidings
Millerhill Up	Pontypool Road	Edge Hill Gridiron
Thornton	Rogerstone	Banbury Hump Yard
Margam	Llandeilo Junction	Bescot Up
Temple Mills	Jersey Marine	Washwood Heath Up
Ripple Lane	Doncaster Bank	Washwood Heath Down
Tinsley	Doncaster Belmont	Crewe Basford Hall Down
Whitemoor Up	Worksop Up	Nuneaton Upside
Whitemoor Down	Wath Up	Mottram
Carlisle Down	Wath Down	Gowhole
Carlisle Up		
Toton Down		
Toton Up		
Bescot Down		

Right:- It was in 1963 that Beeching suggested moves be made to air-brake all freights and invest in high capacity wagons and container terminals, yet it was not until the early 1980s that these changes finally permeated the whole BR network. Thus in 1980, there were still many unfitted mixed freights between major marshalling yards around the country, like this Toton to Tinsley service seen passing Barrow Hill behind Class 44 No. 44004 in June 1980. (M. Rhodes)

CONCLUSION

The 1955 Modernisation Plan envisaged a railway network with 100 or so modern goods depots and approximately 30 mechanised hump yards to efficiently handle wagonload freight traffic. This plan was diligently implemented from 1955 to 1962. Then everything changed with the Beeching Report which emphasised block train working and containerisation. This inevitably signalled a change in policy towards freight train marshalling and after 1963 the schemes for new hump yards at Tonbridge, Gloucester and Shrewsbury were never mentioned again in British Railways' literature. Then the 1967 study on marshalling costs signalled the beginning of the end for Britain's yards. It was in 1969 that the first of the Modernisation Plan hump yards closed, at Ripple Lane. Closure the result of increased block train working from the refineries and industrial complexes along the north bank of the Thames. A relentless stream of closures and downsizing then took place from 1970 until, at the end of 1985, just one hump yard remained in operation at Scunthorpe West. This eventually closed in 1990 signifying the end of an era in Britain. The country, so crucial in the invention and development of gravity-assisted shunting, turned to exclusively block train working. Elsewhere in the world, as we shall see in Chapter 8, there are almost 300 mechanised hump yards still in operation, with new yards being built every year in China and the USA.

References

1   Modernisation and Re-equipment of British Railways, British Transport Commission, 1955.

2   Re-appraisal of the Plan for the Modernisation and Re-equipment of British Railways, British Transport Commission, 1959.

3   The Reshaping of British Railways, British Railways Board, 1963

4   Rhodes M. Beeching, The Impact on Freight, Steam World, November 1990; 5–13.

5   Rhodes M. Wembley: Britain's Busiest Yard, Rail Express 1999.

6   Harvey RF. Marshalling Yards Panel - Progress Report. British Transport Commission, 30 November 1957.

7   Rhodes M. The Illustrated History of British Marshalling Yards. OPC/Haynes 1988.

8   Robertson BH. BTC Re-appraisal of the Plan for Modernisation and Re-equipment of British Railways. HMSO 24 June 1959.

9   Howes DM. Marshalling Yards - an Operating View. Modern Railways, April 1963; 254–259.

10   BR Modernisation Progress Report. pages 36–42. British Transport Commission, 1961.

11   British Railway Progress - May 1962. pages 35–41. British Transport Commission, 1962.

12   The Reshaping of British Railways. Part 1 - Report. HMSO, 1963

13   Rhodes M. Beeching - Part 2: The Impact on Freight. Steam World, November 1990; 6–13.

14   BRB Costings Department. A Study of Marshalling Yard Costs, Capacity and Utilisation. BRB August 1967.

15   Freeman Allen G. Towards Reliable BR Wagonloads. Modern Railways, June 1966; 296–300.

Below & previous page:- *Another ambitious scheme to fall by the wayside, as pit closures and block working took hold, was the yard at Alloa. Plans for the track recovery, dating from 1970, show the once extensive layout which had handled 6173 wagons in a week during 1966. By 1986, when the two images were taken, the remnants of the yard were simply used as a run-round facility for the daily Grangemouth to Menstrie trip freight. Here, taken from up one of the rotting lighting masts, Class 27 No. 27059 runs round the 6N06 from Grangemouth to Menstrie.* (**Both M. Rhodes**)

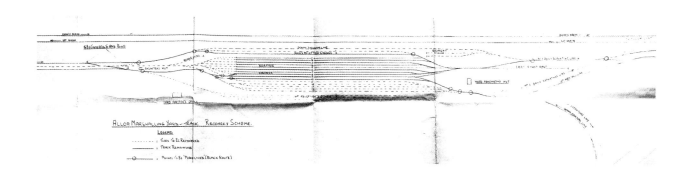

CHAPTER 3

BRITISH RAILWAY MARSHALLING YARD RESEARCH
1955–1970

From Wagon Chaser to the Automatic "Prediction Yard"

Automatic Marshalling Yards by Ian GT Duncan[1] is perhaps the most comprehensive review of "continuous wagon handling" ever produced. It documents 20 different potential methods for controlling freight wagons throughout the marshalling process. The impetus for this detailed BRB report was the realisation that in the 1960s, the traditional automated hump yard with a single set of retarders, was failing to prevent cargo damage and was inefficient because of the insoluble problem of varying wagon rolling resistance. It was noted in this 1963 report that until "relatively recently" retardation of wagons in hump yards around the world was achieved either by slipper brake shoes thrown in front of the wagon or by men known as runners who applied the wagon hand brakes during descent from the hump. Another report from the same era[2] lays out the problem of cargo damage starkly. "Present yards such as Toton and Whitemoor are able to operate because of three factors":

i) Use of wagon chaser (note the idea of introducing retarders to the UK in 1929 at March Whitemoor was supposed to eliminate the need for chasers or brake men, but it was found that with just the one set of retarders there was still the need for one brake man per group of sorting sidings, or four for each yard).

ii) Unproductive time spent in "pushing down". This was the manouveure needed to push wagons along the sorting siding when they stopped short of their intended position next to the wagons already in the siding.

iii) High impact speeds and consequent damage to goods. This was regarded as OK when it was mainly mineral traffic such as at Toton and March, but far more problematic in yards which handled steel goods and general cargo in vans.

The research and development of the 1940s and 1950s was aimed at developing a "prediction yard". The idea of a prediction yard was to measure the speed and acceleration of a wagon automatically and feed the data into a suitable computer. Along with information about the weight of the wagon, precise distance to be travelled, rail curvature, gradient, wind speed and wetness of the rails the idea was to overcome the unpredictability of shunting in yards such as Toton and Whitemoor. The target buffering speed in the UK during the 1950s was 4 mph as compared to 3 mph in Germany and 6 mph in the USA. Even so, much cargo was damaged, not to mention the wagons themselves.

As far back as 1938 a railway engineer called Kriesche predicted that such single retarder yards would not function well because of the problem of both wagon variability and weather changes. It is fascinating to move the clock forward and note that because of strong westerly winds at North Platte in Nebraska (the world's largest hump yard) the traffic from east to west is actually hump shunted from west to east to overcome the uncontrollable variable of strong prevailing winds. Even the newly enlarged Moorman Yard in Ohio (which shunts from east to west) has had to put up special wind breaks because of prevailing westerly winds.

The first solution suggested was to provide two sets of retarders and combine this with weight, speed and wind sensors. The first yard in the world to employ this "total automation" with two sets of retarders was Kirk Yard built by the Elgin, Joilet and Eastern Railroad in Kirk, Indiana in 1955. This idea was first introduced in Britain not much later, in 1956, at Thornton Yard in Fife. The idea behind a secondary set of retarders was to reduce the distance a wagon had to run from the last retarder to its designated siding and thereby reduce the variability introduced by rollability and prevailing winds. An additional benefit was the tighter control of the entrance speed to the sorting sidings afforded by two sets of railbrakes. After trialling various shunting speeds and different entry speeds for wagons at the new Thornton Yard it was concluded that:

i) the difficulty of obtaining and applying accurate resistance measurements

ii) the need for low buffering speeds

iii) the occurrence of overtaking

all appear to be incompatible with using a traditional hump yard without the continued use of chasers and pushing down. In this context the research endeavours turned away from designing the perfect "prediction" yard and towards what became known as "continuous wagon handling" in marshalling yards.

Continuous Wagon Handling

Broadly speaking three methods were considered. First, keeping the 1950s era "prediction" yards with their weighbridges, radar and wind detectors, but adding small retarders and boosters to each sorting siding to propel a wagon or wagons along the siding at a constant (much reduced) speed to buffer up to wagons already in the siding. The second idea was the same as the first option insofar as the prediction yard was to be kept but all wagons would be brought to a stop at the entrance to the sorting siding at which point they would be propelled down the siding by a mechanical pushing device or mule. The third option was to use small retarders and boosters throughout the yard with the addition of pushing devices or mules as required. This third option encompasses what we now know as the Dowty system but also is interesting in that the suggestion was made that mules might also be needed in the sorting sidings. If we look at modern marshalling yards around the world, the Dowty system has been very successful in Austria (Villach and Wien Kledering) and also the USA (Roseville and Memphis Davidson). In contrast large modern yards in Germany have adopted the second option with state of the art "prediction" yards like München Nord and Maschen which use mules to propel wagons along the sorting sidings. Before looking at examples of these two options in use in the 21st century it is perhaps helpful to examine the twenty different technical solutions offered for continuous wagon handling, in the 1963 BRB report.

The remit of the research was a wagon handling system that met nine requirements or performance specifications.

1. To sort at least 7.5 wagons per minute

2. Avoid collisions due to wagons catching up with each other

3. Reduce buffering-up impacts to 3 mph or less

4. Capable of handling wagons of all rollabilities

5. Capable of handling cuts of up to six wagons

6. Capable of handling even the longest wheelbase wagons (Borail at 46 feet) and even the standard BR coach (46 feet and 6 inches)

7. Capable of handling up to a maximum axle weight of 17.5 tons

8. Capable of handling a maximum overall length of 69 feet and 6 inches (Borail) and also continental wagons

9. Any equipment should be compatible with existing balloon yards and locomotives should be able to traverse any part of the yard

Below:- *By the 21st century, all evidence of the 1950s "Gremberg Siding" experiment had vanished at Köln Gremberg Yard. By 2007 when this image was taken, the yard was the third busiest in Germany after Hamburg Maschen and Mannheim. Two humps handled 5000 wagons each day. Here Class 296 No 296 059 finishes humping an arrival in the south-north system. Interestingly, the humping of container wagons is widespread in Germany with one of the newest yards in Germany at Hamburg Waltershof dedicated almost exclusively to the hump shunting of container wagons. In Köln, there are two hump yards at Gremberg and Kalk Nord. Gremberg is the major yard with a north-south system containing 12 arrival sidings, 32 sorting sidings and 12 departure roads. The south-north system, seen here is fractionally bigger in that it has 14 departure sidings with identical arrival and sorting sections.* **(M. Rhodes)**

Retardation with Graded or Sloping Sorting Sidings

1. Gremberg Siding

This method was trialled at Köln Gremberg Yard as the name suggests. With a sorting siding graded for the first quarter at 1 in 125, the entrance to the siding was controlled by retarders at close intervals. It is thought that the purchase of 100 Dowty retarder units by Deutsche Bundesbahn in the late 1950s was for use at Gremberg. Other control units were proposed for this method of total wagon control including the hydra-brake made by Strachan and Henshaw. The success of the Dowty retarders was such that the Gremberg Siding never progressed as an idea and today's Gremberg Yard is controlled by two sets of retarders and mules at the entrance to each sorting siding. Meanwhile the use of Dowty retarders has become widespread around the world. Interestingly in Nürnberg Yard, rebuilt in 1988, the Dowty was used in this fashion alongside three primary, ten secondary and 56 sorting siding retarders. 42,000 units were used in the sorting sidings giving "total wagon control"[3].

2. Brunswick Siding

The Brunswick siding is named after Braunschweig, where it was introduced and trialled in the late 1950s.

The idea here was for each siding to have an entrance retarder at the start of a graded sorting siding. The retarder at the top end was used to "hang" or suspend wagons beyond it, into the siding. The retarder was placed several wagon lengths into the sorting siding and on the yard end of the retarder the last wagon shunted was held firmly, coupled to the rest of the wagons in that siding, which effectively hung from it down the gently sloping sorting siding. New arrivals in the siding were retarded to a halt, buffered up against the wagon which was held in the yard end of the retarder. Once five or six wagons had arrived, these were coupled together and the retarder was opened slightly to allow the wagons to move, six wagon lengths along the siding. The retarder was then closed to secure the last wagon into the siding. This then made space for 5 or 6 more wagons to be shunted into the siding. The process was then repeated as these new arrivals were coupled up and gently allowed to roll a couple of hundred yards into the sorting siding before the process was repeated. The gradient for this system was typically 1 in 125 for the first quarter of the siding and level thereafter. The system could also work with a continuously graded siding with a stop mule which started its shift at the entrance to the sorting siding and was gradually moved away from the hump as more wagons arrived in the siding. The use of a stop

Above:- Another German innovation was the "Brunswick" or Braunschweig siding trialled in the 1950s in Braunschweig. Sadly there is no trace of this at today's Braunschweig hump yard. Indeed the retarders here have been silent for over a decade. Here, in 1993, Class 140 No.140 539 passes the hump, having arrived with a freight. At this time the yard continued to function, handling over 1500 wagons a day and with five groups of sidings, each with a secondary retarder to control entry into them. (**M. Rhodes**)

mule in this way had been trialled in some UK colliery sidings in the 1940s and 1950s with gradients of 1 in 55, but generally only with small yards and short sidings.

The disadvantages of this system were several. First and foremost, the earthworks needed to create large yards with continually falling grades in the sorting sidings were considerable. Second, operational limitations, particularly pertaining to the size of a single cut destined for a siding are obvious. The arrival of the Dowty system in the late 1950s, where retarders could slow and accelerate wagons, rendered the Brunswick siding redundant and needless to say the modern day Braunschweig Yard shows no signs of this 1960s experiment. The idea of entrance retarders on each sorting siding was however widely adopted in Germany, notably in Hamburg Waltershof, opened in 1994, and the modernised yard at Berlin Seddin. This method of retardation was also used in North America at the rebuilt Chicago Bensenville, operated until last year by CP.

Retardation and Acceleration with Slightly Sloping or Flat Sidings

3. Dowty Retarders/Boosters

This method of total wagon control involves the use of hydraulic devices bolted to the inside of the running rail and powered by an oil hydraulic main at a pressure

Above & below:- Of all the innovations mentioned in the 1963 British Railways Research document, the Dowty retarder has been the most successful and the most durable. This June 2015 view shows the rows of Dowtys at Memphis Harrison Yard. The yard here had been owned by the Illinois Central and called Johnson Yard until its rebuild as a 45-track Dowty yard in 2009 by CN, who named it after their president. The first image shows a maintenance crew attending to Dowty retarders about 100 yards from the hump, whilst the second image gives an overall view of the hump area. The striking thing in the second image is the low profile of the hump (on the right of the picture) as compared to other "total wagon control" yards which tend to have much higher hump earthworks, followed by primary, secondary and sorting siding entrance retarders to which mules are often added. (**Both M. Rhodes**)

Left:- *This May 2013 image shows the sorting sidings at Berlin Seddin, the main marshalling yard for the German capital. On the left of the image the individual sorting siding entrance retarders can be seen on the right hand running rails. Beyond that are mules used to ease wagons forward in the siding driven by wires which as can be seen stretch as far as half way down the sorting siding. The sidings on the right of the image are being fitted with mules, a multi million Euro investment, reflecting the importance of Seddin as one of the key Deutsche Bahn "Network" yards.* (**M. Rhodes**)

of 1450 pounds per square inch. The small hydraulic rams have a maximum vertical travel of 3 inches and can exert a maximum upward pressure of 1.5 tons (any more and empty wagons might leave the track). They are designed to retard any wagon moving at more than 3 mph, but boost or accelerate any wagon moving more slowly than this. The spacing of the hydraulic units can be varied depending on the requirement of a given yard and the slope of the track. The system has the advantage of total control and not only solved the problem of heavy impacts that damaged goods, but also the problem of short runners because of its ability to boost slow running wagons. The one down side to the idea was cost, but it was noted during early development that the number of units needed in a yard could be reduced if wagons became heavier, because the maximum force that a single unit could deliver would be increased without the risk of derailments. The reliability and flexibility of the system is reflected in its use in 17 countries worldwide.

4. Electrical Retarder/Booster

Research was conducted to see if a device similar to the Dowty could be built, but using electromagnetic energy. Calculations suggested that it would need to generate a force of up to 3140 lbs and it proved impossible to design something of this power which was small enough to fit alongside the track like the Dowty did. The idea was abandoned.

5. Coyne Weight-Sensitive Retarder

This simple idea was remarkably similar to the Dowty retarder in that small hydraulic units filled with compressed air were bolted to the inside of the running rail. The resistance they offered an approaching wagon was proportional to its speed and weight and but for the fact that the Dowty did the same, but also offered the possibility to speed a slow moving wagon up, they might have caught on. The idea never left the design

stage and the lack of a boosting capacity consigned this idea to the history books.

6. Electromagnetic Means

This idea involved placing a series of electromagnets along the siding which could be switched on or off as required in order to accelerate or decelerate a wagon. Calculations by the boffins in the Derby Railway Technical Centre estimated that for a 35-ton wagon with average rolling resistance, a force of 710 kg would be required to keep it rolling at a constant speed along a level piece of track. It was calculated that each magnet would need to be 27 kW in power and that the switching and wiring issues to route this amount of power to magnets placed every five to six feet along a siding were extremely complex. The idea progressed no further than the laboratory.

7. Linear Motor (Electro-Dynamic)

The principle of this remarkable idea (tested in Switzerland[4]) was to pass large currents of electricity through sections of the siding so that an electromotive force is applied to the wheelset and thereby provide acceleration or retardation. Obviously because of the need for a closed circuit, this idea could only be applied to plain track. The advantage of this method is the complete lack of moving parts, but the downside is the need to pass massive currents (20,000 amps) through the tracks and the consequent danger of heating and welding the wagon wheels to the rails! The idea never caught on.

8. Undulating Rails

This idea is one of my favourites for its sheer madness! The suggestion here is that along each siding the track should have breaks every 26, 42 or 67 feet. Underneath either end of the track would be hydraulic rams which could lift the track by 2 inches. At the hump end this

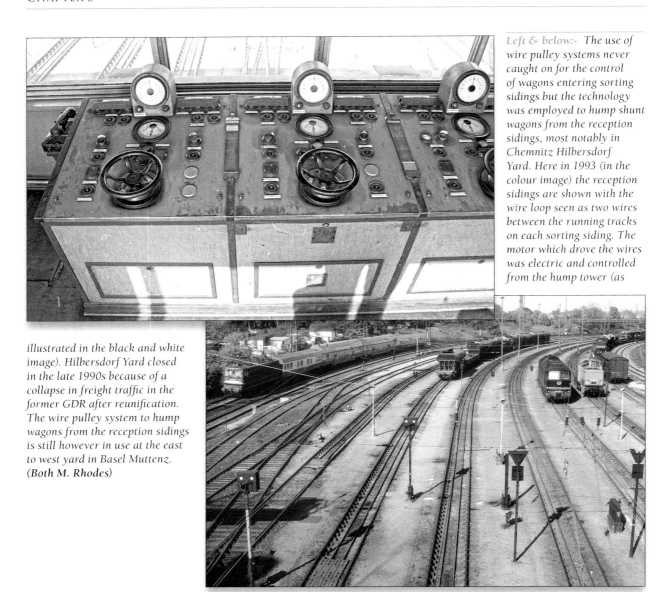

Left & below:- *The use of wire pulley systems never caught on for the control of wagons entering sorting sidings but the technology was employed to hump shunt wagons from the reception sidings, most notably in Chemnitz Hilbersdorf Yard. Here in 1993 (in the colour image) the reception sidings are shown with the wire loop seen as two wires between the running tracks on each sorting siding. The motor which drove the wires was electric and controlled from the hump tower (as illustrated in the black and white image). Hilbersdorf Yard closed in the late 1990s because of a collapse in freight traffic in the former GDR after reunification. The wire pulley system to hump wagons from the reception sidings is still however in use at the east to west yard in Basel Muttenz. (Both M. Rhodes)*

would speed a wagon up, at the exit end of the siding this would slow the wagon down. Ten pages of the BRB Research Centre document are taken up with calculations for this idea. In the end the conclusion is that "the mechanical construction would appear to be somewhat elaborate, and hence expensive, whilst a considerable amount of installed power would be necessary." Not only that but issues of metal fatigue in the running rails which would be jacked up and down as often as a thousand times each day meant this was another glorious non-starter.

9. Servo System with Moving Belts

The idea behind this suggestion was to have moving belts, in contact with the wheel flanges along the siding. These belts would chivvy a wagon along or slow it down. I use the word chivvy because it became clear during the initial mathematical calculations that the co-efficient of friction between the belt and the wheel flange meant that the amount this system could influence a standard 35-ton wagon was minimal. It was a non-starter because it hardly influenced the transition of a standard wagon along the siding.

Constant Speed Propulsion with Slightly Graded or Flat Sorting Sidings

10. Rope-Hauled Mules

Mules are small mechanical devices which commonly run on a narrow gauge track in the six foot gap between sidings and have a retractable arm which propels a wagon forwards along the siding. The simplest method is to place continuously moving steel ropes to which the mules can attach and detach. The original idea to use mules throughout a marshalling yard relied on a ladder style yard with a single mule used to move wagons from the track that exited the reception area all the way along the ladder track from which up to 20 sorting sidings branched (see diagram). Wath Yard was laid out like

Above:- All of the innovations discussed in this chapter were attempts to guarantee total wagon control from the hump crest to safe arrival in the sorting siding. The problem still exists today as demonstrated in the newest hump yard in the world at Bellevue, Ohio. Opened in November 2014, Moorman Yard has 80 sorting sidings, seen here in June 2015. The problems of curvature and increased distance to the outer roads are solved by the "Train Tech" system which Norfolk Southern employ but weather is still a problem. Strong prevailing westerly winds can stop a lightly loaded wagon on the hump and so a wind break has been constructed to help with this problem (seen on the right of this image taken from the hump crest). Debate still rages as to whether a bigger hump and complex primary, secondary and sorting siding retarders with mules are better than the Dowty system. This is evidenced by the fact that the last two large marshalling yards built in the Western world were in Memphis by CN (Dowty) and Bellevue by NS (traditional). **(M. Rhodes)**

this, but nearly all subsequent marshalling yards in the UK were constructed on the balloon principle where tracks split and then split again so that from the hump apex there are 6 or 8 tracks which each divide into between 4 and 8 sorting sidings. Unfortunately this track layout necessitates 8 separate mules to move wagons through the sorting area as opposed to just a single mule in a ladder yard. Then each siding has a mule which picks wagons up as they enter and propels them to buffer up to traffic already in the siding.

The Railway Technical Centre at Derby concluded it was unwise to try and rebuild the many balloon yards that

had just been constructed and suggested that combining a hump with retarders and mules along the individual sidings might be a possible design for total wagon control. Calculations were made and it was found that 110 hp would be needed to propel a cut of six wagons along a level siding. This high horsepower for every siding and concerns about applying this technology to a balloon yard led to it being put to one side.

11. Linear Induction Motor Powered Mules

In the 1940s Eric Laithwaite from Imperial College developed a linear induction motor and by the

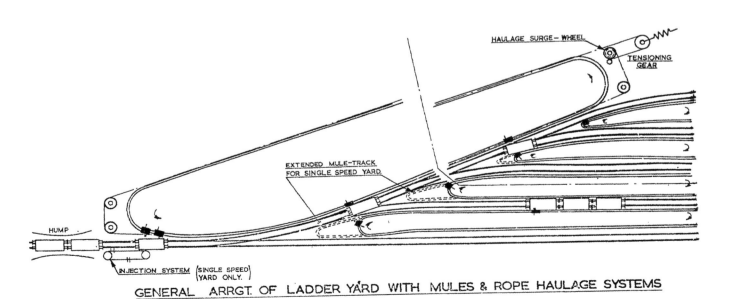

1960s, when railway engineers in Derby developed the MAGLEV, researchers could see a potential application in the marshalling yard. The concept was to place a continuous strip of metal alongside the track and have the mules levitate above the strip and move slowly as the linear induction current was altered. The idea was that because the linear induction motor would only consume power whilst it was running, as compared to the rope system which would require continuous power input, it would be cheaper and also easier to maintain because of the lack of mechanical moving parts. It was proposed that this idea should be installed in some sidings in an operating yard to assess its usefulness. The MAGLEV never fulfilled its potential with just the 1984 line at Birmingham airport built in the UK. This closed in 1995. As for use in marshalling yards, this never happened and MAGLEV mules remain a "what might have been" idea that was never put to the test.

12. Oscillating Mules

The idea behind this invention, which is widely used in Germany today, is that the mule moves back and forth along a short section of the sorting siding. This design does not allow mules to operate across points and is therefore only suitable for the straight track in the sorting sidings. The current systems used in Germany have the mule mounted between the rails of the track and controlled by two pulleys which can move it into or back to the start of the siding.

13. Self-Powered Haulage Mules

The idea behind this suggestion was to abolish the need for a continuously moving rope, or linear motor, but have each mule mounted on a rail with internal power. Because each mule has its own electric motor, the idea was deemed too expensive and discounted except for use in some loading or unloading sidings.

14. Continuously Running Wire Ropes

This idea suggested the placement of continuously running wire ropes (as would have been used to move the mules in the rope powered mules option described above). Here however, each wagon would have a clip which would grip or ungrip the ropes. Such systems were in operation in many mines around the UK to move small mine "tubs" around the colliery. The problem was in scaling up the idea to equip the 900,000 wagons on the national network at the time of the suggestion. This was deemed unrealistic and this idea was shelved.

15. Pushing Rakes into Siding One by One from Top using a "Charger"

This idea necessitated bringing each wagon, or cut of wagons to a complete stop at the entrance to the siding. At this point a mechanical "charger" would pop up and push the wagon into the siding. Of course once the siding was approaching capacity, the charger would have to propel a rake of up to 70 mineral hoppers. Not

Above:- München Nord Rangierbahnhof (marshalling yard) was opened in 1991 to concentrate all wagonload traffic in the Munich area on one yard. As can be seen from this picture, taken in 2013, the yard employs oscillating mules. Unlike Berlin Seddin, each sorting siding has several mules covering approximately 100 metres of siding, after which a second mule takes over. (M. Rhodes)

only that but each siding would need an entrance retarder to ensure wagons stopped before the charger was engaged. Although an academic paper on this idea was presented in 1958[5] it was never developed for a full scale marshalling yard and remained an idea for potential use in small goods depots and industry sidings.

16. Tractors on Road Wheels

The idea here was to have a rubber tyred road vehicle with an operator to zip between sorting sidings and push wagons down the tracks. The idea was this might be cheaper and more efficient than providing each individual siding with a wagon charger. On the other hand the possibility of collisions between road vehicles zigzagging across the shunting neck as wagons whistled past every 10-20 seconds was regarded as making this a retrograde step.

17. Linear Induction Motor

The fascination with linear induction motors extended to suggestions that special rails wound with coils could be installed and the wagon wheel could then be controlled as the "rotor" of the linear induction motor. Apart from the fact that this "short rotor" design is very inefficient and can only exert relatively small amounts of power, it was also prohibitively expensive.

Other Systems

18. Slipper Brakes and Proximity Detectors

This method of controlling wagons involves fitting every wagon with a proximity detector. Once triggered as it approaches the next wagon in the siding, a slipper brake is released. The suggestion was that rather than refit the entire wagon fleet, a design of slipper brake could be made which was attached to each wagon as it passed over the hump. The problem was that tests showed that a single design of slipper brake was inconsistent in stopping the widely differing wagons on the network. Lighter empty wagons were halted almost immediately, whilst heavy steel or aggregate carrying wagons were not stopped quickly enough.

19. Traverser

This idea involved the provision of a metal framed traverser, 50 feet across and 600 feet long. The idea being to "inject" wagons at 4 second intervals onto a continuously moving traverser set across the top of 50 sorting sidings. It was noted in the understated way of many scientific papers that "A large amount of development must be undertaken in order to produce an injector system, an extracting device, a durable conveyor belt and an optimum design for the transfer guides". In other words it's a great idea but we haven't got a clue what it would look like in real life! On top of this blue sky thinking it was noted that the conveyor would have to be very heavy duty in order to hold up to 50 wagons making

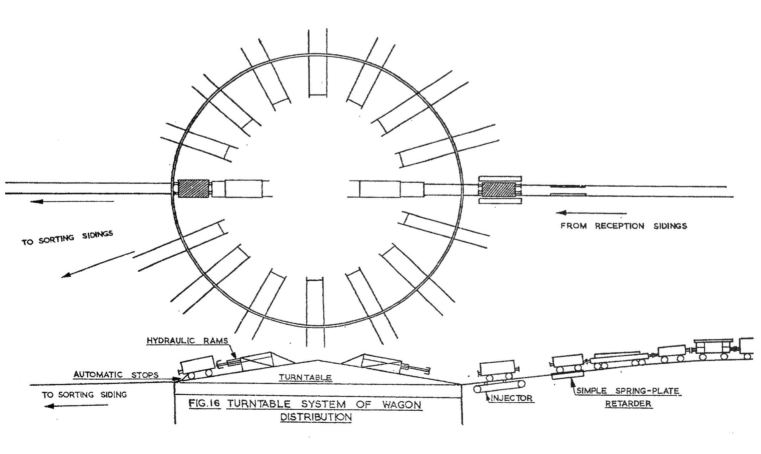

FIG.16 TURNTABLE SYSTEM OF WAGON DISTRIBUTION

up to 1500 tons in the 1960s. It would also, whilst saving approximately 8 acres of land, by getting rid of the points between the hump and sorting sidings, need to be combined with a wagon control system in the sorting sidings. This Heath Robinson idea for a 50 track hump yard never got past the design board.

20. Turntable

Back in the 19th century, turntables were used to save space when sorting wagons in goods yards, such as St.Pancras. The idea here would be to have a reception yard with a single lead to the turntable. One wagon at a time would be fed onto the massive turntable, or it would need to be huge if it were to serve a 50 track yard. As the turntable rotated, new wagons would be added as on the other half of the massive circle, wagons would be ejected into the correct siding (see diagram). Because of the sheer size of a turntable to feed 50 sidings, it was suggested that maybe a turntable would replace king, queen and jack points and feed just 6-8 sorting sidings. This was found to be exceptionally expensive for no perceived benefit over traditional points.

Above:- One aspect of wagon control not dealt with by the Railway Technical Centre in Derby was the East German "screw retarder", seen here in Leipzig Engelsdorf during a visit in 1993. This particular design of rail brake seems to have been confined to countries behind the iron curtain and was designed to be used as an entrance retarder on individual sorting sidings. The flange of a wagon's wheel pressed down on the reciprocating flange on the retarder and this provided retardation. (**M. Rhodes**)

References

1   Duncan IGT. Automatic Marshalling Yards. British Railway Board Report No. E453, 1963

2   Report No. E188, British Railways Research Department Engineering Division, Derby.

3   Lorenzen C. Rangierbahnhof Nürnberg 1903-1988. Hestra Verlag, Darmstadt 1988.

4   Huber & Brimer. Electrodynamic Linear Motors for Modern Shunting. Eisenbahntechnische Rundschau, 1954; 8: 343–348.

5   Grossmith GW. Mechanical Marshalling of Railway Wagons in Works Sidings. Proc I Mech E, 1958; 172: No.37.

CHAPTER 4

BRITAIN'S EARLY YARDS
1880–1955

INTRODUCTION

In this chapter we shall survey the major, non-mechanised hump yards constructed around Britain between 1882, when the Edge Hill Gridiron sidings were opened, and 1955 when the Modernisation Plan appeared and mechanised hump yards were built at over 20 locations. The Edge Hill Gridiron was hailed as one of the first "gravity" yards in the world; it was certainly the first purpose-built gravity yard in the UK. Following on from the success of the Gridiron, hump yards were built at Stockton, York, Hull and Gascoigne Wood on the North Eastern Railway. Similar hump yards were built at Wembley (Sudbury) and Nuneaton by the London & North Western Railway.

The first milestone in yard construction after the Gridiron was in 1907 when the sidings at Wath were opened by the Great Central Railway. With their automatic points, hump shunting was greatly speeded up and even though control of wagons was still undertaken by shunters chasing after them, mechanisation had arrived. A similar double hump yard was built by the LSWR at Feltham in 1923 but it wasn't until March 1929 that full mechanisation arrived in the UK with the opening of March Whitemoor "up" yard by the Great Eastern Railway (described in chapter 5).

The GWR building works of 1931 saw the construction of four new hump yards at Rogerstone, Banbury, Severn Tunnel Junction and Swansea Burrows. These were the last non-automated hump yards to be built in the UK. There followed in 1935 the mechanised hump yard at Hull and then the yards at Toton in 1939 and 1950 (all covered in chapter 5).

There were of course many other major hump and flat-shunted freight yards around the UK. This chapter details the life and times of most of these, one or two of which have survived into the 21st century, but most of which have sadly disappeared.

Left:- By 1992 when this picture was taken, very little was left of the once extensive yards at Rose Grove. Class 60 No. 60071 passes the station at Rose Grove with a train of empty coal wagons from Padiham Power Station to the rapid loader at Maryport. The eastbound yards are now covered by the motorway whilst the westbound sidings are wasteland. (M. Rhodes)

Non-Mechanised Hump Yards

Table 1. Non-Automated Hump Yards - Summary of Major Pre-Modernisation Yards

Yard	Tracks	Throughput in sample week October 1966	Status
Feltham	"up" - 8 reception, 18 sorting "down" - 6 reception, 16 sorting	11000 wagons	Closed 1970, land redeveloped
Banbury	18 + 8 sorting	Up yard - 3774 wagons Down yard - 3112 wagons	Closed as hump 1960s, used for Speedlink until 1990, now redeveloped land
Stonebridge Park (Sudbury)	7 reception, 20 sorting	7942 wagons	Closed as hump 1970s, redeveloped as Wembley Yard 1993
Colwick, Nottingham	"up" - 12 reception, 50 sorting "down" - 6 reception, 31 sorting	Up yard - 6928 wagons Down yard - 4427 wagons	Closed 1970, all work transferred to Toton, now trading estate and derelict land.
Neilson's Sidings, Wellingborough	24 sorting	Up yard - 5276 wagons Down yard - 4780 wagons	Hump closed 1981, much of yard still used for engineers' traffic
Chaddesden, Derby	8 reception, 30 sorting	8444 wagons	Closed 1970 as a hump when all work transferred to Toton. 7 sidings used by Network Rail in 2015.
Beeston	"up" - 6 reception, 20 sorting "down" - 9 reception, 20 sorting	7741 wagons (including Nottingham)	Redeveloped for housing in 2016
Stanton Gate	3 reception, 20 sorting	Not recorded	Returned to woodland in 2016
Barrow Hill	"up" - 3 reception, 12 sorting "down" - 12 sorting	17173 wagons (including up, down and Seymour Junction)	In 2016 three tracks on "up" side still used by Freightliner
Washwood Heath, Birmingham	"up" - 3 reception, 23 sorting "down" - 3 reception, 25 sorting	Up yard - 7720 wagons Down yard - 10664 wagons	In 2016, "up" yard is a stone terminal and "down" yard is mothballed and stores wagons
Mottram	8 reception, 20 sorting	7974 wagons	Downsized 1970s and closed completely 1981
Basford Hall, Crewe	"up" - 20 sorting "down" - 30 sorting	Up yard - 6225 wagons Down yard - 9385 wagons	Most of sidings still in use as flat yard by Freightliner in 2016
Belmont, Doncaster	"up" - 18 sorting "down" - 25 sorting	Up yard - 5239 wagons Down yard - 2901 wagons	In 2016, "up" yard returned to woodland and "down" yard used by wagonload traffic and Network Rail
Dringhouses, York	19 sorting	6446 wagons	Closed in 1990 at end of Speedlink, now housing estate.
Alloa	19 sorting	6173 wagons	Closed 1981, now returned to woodland
Cadder	22 sorting	10297 wagons	Opened 1901 by NBR, closed 1970s, now returned to woodland
Rose Grove	"up" - 12 sorting "down" - 20 sorting	3762 wagons	Closed 1971, now covered by motorway.

Right:- In July 1984, in the middle of the miners' strike, traffic north from Toton was sparse. Class 31 No. 31218 passes Stanton Gate with empty steel wagons which had been used to bring rails south from Scunthorpe. Above the locomotive are the former "down" sidings at Stanton Gate which numbered just six tracks and had the capacity to hold 259 wagons. Above the rear of the train is the land formerly occupied by the much larger "up" yard which had 3 reception sidings and 22 sorting sidings with the capacity to hold 1440 wagons. The yards closed in the late 1970s and by 1984 were returning to woodland. (M. Rhodes)

Above:- This aerial view taken by the NCB when surveying the land upon which Selby Drift Mine was to be built, shows the yards at Gascoigne Wood. Although the trackwork has clearly been much reduced by the time of this 1970s image, the outline of the hump yard to the north of the main line can clearly be seen. Five rows of wagons remain in what must have been a 28 or 30 track classification bowl, shunted from the far end. The smaller westbound yard has just two rows of what look like ballast wagons, still in the yard. (NCB)

EDGE HILL GRIDIRON [1]

Opened: 1882
Closed: 1969–1970
Classification tracks: 24
Capacity in 24 hours: 2000 wagons

In 1873 it was decided that a new yard was needed at Edge Hill, just outside Liverpool. In 1850 there had been sidings with room for 1782 wagons and the yard had dispatched 257,025 tons of goods. Compare that to 1873 when the sidings had expanded to accommodate 3215 wagons but freight forwarding had risen to 1,032,853 tons. Thus the siding capacity had doubled but freight forwarding had quadrupled. In this context, 70 acres of land to the north of the Liverpool to Manchester main line were earmarked for a new yard. The new yard brought the total area covered by sidings at Edge Hill to 200 acres, with 57 miles of tracks and capacity to hold 6500 wagons. Amazingly in 1889 there were 273 arrivals and 261 departures every 24 hours at Edge Hill - 534 freight trains in 24 hours!

Whilst gravity had been used for shunting before the construction of the yard at Edge Hill, the engineer who built the yard, Mr. Footner, claimed several firsts for the Gridiron Yard. Prior to 1873, gravity was used to shunt coal wagons, loading ships on the Tyne and also to sort mineral wagons in Darlington, but the new Gridiron Yard in Edge Hill was the first location where gravity allowed the sorting of wagons without the need for horses or locomotives. By building the entire yard

on a continuously falling grade which varied between 1 in 60 and 1 in 115, wagons could be released from the reception sidings and make their way through the sorting sidings and Gridirons, arriving in the departure yard, without the need for propulsion. This was revolutionary, not least because in 1889 the LNWR employed 228 shunting locomotives every day and estimated that 1,989,751 hours were spent shunting every year at a cost of over half a million pounds.

The engineers on the LNWR noted that when they surveyed the options for a new yard at Edge Hill there were several large yards elsewhere in the UK already using gravity, but not without the need for shunting locomotives or horses. Camden Yard in London had adopted parallel tracks linked by large turntables, used to transfer wagons. The yards at Willesden and Stafford were arranged with "fans" of sidings from a single shunting neck. Gravity was used at larger yards like Shildon and Blaydon on the North Eastern and at Chaddesden and Toton on the Midland Railway.

Shildon[2] was a particularly interesting yard, built in 1869 and on a continuously falling grade of 1 in 144, it could lay claim to be one of the first "gravitational"

Below:- This view was taken in 1970, after the sorting sidings at Edge Hill were finally closed. Partly they closed because of a fall in traffic, but also because the revolutionary yard here proved one of the most expensive on the network. In 1966 only the newly refurbished and expanded Hither Green Continental Sidings was more costly. The weeds are beginning to appear as traffic has departed. (C. Coulter)

*Above:- Hidden away in the store room located next to the Great Hall in the National Railway Museum, is this wonderful model of "H. Footner's System of Sidings for Marshalling Trains by Gravitation". It was built to celebrate the opening of the yard in 1882 by the LNWR and gives an excellent impression of the revolutionary yard at Edge Hill. (**M. Rhodes**)*

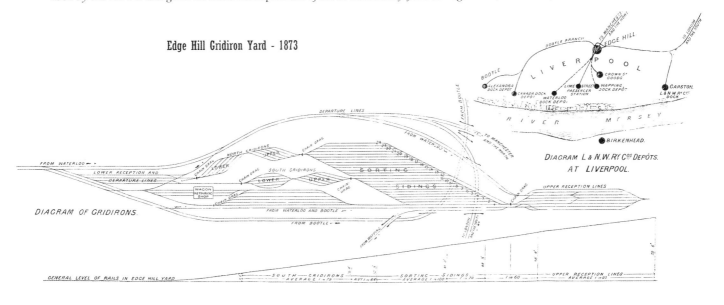

*Above:- This plan from the 1889 book by Findlay shows the original 1873 design for the Gridiron yard which was pretty much the track layout until its closure in 1969. (**M. Rhodes collection**)*

marshalling yards in the world. Unlike the Edge Hill Gridiron however, horses and later locomotives were used to propel the wagons into the sidings. The yard handled 2000 wagons a day when it opened and this increased dramatically as coal traffic from the West Durham Coalfield, combined with limestone and iron ore rose from 20 million tonnes in 1870 to 49 million in 1910. This dramatic rise was the reason for the 1913 electrification of the line from Shildon to Erimus Yard (the site of the Thornaby Yard built in the 1960s). The depression of the 1930s led to a virtual collapse of the mineral traffic that had supported not only the construction of a gravity yard in Shildon and electrification of the line to Middlesbrough, but also the construction of three separate hump yards in Thornaby.

Shildon Yard was closed and the electrification removed in 1935.

The unique feature at Edge Hill was that once the locomotive was detached from an arrival in one of the six reception sidings, no further motive power was needed before a locomotive was attached to a departure at the other end of the complex. The standard of the day was to use "chasers" or "shunters" to apply the wagon brakes manually. Footner tried to make their jobs easier by making sure that all curves were 7 chains in the yard at Edge Hill and that distances from the shunting neck to each siding were approximately the same. Even so, he recognised that some wagons might run away from the shunters, especially with a continuously falling grade. He

Above:- This view, shows the Edge Hill area in 1970. The railways were not the primary purpose of the photograph, but the yards around Edge Hill have been selected from a larger print. By this stage the locations of the sorting sidings and reception yard are empty ballast whilst some tracks remain at the western end of the yard in the form of the Gridirons themselves and Tuebrook Sidings (illustrated below). **(M. Rhodes collection)**

Above:- Looking east in the early 1960s, before the wires reached Liverpool, this view shows the western exit from the Gridiron Sidings in the left foreground. To the left of the main running lines are the Tuebrook Sidings which survived well into the 1980s. **(K. Parker)**

developed an ingenious system of chain drags, marked on the plan on page 57. These devices were activated by the shunter when a wagon wasn't stopping in time. Using a lever in the "four foot" between the tracks, a hook which was attached to a heavy chain (like the anchor chain on an ocean liner), was raised and would catch on the axle of the errant wagon. The sheer weight and frictional force of the massive chains would slow the wagon quickly avoiding runaways. Records from the yard reveal that the chain drags were only deployed 135 times in the first 12 years of the Gridiron's operation.

Once opened the yard employed 83 men and in 1887 it handled 626,000 wagons. 510,000 were loaded, bound mainly for the thriving docks in Liverpool and 108,000 were empties. The average daily throughput was 2000 wagons which equated to an average of 50 trains. The six reception sidings could hold a total of 294 wagons. These led through a shunting neck to 24 sorting sidings with a capacity for 1065 wagons. The sorting sidings were in two groups, each group having a Gridiron for a second round of marshalling to make sure that all departures were put together in the correct order for their destinations. It was noted that the capacity of the Gidiron was never reached

and it was felt that up to 50% more wagons could use the facility without needing to change the layout, or employ extra staff.

After much fanfare at the opening, not much is known about the Gridiron except that it continued to be busy right up until 1966. It was noted to have handled 8050 wagons in a week during the national yard survey but interestingly the cost per wagon marshalled was much higher than the national average at 79 pence per wagon. This made it, by far and away, one of the most expensive yards on the network apart from the newly built Continental Sidings at Hither Green and considerably more expensive than the modern mechanised hump yards, let alone the older flat yards. The cost of the facility, coupled to the demise of Liverpool Docks because of the failure to embrace container traffic and the general decline in general goods traffic, meant the Gridiron was closed completely in 1969 and by the time of our aerial photograph in 1970, nothing but an expanse of ballast was left of this unique yard. The construction of the yard is celebrated in a wonderful model, exhibited in York at the National Railway Museum, but sadly buried in the massive storage room adjacent to the Great Hall.

Above:- This image, credited to a photographer called "King of Edge Hill's brother", shows long term resident of Edge Hill shed, Jinty No. 47357 shunting the hump at the Edge Hill Gridiron Yard. The locomotive was allocated to Edge Hill from 1950 until withdrawal in 1966 and it is probable this image is taken around 1965. (**Photographer unknown**)

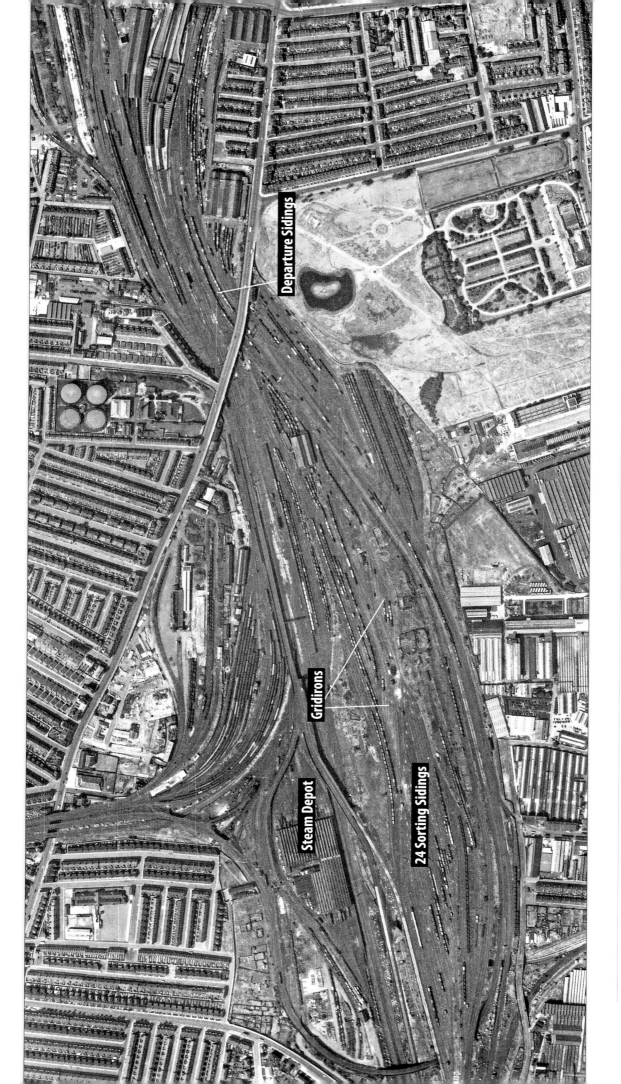

Departure Sidings

Gridirons

Steam Depot

24 Sorting Sidings

Above:- In this 1945 view taken by the RAF, the sorting sidings at Edge Hill are on the left of the image whilst Edge Hill passenger station is on the right. The Gridirons were still in use at this stage and wagons can be seen in both the upper and lower Gridirons. (English Heritage)

CREWE BASFORD HALL [34]

Opened: 1900
Closed: 1972
Classification tracks: 30 + 20
Capacity in 24 hours: 3500 wagons

The sidings at Crewe Basford Hall were always the most important in Crewe, serving the main line from London Euston to Scotland. Built around 1900 they were listed as one of the major yards in the UK in 1910. Gravity was said to be a factor in the yard but there was no hump as such, rather a falling grade which ironically worked against the shunter in both "up" and "down" yards, as these were shunted from south to north and there was a gentle falling grade from north to south. With the electrification of the Euston to Manchester and Liverpool routes, a cornerstone of the 1955 Modernisation Plan, the opportunity was taken to modernise the yards here.

The creation of a new hump yard on the "down" side (albeit, not a mechanised one), allowed the closure of yards at Chatterley and Alsager as well as Crewe North Stafford "up" yard. The "up" yard was also remodelled but without a hump. The "up" yard had 3 reception roads and 20 sorting sidings (all single ended) as compared to 4 reception sidings and 30 sorting sidings on the "down" side. The hump on the "down" side was different from all previous humps around the UK in that its vertical curvature had to allow the passage of the new Class 40 locomotive with its 1-Co-Co-1 wheel arrangement. Three new signal boxes were constructed (SS Middle Up, SS Middle Down & SS North) to control the yard and these opened between October 1961 and June 1962.

The importance of Crewe Basford Hall (and indeed all the yards in Crewe) was short lived. In 1971, restructuring of freight traffic relocated many wagonload services to Warrington and Bescot on the West Coast Main Line. Similarly services from the South West and South Wales were marshalled either

Left:- After the closure of the hump at Basford Hall in 1972, right through the 1970s and 1980s, the yard at Basford Hall fell into disrepair and was used largely for engineers' traffic and rolling stock storage. The reintroduction of freightliner services after 1990 led to investment but one other traffic used the yard during these barren years and that was coal traffic. In July 1991, Class 20 Nos. 20090 & 20015 are seen going away from the camera with an empty MGR from Rugeley Power Station to the Maryport coal loader in Cumbria, whilst Class 20 Nos. 20215 & 20169 are about to depart No. 3 sorting siding in the "down" yard with an empty MGR from Crewe to Silverdale Colliery. (**M. Rhodes**)

Right:- It was really the intense evening and overnight portion swapping of freightliner services from Liverpool, Manchester and Glasgow that breathed new life into Basford Hall yards. Once these trains were taken over by Freightliner in 1996[5], it was natural that the infrastructure assets at Basford Hall would be managed by the newly formed company. Here, back in 1991, Class 90 No. 90047 arrives with 4Z63, an extra service from Carlisle to Southampton. Of course as well as co-ordinating portions from the large northern terminals, Crewe attached portions to southbound services headed for Southampton, London and Felixstowe terminals. (**M. Rhodes**)

Above:- Staff are clearing weeds from Basford Hall in this 1990 view. The location of the trolley is where the king points used to be situated on the "down" hump; the 30 sorting sidings of the "down" yard can be seen, disconnected on the left and three fans still connected on the right. At this time the yard was increasingly important for the swapping of sections from Freightliner services and considerable remodelling and track laying were taking place to accommodate the new traffic. (**M. Rhodes**)

Above:- Class 66 No. 66560 shunts ballast wagons in Basford Hall "up" yard. The majority of the land formerly occupied by the "up" yard is a virtual quarry with just eight tracks left for marshalling container trains. In the left background is the old "down" yard which has been rebuilt with 24 through sidings, but without the old hump. Abolishing the hump and reducing the number of tracks has allowed the sorting sidings to be made longer to cater for the lengthier trains of the 21st century. (**M. Rhodes**)

in Bescot or Warrington. The fall in traffic led the hump at Basford Hall to close on 5 May 1972. Within the five years between the national marshalling yard survey of 1967 and the closure of the hump at Basford Hall, the wagonload traffic had fallen from an amazing 15,610 wagons a week to virtually nothing. Similarly, the marshalling of 7096 wagons a week at nearby Crewe Gresty Lane Yards had also fallen to nearly nothing.

Above:- *This wonderful Aerofilms image dating from 1954 shows the yards at Basford Hall in all their glory. At this stage the hump had not been built and the wires were still nearly a decade away.* (**English Heritage**)

Crewe Basford Hall Departures - 1967

Headcode	Departure time	From	To
4O12	0005	Heysham Moss	Basingstoke
5A29	0050	Warrington	Willesden Sudbury Yard
6F88	0057	Crewe	Birkenhead
5P01	0111	Aston Goods	Heysham Harbour
7D55	0125	Crewe	Mold Junction
5G03	0125	Warrington	Bescot
7G10	0129	Stanlow	Kings Norton
5J75	0152	Camden Yard	Brewery Sidings
5G54	0200	Crewe	Washwood Heath
3M29	0219	Glasgow College	Hendon
4M42	0220	Southampton New Docks	Edge Hill
4P10	0230	Camden Yard	Carnforth
5F53	0241	Camden Yard	Edge Hill
7G04	0245	Ellesmere Port	Bescot
4M20	0247	Dagenham Dock	Ford's Sidings (Halewood)
4H20	0252	Crewe	Adswood Sidings
5F06	0255	Crewe	Warrington

Headcode	Departure time	From	To
3M04	0300	Johnstone High	Gosford Green
5D79	0301	Camden Yard	Mold Junction
6F89	0330	Aston Goods	Birkenhead
3E31	0339	Garston Speke Sidings	Ripple Lane
5F02	0350	Willesden Brent Sidings	Runcorn Folly Lane
5M52	0352	Glasgow Sighthill	St. Pancras
4G07	0408	Ellesmere Port	Anglesea Sidings
6P01	0410	Crewe	Wyre Dock
5L03	0425	Willesden Brent Sidings	Carlisle
4M74	0441	Dunton Green	Croess Newydd
5F51	0505	Camden Yard	Warrington
7K70	0505	Crewe	Stoke on Trent
4F82	0510	Coleshill	Stanlow
8F00	0515	Crewe	Northwich Sidings
7F49	0517	Crewe	Garston
8F82	0520	Crewe	Mold Junction
6F47	0542	Crewe	Warrington

Headcode	Departure time	From	To
7N67	0604	Bescot	Tees
7K27	0605	Crewe	Nuneaton
4F10	0609	Tipton Gas Sidings	Stanlow
8K22	0612	Crewe	Stafford
5L00	0614	Bescot	Carlisle
4M86	0635	Glasgow College	Aston
3E33	0639	Garston Speke Sidings	Ripple Lane
8F82	0641	Oldbury	Northwich Sidings
4E09	0648	Ford's Sidings (Halewood)	Dagenham Dock
8K54	0730	Crewe	Waverton
6J77	0739	Bescot	Weaste Junction
8H06	0741	Bescot	Addswood Sidings
6F85	0830	Crewe	Stanlow
6G00	0830	Stott Lane	Bescot
7F71	0840	Crewe	Northwich
7K40	0908	Northwich Sidings	Silverdale
7K20	0910	Crewe	Whitchurch
6G02	0929	Carnforth	Bescot
5M43	0937	Eastleigh	Carlisle
4G05	1011	Ellesmere Port	Albion
7F56	1038	Crewe	Warrington
7F48	1113	Crewe	Garston
4G04	1142	Stanlow	Tipton Gas Sidings
8K42	1202	Crewe	Mold Sidings
6F91	1210	Crewe	Birkenhead
5H04	1234	Carlisle	Banbury
8A09	1240	Crewe	Willesden Sudbury Sidings
8F06	1316	Silverdale	Northwich Sidings
7D61	1320	Crewe	Mold Junction
7F65	1410	Crewe	Bamfurlong Sidings
4G02	1428	Ellesmere Port	Albion
5A09	1440	Carlisle	Willesden Sudbury Sidings
4M09	1445	Dagenham Dock	Ford's Sidings (Halewood)
5H18	1517	Warrington	Banbury
7G02	1552	Carlisle	Bescot
4F55	1554	Anglesea Sidings	Ellesmere Port
4A18	1600	Holyhead	Broad Street North
3M31	1614	Dagenham Dock	Garston Speke Sidings
6F87	1618	Nuneaton	Ellesmere Port
5M45	1620	Basingstoke	Trafford Park
4G06	1626	Stanlow	Coleshill
6M26	1628	Cliffe	Ditton Junction
5A13	1633	Crewe	Willesden Sidings
7F45	1718	Washwood Heath	Stanlow
4M18	1720	Dagenham Dock	Ford's Sidings (Halewood)

Headcode	Departure time	From	To
6F56	1734	Crewe	Garston
3S49	1747	Kings Norton	Bathgate
4F81	1758	Albion	Ellesmere Port
7K30	1810	Crewe	Nuneaton
7P31	1815	Crewe	Chaddesden
3E34	1819	Ford's Sidings (Halewood)	Ripple Lane
4E76	1902	Ford's Sidings (Halewood)	Dagenham Dock
3S40	1905	Gosford Green	Johnstone High
7G39	1905	Stanlow	Coventry Goods
8F02	1936	Crewe	Northwich
4F02	1940	Tipton Green	Stoke on Trent
3S25	1941	Morris Cowley	Johnstone High
4O03	1945	Croess Newydd	Dunton Green
3M30	2023	Dagenham Dock	Garston Speke Sidings
5A16	2027	Carlisle	Willesden Acton Lane
7F70	2040	Crewe	Bamfurlong Sidings
3M45	2052	Bathgate	Kings Norton
8D73	2122	Crewe	Mold Junction
4S70	2125	Aston	Glasgow College
6F49	2140	Crewe	Warrington
5A19	2150	Edge Hill	Camden Yard
8F84	2200	Crewe	Birkenhead
8F75	2211	Crewe	Garston
5G50	2224	Edge Hill	Bescot
6F69	2230	Crewe	Edge Hill
5A02	2234	Runcorn Folly Lane	Willesden
5A17	2251	Mold Junction	Camden Yard
5A20	2302	Moston	Willesden Sudbury Sidings
4G14	2310	Stanlow	Tipton Gas Sidings
3E30	2314	Garston Speke Sidings	Ripple Lane
3S60	2334	Hendon	Glasgow College
5L42	2340	Crewe	Carlisle
5G01	2358	Preston	Curzon Street

Above:- This table of departures from Crewe Basford Hall was constructed using the summer 1967 working timetable for mandatory freight trains (LMR section A). At this time the yards at Basford Hall were marshalling a total of 9385 wagons on the "down" side each week and 6225 on the "up" side. The total of 15,620 wagons a week translated to nearly 3000 wagons a day, making the yard one of the busiest in the UK. It is fascinating to note that the sidings at Crewe Gresty Lane were studied at the same time and they handled a total of 5310 wagons on the "down" side and 1786 on the "up" side; a total of 7096 wagons per week which was reflected in the wide range of departures from here to Shrewsbury, Pontypool Road, Cardiff, Margam, Bristol and the South West. Indeed there were several dozen long distance freights every day in and out of the cramped and flat-shunted sidings at Gresty Lane. Crewe in total handled nearly 23,000 wagons a week in 1967 when this working timetable was extant.

Below:- This file from the depths of Network Rail's archives, shows how the shunting neck at Basford Hall was modernised in 1962 to create 4 reception sidings and a hump leading to 30 sorting sidings. **(BR LMR - M. Rhodes collection)**

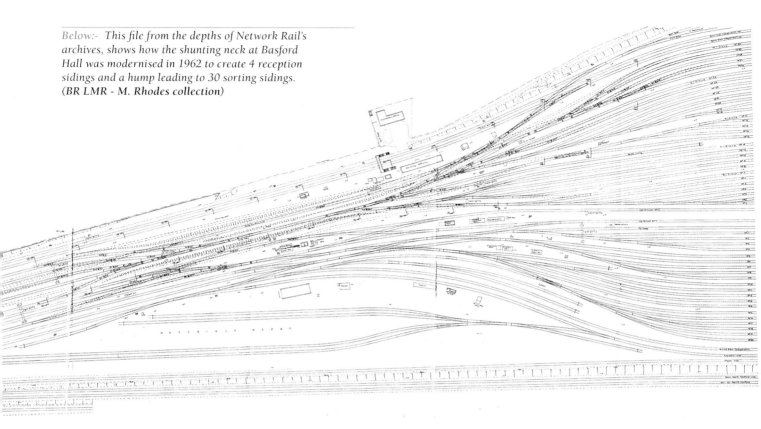

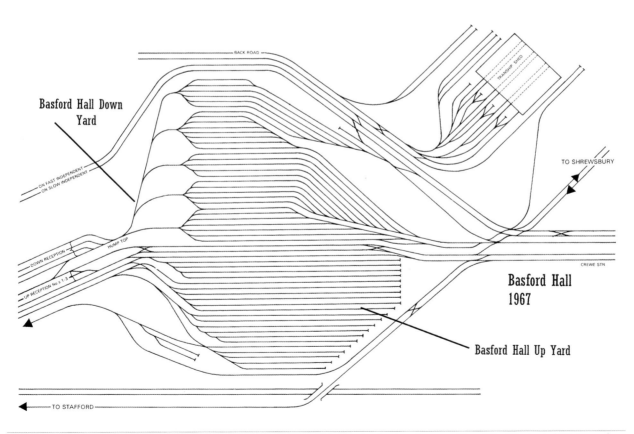

Above:- Redrawn by a friend who used to work for the Ordnance Survey, back when I was writing 'The Illustrated History of British Marshalling Yards', this actually represents the track layout in "post-1962" hump yard guise. This was how the yard appeared in 1967 at the same time as our sample freight departures timetable was in operation. **(M. Rhodes)**

COLWICK [67]

Opened: 1890–1900
Closed as hump yard: 1970 (actually closed completely)
Classification tracks: 50 + 31
Capacity in 24 hours: 6000 wagons

The construction of a major marshalling yard at Colwick, east of Nottingham, dates back to 1872 when the GNR acquired 150 acres of land for railway sidings in the area. By 1876 there was room for 1150 wagons in the newly constructed sidings as well as houses and a small 4-track locomotive depot. By 1881, the Leen Valley line to the north gave access to collieries around Newstead and Annesley. Traffic to the south and east via the GNR line to Melton Mowbray was booming and significant expansion of the yard at Colwick was therefore undertaken. By 1900 the "up" yard had 12 reception sidings, split into six for general goods and six for minerals. These led to 29 and 21 sorting sidings respectively. On the "down" side, six arrival sidings led to 31 sorting sidings. Both humps were manual, without retarders, and as a result the yards employed a total of 52 class three shunters or chasers who followed the cuts of wagons "down" from the hump and manually applied the hand brakes to slow the wagons into the appropriate siding.

Traffic through the yard was at its zenith during the inter-war years. In 1925 throughput was recorded as 147,913 wagons in a month. This fell to 89,815 in 1957, 55,979 in 1961 and by 1967 the figures recorded during the 1967 British Railways marshalling yard audit[8] were 4427 per week in the "down" yard and 6928 per week on the "up" side. This made a monthly total of approximately 45,000. The capacity of the yard to handle 6000 wagons per 24 hours made it the largest on the GNR, handling more traffic than the other major yards at Peterborough, Doncaster and Wath.

Decline began at Colwick as long ago as 1948 when most of the collieries it served were allocated to the London Midland Region in the nationalisation of the railways. Colwick on the Eastern Region had access to many of the collieries to the north of Nottingham, but not as many as the London Midland Region yards at Toton. This access decreased greatly in 1960 with the closure of Mapperley Tunnel. Collieries north of Nottingham had to send traffic to Colwick via Nottingham Victoria and Netherfield, a more circuitous route than to the LMR yards at Toton. After 1960, No. 3 yard at Colwick was lifted and traffic continued to fall. During the same decade, traffic rose at Toton. In

Above:- All that remains of the vast expanse of Colwick Yard are two of the former reception sidings of the "down" yard which lead to Rectory oil terminal, seen here on the right of this image at Rectory Junction. Taken with the aid of a pole (there are no convenient over-bridges next to the River Trent here), it shows Class 56 No. 56078 with 6E07, the 1108 Washwood Heath to Boston steel train on 18 April 2015. (**Paul Robertson**)

To Gedling and Leen Valley

To Nottingham

Above:- Taken in 1945, this shows the full extent of the yards at Colwick. With Rectory Junction in the bottom right hand corner, the yards stretch north towards Gedling and the Leen Valley via Mapperley Tunnel. (English Heritage)

Rectory Junction Signal Box

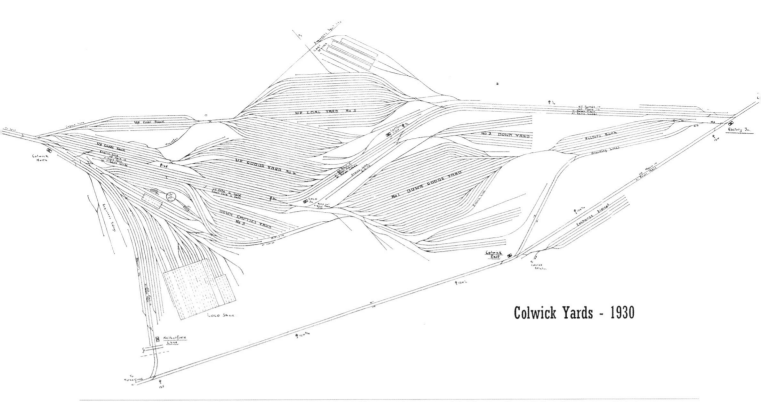

Colwick Yards - 1930

*Above:- On the far right of this plan is Rectory Junction, illustrated on page 66. The yards at Colwick were at their largest between the 1920s and 1960. (**GNR - D. Pearce collection**)*

*Above:- Heading south from the yards is a WD 2-8-0 Austerity locomotive with an "up" goods train. Taken in 1952, this shows the "down" reception sidings in the foreground. (**David Ford**)*

1966, Colwick was reallocated to the London Midland Region and in August 1966 most remaining colliery traffic was routed via Toton and onwards to London via Wellingborough, rather than via Colwick and the route to Melton Mowbray and via Manton Junction to London. The yard finally closed on 13 April 1970.

*Left:- By 1974, all of the track had been lifted at Colwick and the site of the yards was rapidly returning to nature. (**David Ford**)*

Proposed new hump yard at Colwick - 1955

*Above:- This exceptionally rare document, discovered with the help of railway author Alex Fisher, shows what might have been at Colwick. There were detailed plans for a new mechanised hump yard on the site with 15 reception sidings, 48 sorting sidings and 12 departure roads. Drawn up in 1955 as an early design undertaken as part of the 1955 Modernisation Plan, the rebuild never progressed and was shelved by 1960 when Mapperley Tunnel closed. (**M. Rhodes collection**)*

*Right:- Taken just after closure in 1970, this scene is looking north over the 32 tracks of the "down" sorting sidings. The yard is full of surplus wagons for coal, as well as a rake of iron ore wagons on the right and dozens of guards vans. (**Photographer unknown**)*

WILLESDEN YARDS - (SUDBURY TO BRENT TO WEMBLEY) [9]

Opened: 1900
Closed: 1971
Classification tracks: 20
Capacity in 24 hours: 1500 wagons

The yards at Wembley are a complicated matrix of sidings, but prior to 1971 the yard at Sudbury had been the main hump yard for LNW traffic from Birmingham and beyond. The manual hump yard here (as can be seen from the plan on page 72), contained seven reception sidings and 20 sorting sidings. Built around 1900, and an effective replacement for the more cramped yards at Camden, it remained busy right until the end of the 1960s. Indeed in the 1966 yard survey it handled 7942 wagons in a week. This compared to 5881 wagons marshalled in the flat-shunted Brent Sidings and just 857 in the High Level Yard (which had 5 reception and 24 sorting sidings). The tiny "F" sidings on the down side of the main line, with just 12 sidings handled 1200 wagons in the week and the

compact sidings at Willesden Acton Lane (illustrated on page 73), an incredible 1712.

The hump at Sudbury closed in 1971 and all wagonload marshalling was transferred to Brent Yard. This flat-shunted yard became the focus for wagonload traffic in north London and was by far and away the busiest Speedlink yard in 1989/90 when the wagonload service in the UK finished and Speedlink was disbanded. Enter Wembley Yard, built on the ground formerly occupied by Sudbury Yard! To quote a senior Railfreight Executive back in 1993, "It wasn't meant to be designed like this, and it wasn't supposed to handle wagonload traffic, but apart from that it's fine!". The yard, built with a view to serious tonnages

Left:- The yard foreman (in a top hat) looks north to the reception sidings at Sudbury Yard. This image, taken in the 1950s, shows the early introduction of diesel shunting locomotives, especially common in the London area because of worries about pollution. (BR – M. Rhodes collection)

Below:- The 20 sorting sidings at Sudbury Yard are seen from above the hump. Grouped in three sets, they were the major wagonload yard for the LNW from the time of their construction until closure in 1971. (BR – M. Rhodes collection)

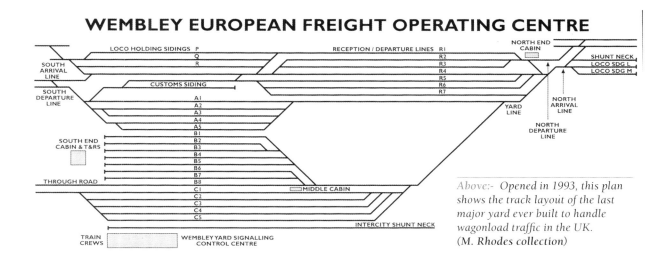

WEMBLEY EUROPEAN FREIGHT OPERATING CENTRE

Above:- Opened in 1993, this plan shows the track layout of the last major yard ever built to handle wagonload traffic in the UK. (M. Rhodes collection)

of cross-channel traffic and owned by Railfreight Distribution was the UK railways last "hurrah" as far as wagon marshalling was concerned. Hopefully the images in this illustrated guide bear testament to that. The yard was taken over by EWS from 1998 and was effectively the only wagonload marshalling yard in the UK. The departure schedule, if one included trains calling for a crew change, listed over 100 freight workings each 24 hours between Monday and Friday. Even now in 2015, this is the yard most likely to witness the passage of a revenue earning wagonload freight train. The sidings at Wembley were divided into groups. Group A was designated for intermodal traffic, whilst group C was for "Enterprise" traffic, or the remnants of UK wagonload services after Speedlink was abolished. Group B was for the storage of crippled or empty wagons, awaiting either repair or orders. When I visited in 1998 the staff were of the opinion that life would be much simpler if they had a "good old fashioned hump yard" - a sentiment reflected by railway practice in the USA and elsewhere in 2015!

Above:- Taken in 1993, just before the yard at Wembley was completed, this view shows the shiny new yard and behind it the Wembley carriage sidings. (BR – M. Rhodes collection)

Above:- In July 1999, Wembley was by far and away the busiest yard in the UK with over 100 trains a day. Even with the demise of Speedlink, nearly a decade earlier, there was still considerable wagonload and Continental traffic thanks to the then enthusiastic EWS led by Ed Burkhart. Here Class 66 No. 66025 stands awaiting its next duty on a rainy July day in 1999 whilst Class 66 No. 66129 has just arrived with the 4A36 freight from Hams Hall. (**M. Rhodes**)

Again in July 1999, this shows the 6B45 evening departure to Dollands Moor behind Class 92 No. 92023. Three fellow Class 92s await work, something which never really arrived for the class over the next 15 years! (**M. Rhodes**)

Below:- As can be seen from this 1970s plan of the complex of yards that stretched from Willesden to Wembley, there were two manual hump yards at Sudbury and then at the "High Level" sidings where 5 reception roads led to 24 sorting sidings. Brent Yard with its 26 tracks was the main revenue-earning wagonload yard from 1971 to 1993. (**M. Rhodes**)

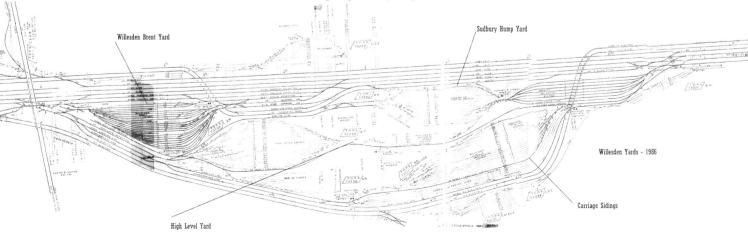

Willesden Brent Yard

Sudbury Hump Yard

Willesden Yards - 1986

Carriage Sidings

High Level Yard

Above:- Acton Lane Sidings at Willesden used to be an important wagonload yard and still handled several hundred wagons each day in 1979, when this view was taken. Class 47 No. 47239 passes Acton Wells Junction with a Willesden to Southampton freightliner service. (**M. Rhodes**)

Left:- In January 1993, the sidings at Wembley were completed and awaiting commissioning. This view is looking south from approximately the same position as that of the Sudbury hump, taken 40 years earlier. (**M. Rhodes**)

Right:- After the closure of Sudbury Yard in 1971 and before the opening of Wembley Yard in 1993, all wagonload marshalling was undertaken in Willesden Brent Sidings, a flat-shunted yard which became extremely busy. Here in 1993, Class 47 No. 47114 and Class 08 Nos. 08926 & 08653 are stabled at the south end of the yard which is still being used for what remains of wagonload traffic to the capital. (**M. Rhodes**)

WASHWOOD HEATH

Opened: 1900
Closed as hump yard: 1975–1982
Sorting sidings: 23 + 25
Capacity in 24 hours: >5000 wagons

Prior to the rebuilding and modernisation of Bescot, completed in 1966, the yards at Washwood Heath were by far the largest and busiest in the Birmingham area. Built around the turn of the century, there were two hump yards either side of the main line from Birmingham to Derby, but also many other sets of sidings between Water Orton and Lawley Street at which point the Birmingham avoiding line via St. Andrew's Junction and Camp Hill diverged away from the main passenger route to Birmingham New Street.

The sidings at Washwood Heath, when combined with the yards at Lawley Street and Water Orton had the capacity to hold nearly 9000 wagons, making this combination of marshalling yards as large (or slightly larger) than the modernised hump yards at Toton and March Whitemoor. At Washwood Heath itself, the "up" yard had 3 reception tracks with a capacity of 287 wagons, situated parallel to the sorting sidings. Hump shunting was undertaken by using a head shunt and wagons were pulled back along it before being propelled over the hump and into the 23 sorting sidings (with a capacity of 1582 wagons). On the "down" side there were again 3 reception sidings, leading directly to the hump which fed 25 sorting sidings with a capacity for 1739 wagons. The yards further south at Lawley Street and Duddeston Sidings had room for over 1900 wagons, whilst the marshalling yard at Water Orton could hold nearly 1600 wagons and was used for quite a number of long distance northbound departures.

The table below lists the departures and passing freight at Washwood Heath in the summer of 1961 and gives an idea of the crucial role the two hump yards here played on the network. By the 1967 freight traffic survey, Washwood Heath "down" yard handled 10,664 wagons in a week as compared to the newly built "down" hump at Bescot which handled 8062 wagons. The "up" side at Washwood Heath was busier too with 7220 wagons sorted as compared to 6485 on the "up" side at Bescot. Added to that were a further 3392 wagons shunted at Water Orton. By 2016 the yards at Water Orton are a distant memory covered in trees and industrial units as the picture of the Washwood Heath to Peak Forest stone train shows. Washwood Heath "down" yard was still configured as a hump yard, but shunted like a flat yard in 1982, whilst the "up" sidings had largely been

removed. Today the Washwood Heath Stone Terminal stands where once the "up" sorting sidings were, whilst the "down" yard, having seen much use for the last 20 years for block trains from MGR coal traffic to automotive services, is now out of use with its 25 sidings still in place, but covered in rust.

Washwood Heath Yard

Southbound Departures - Summer 1961

Headcode	From	To	Dep.	Pass
4O11	Washwood	Southampton	0110	
Target 47	Washwood	Camp Hill	0115	
Target 73	Washwood	Selly Oak	0130	
8V12	Washwood	Redditch	0157	
Target 22	Washwood	Bordesley	0200	
4V42	Bradford	Westerleigh		0215
4V37	Washwood	Westerleigh	0245	
4O06	Washwood	Basingstoke	0250	
9V19	Washwood	Gloucester	0255	
Target 23	Washwood	Bordesley	0335	
4M78	Sheffield	New Street (fish)		0410
Target 42	Washwood	St. Andrew's Exchange	0410	
4V43	Washwood	Gloucester	0415	
9V21	Washwood	Westerleigh	0500	
Target 19	Washwood	Bordesley	0507	
5V11	Washwood	Westerleigh	0550	
5V12	Washwood	Worcester	0555	
Target 32	Washwood	Selly Oak	0625	
8V14	Washwood	Worcester	0640	
Target 30	Washwood	Kings Norton	0650	
4V45	York	Bristol		0709
Target 22	Washwood	Bordesley	0720	
8V16	Washwood	Westerleigh	0730	
9V23	Washwood	Redditch	0755	
4V46	Washwood	Severn Tunnel	0815	
Target 23	Washwood	Bordesley	0820	
9V24	Washwood	Gloucester	0830	
Target 28	Washwood	Rubery	0845	
Target 49	Washwood	Selly Oak	0900	
Target 38	Washwood	St. Andrew's Exchange	0930	
4O19	Bromford	Fawley		0940
5M88	Carlisle	Kings Norton		0948
Target 39	Washwood	Kings Norton	1005	
8V18	Washwood	Westerleigh	1030	
4V50	Bromford	Avonmouth		1040
Target 47	Washwood	Camp Hill	1055	
4V48	Washwood	Westerleigh	1118	
4V49	Edinburgh	Bristol		1155
5O12	Washwood	Eastleigh	1215	
Target 22	Washwood	Bordesley	1235	
5V15	Washwood	Worcester	1250	
5V16	Washwood	Gloucester	1300	
8V21	Washwood	Westerleigh	1330	
Target 42	Washwood	Longbridge	1340	

Headcode	From	To	Dep.	Pass
Target 38	Washwood	St. Andrew's Exchange	1350	
Target 23	Washwood	Bordesley	1405	
4O14	Bromford	Fawley		1508
9V25	Washwood	Gloucester	1515	
9V26	Washwood	Westerleigh	1525	
Target 66	Washwood	Bournville	1550	
6V04	Washwood	Severn Tunnel	1630	
Target 22	Washwood	Bordesley	1705	
4V54	Horninglow Bridge	Bristol West		1742
9V27	Washwood	Westerleigh	1755	
Target 44	Washwood	Kings Norton	1810	
4V56	Washwood	Bristol	1830	
7V40	Washwood	Morris Cowley	1850	
8V25	Washwood	Bromsgrove	1855	
Target 20	Washwood	Lifford Station	1905	
Target 23	Washwood	Bordesley	1910	
8V26	Washwood	Westerleigh	1930	
4V36	Bromford	Avonmouth		2005
Target 47	Washwood	Bordesley	2005	
9V28	Washwood	Westerleigh	2015	
Target 29	Washwood	Hazelwell	2100	
7O66	Spondon	Eastleigh		2106
Target 22	Washwood	Bordesley	2147	
9V30	Washwood	Westerleigh	2210	
8V31	Washwood	Worcester	2300	
4V34	Derby St. Mary's	Gloucester		2340
4V35	Nottingham	Bristol		2354

Washwood Heath Yard

Northbound Departures - Summer 1961

Headcode	From	To	Dep.	Pass
7M61	Barnwood	Branston Junction		0008
Empties	Washwood	Branston Junction	0035	
5C30	Lawley Street	Brent		0108
6D81	Washwood	Beeston	0155	
7M48	Didcot	Spondon		0210
Target 37	Washwood	Water Orton	0220	
Empties	Washwood	Beeston	0230	
4M32	Avonmouth	Water Orton		0237
Empties	Washwood	Branston Junction	0255	
Empties	Washwood	Masborough	0325	
6J77	Washwood	Weaste	0405	
Target 37	Washwood	Water Orton	0440	
Empties	Washwood	Toton	0500	
Empties	Washwood	Barrow Hill	0520	
6D92	Washwood	Toton	0645	
5M14	Westerleigh	Water Orton		0650
Target 34	Washwood	Bromford Tube	0710	
Empties	Washwood	Blackwell	0715	
Target 58	Washwood	Kingsbury	0725	
Empties	Washwood	Toton	0820	
Target 37	Washwood	Water Orton	0830	
Empties	Washwood	Toton	0850	
Target 34	Washwood	Bromford Tube	0915	
Empties	Washwood	Hugglescote	0915	
Target 59	Washwood	Kingsbury	0955	
6D84	Washwood	Beeston	1055	
6M05	Westerleigh	Toton		1128
No Headcode	Washwood	Corby	1220	
Target 49	Selly Oak	Water Orton		1307
Empties	Washwood	Overseal	1315	
Target 37	Washwood	Water Orton	1323	
Target 66	Bournville	Water Orton		1350
Target 34	Washwood	Castle Bromwich	1400	
Target 39	Kings Norton	Water Orton		1400
5M19	Bristol	Water Orton		1407
Empties	Washwood	Chaddesden	1445	
Empties	Washwood	Little Eaton Jn	1500	
Target 29	Lawley Street	Water Orton		1510
Target 50	Washwood	Kingsbury	1525	
4M34	Evesham	Water Orton		1533
Target 20	Lawley Street	Water Orton		1540
Target 37	Washwood	Water Orton	1613	
4M36	Avonmouth	Water Orton		1639
6P07	Lawley Street	Rowsley		1715
Target 38	Lawley Street	Water Orton		1725
Target 29	Washwood	Kingsbury	1730	
6D91	Washwood	Toton	1835	
4N57	Bristol	Dringhouses		1843
Empties	Washwood	Branston Junction	1900	
Target 38	Washwood	Water Orton	1920	
Target 59	Washwood	Kingsbury	1935	
Target 56	Lawley Street	Water Orton		2001
4C13	Lawley Street	Brent		2008
5M08	Lawley Street	Hinksey		2020
No Headcode	Lawley Street	Whitemoor		2023
4M37	Avonmouth	Water Orton		2030
4N58	Bristol	Hunslet Lane		2049
No Headcode	Lawley Street	York		2058
Empties	Washwood	Saffron Lane	2100	
5M25	Bristol	Water Orton		2115
Target 84	Washwood	Stockingford Tunnel Pit	2140	
No Headcode	Lawley Street	Normanton		2154

Headcode	From	To	Dep.	Pass
No Headcode	Lawley Street	Hunslet		2202
4P01	Lawley Street	Rowsley		2222
Target 44	Longbridge	Water Orton		2247
4M38	Avonmouth	Water Orton		2258
6P28	Lawley Street	Derby St. Mary's		2303
5M27	Bristol	Derby St. Mary's		2333
No Headcode	Lawley Street	Sheffield		2336

Below:- During a snow flurry in March 1984, Class 47 No. 47113 departs from the north of Washwood Heath "down" yard with 7T50, the morning trip freight to Bescot. The yard is full of oil tanks used to bring fuel oil to the nearby Bromford Bridge terminal and MGR wagons still used to carry coal from Warwickshire pits. On the left of the horizon, Washwood Heath No. 5 Signal Box can be seen next to the modern lighting mast, standing tall above the disused hump. (**M. Rhodes**)

Notes on Washwood Heath tables.

The sheer volume of freight traffic dealt with at Washwood Heath and neighbouring yards is quite staggering. On an average weekday in 1961 there were no fewer than 58 southbound departures and 36 northbound departures. As can be seen from the table for northbound traffic, there were a minimum of 15 mandatory paths every 24 hours for empty mineral wagons returning to the pits of Leicestershire, Derbyshire and Nottinghamshire. There were also six daily return pairs of trip freights linking Washwood Heath to the yards at Water Orton. The sidings at Water Orton handled quite a number of long distance freights themselves. Then of course there was the sundries traffic from Lawley Street Goods Depot and Sidings with eight express freights leaving northbound each evening - interestingly without headcodes in my copy of the 1961 working timetable.

Left:- Looking north, through the window of Washwood Heath No. 5 signal box, the remains of the 25 track "down" sorting sidings can be seen. By 1984 when this view was taken, the majority had been disconnected from the hump and the yard was mainly flat-shunted from the north end. (**M. Rhodes**)

Below:- This view is taken from the old hump crest in the "down" yard and shows Class 47 No. 47186 reversing into the sorting sidings with 6T78, an Ironbridge Power Station to Daw Mill empty MGR service. The train has run via Madeley Junction, Bescot and Sutton Park, arriving just

minutes earlier on the track to the right of the box. The empty wagons were deposited in the old sorting sidings where they waited overnight before heading with a new locomotive and crew to Daw Mill Colliery for reloading. During the late 1970s and early 1980s, several long distance MGR services failed to meet the aspiration of direct services from pithead to power station, instead taking much longer to complete the loop because of stabling in yards such as Washwood Heath, Toton and Barrow Hill. Gradually such inefficiencies were reduced and timetables introduced which avoided staging in yards as seen here. (**M. Rhodes**)

Left:- A busy scene at Bromsgrove in 1967 shows (from left to right), a pair of Class 37s awaiting banking duties, Class 25 No. D5183 with 7V23, the 1400 Washwood Heath to Stoke Gifford un-fitted freight, and Hymek No. D7048 with 4V40, the 0840 Washwood Heath to Cardiff express freight. Timekeeping was notoriously poor during the 1960s as this view shows with freights sitting beside each other when they should be nearly six hours apart! Washwood Heath continued to

dispatch a dozen or more freights each day down the Midland Main Line to Worcester, Gloucester, Bristol and Cardiff until 1968 when it became less crucial with the introduction of the National Freight Train Plan. (**A.A. Vickers - M. Rhodes collection**)

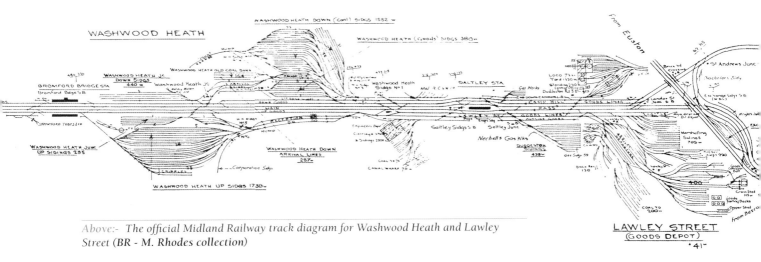

Above:- The official Midland Railway track diagram for Washwood Heath and Lawley Street (BR - M. Rhodes collection)

Above:- Class 60 No. 60049 passes Water Orton on 2 April 2012 with 6M11, the Washwood Heath to Peak Forest freight. The trees and industrial units behind the train occupy the site of the former Water Orton marshalling yard. (M. Rhodes)

Below:- The official Midland Railway track plan for the marshalling yard at Water Orton. (BR - M. Rhodes collection)

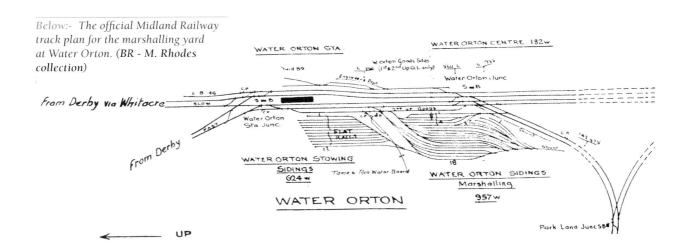

WATH YARD [10 11 12]

Opened: 1907
Closed: 1981–1986
Classification tracks: 2 x 30
Capacity in 24 hours: 5000 wagons

Inspired by a visit to Altoona on the Pennsylvania Railroad, the Great Central started construction of the UK's first purpose-built hump yard at Wath-upon-Dearne in 1905. The contract was awarded to Logan & Hemingway, who had successfully built the London Extension between Annesley and East Leake. The yard opened in 1907 and served 45 collieries in South Yorkshire. It dwarfed the other GC gravity yards at Worksop, Dunford Bridge, Annesley and Warsop in that it had 36 miles of track spread over two classification bowls, each containing 30 tracks. The sorting sidings as they were called in the UK, were unusual in that access to each siding was controlled by two signal boxes and compressed air operated points - the first "automated" hump yard in Britain! The potential capacity at Wath was 5000 wagons per 24 hours.

The sheer size of the new yard posed challenges in many areas. One was the need for a more powerful locomotive to propel long strings of coal wagons over the hump. John G Robinson, the Chief Mechanical Engineer of the GCR, rose to the challenge and designed his now fabled "Wath Daisies". These 3-cylinder, 0-8-4 tank locomotives were built by Beyer Peacock in Manchester and cost just £4,625 each. Sadly none have survived into preservation.

There is no doubt that Wath yard was a great success. With its electro-pneumatic point operation and the economies of scale, one might have thought that hump yards would have taken off in the UK, but they did not. The reasons for this are not immediately apparent. Between 1907 and 1948, hump yards and later automated hump yards sprung up all over Germany, France and the USA, but only three retarder yards were built in the UK at March Whitemoor, Toton "down" Yard (1939) and Hull Inward Yard. The largest of these projects, by far was at March Whitemoor. The "up" yard there, opened in 1929, employed German retarder technology invented by Dr. Frölich, and was by all accounts, extremely efficient. A train of 70 wagons could be shunted in 7 minutes and a record was set on 27th June 1930 when

69 trains made up of 3485 wagons, were handled in 24 hours over the single hump! But before considering March Whitemoor in more detail, why did so few automated yards get built in the UK in the first half of the 20th century?

The first obvious issue with the construction of an automated hump yard is land availability. In the USA, the population density was such that railroad yards were, and can still be built, with impunity. The population density of Germany is also far lower than England, but also the political systems running the country were different to those in the UK, both before the Great War and especially after. The Great War itself would have affected railway investment and building in the UK as compared to the USA and then the Great Depression might also have had an effect. Perhaps the invention of the Frölich "Gleisbremse" or rail brake by

Above:- *It's nearly all over for Wath Yard in this 1985 view as the sidings will close completely in less than 12 months time. Only 15 tracks are left in the eastbound sorting sidings and just half a dozen of those are needed for traffic. Class 20 Nos. 20167 & 20174 await departure with 6T36 to Tinsley. The consist includes 3 HEA hoppers from Manvers Coking Plant to Hull Sculcoates Coal Depot, a further eight hoppers bound for Preston Deepdale Coal Depot and then finally a single HAA hopper at the rear which is a cripple headed to Tinsley for repairs. The yard pilot is Class 08 No. 08782. (M. Rhodes)*

a German was a factor. It is certainly recorded that its use in the 1920s was "fashionable in Germany". It is also interesting that the first major automated hump yard was built in the East Anglian fens, where land is relatively cheap and population density low. Whatever the causes, freight yard development in the UK between 1907 and 1948 was considerably lagging behind the rest of the modern world. This fact is perhaps reflected in the strident tones of the 1955 Modernisation Plan and Dr. Beeching's `Re-shaping of Britain's Railways' plan, at the start of the 1960s. A nation in the thick of two world wars and a Great Depression, and with some of the most densely populated land in the world had been left behind.

Wath Yard meanwhile was a victim of both the collapse of the UK coal industry, but also most crucially, closure of the Woodhead route in July 1981. The yard itself made a sorry sight during its last 5 years and now is unrecognisable, covered with modern housing.

FIG. 23.—STATEMENT SHOWING NUMBER OF TRAINS AND NUMBER OF WAGONS LEAVING YARD A DURING MONTH OF JUNE 1907.

Date.		No. of Trains Leaving Yard.	No. of Wagons Attached in Yard.			Remarks.
			Loaded.	Empty.	Total.	
June 1	.. ..	95	3,608	1,267	4,875	
2	.. ..	82	3,555	1,104	4,659	
3	.. ..	52	2,365	620	2,985	Sunday
4	.. ..	61	2,073	859	2,932	
5	.. ..	86	2,837	1,377	4,114	
6	.. ..	98	3,768	1,260	5,028	
7	.. ..	102	3,994	1,215	5,209	
8	.. ..	102	3,790	1,308	5,098	
9	.. ..	97	3,892	1,139	5,031	
10	.. ..	47	2,287	472	2,759	Sunday
11	.. ..	60	1,977	887	2,864	
12	.. ..	91	3,002	1,231	4,233	
13	.. ..	95	3,424	1,197	4,621	
14	.. ..	102	3,923	1,448	5,371	
15	.. ..	100	3,925	1,385	5,310	
16	.. ..	95	3,962	1,261	5,223	
17	.. ..	46	2,236	623	2,859	Sunday
18	.. ..	57	1,861	786	2,647	
19	.. ..	85	3,011	1,031	4,042	
20	.. ..	103	3,430	1,391	4,821	
21	.. ..	102	3,897	1,280	5,177	
22	.. ..	102	3,944	1,158	5,102	
23	.. ..	95	3,784	1,245	5,029	
24	.. ..	46	2,155	586	2,741	Sunday
25	.. ..	58	2,023	914	2,937	
26	.. ..	94	3,201	1,187	4,388	
27	.. ..	102	3,616	1,378	4,994	
28	.. ..	97	3,721	1,243	4,964	
29	.. ..	102	3,674	1,460	5,134	
30	.. ..	93	3,480	1,236	4,716	
Total	..	2,547	96,415	33,448	129,863	

SUMMARY FIGURES OF A SPECIFIC MARSHALLING YARD.

Year.	Number of Wagons Entering Yard.		Yard Wages per Wagon Entering.	Pilot Working Average No. of Wagons Shunted per Hour.		Remarks.
	Total.	Per Engine Hour.	Pence.	Up Side.	Down Side.	
1912	671,198	28·57	0·71	42	57	National Strike of Miners, March
1913	764,735	28·35	0·71	43	59	
1914	724,653	27·23	0·83	41	55	
1915	699,590	25·41	0·95	37	53	War Period
1916	701,276	24·26	1·09	37	53	
1917	681,006	23·82	1·24	39	55	

Above:- Activity at Wath Yard during June in the first year of its operation.

Left:- Activity at Wath Yard during the First World War.

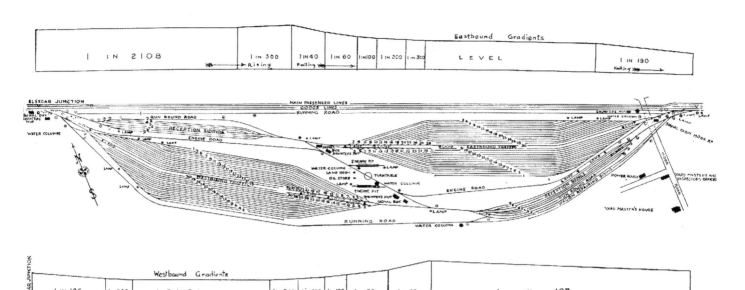

Above:- *Official GC plan of Wath Yard at the time of opening.* (**M. Rhodes collection**)

Below:- *The new diesel depot is seen at the centre of this 1968 image of the south-eastern half of Wath Yard. The top of the railway complex shows the eight reception tracks of the westbound yard. Below these are the 30 sorting sidings of the eastbound yard filled with 16-ton mineral wagons.* (**M. Rhodes collection**)

The morning mist is lifting over the eastbound classification tracks at Wath as Class 08 No. 08050 arrives "engine and van" from Manvers Coking Plant. Behind the shunter are Class 20 Nos. 20059 & 20005 which will depart east with a train of scrap bound for Tinsley. (*M. Rhodes*)

Below:- Class 76 Nos. 76029 and 76030 take the through lines at Elsecar Junction, at the north end of Wath Yard in April 1980. Their short train of "Covhops" is the 8E08 sand train from Wallercote to the glassworks at Rockware. The branch to the left, beyond the crossing is to Corton Wood Colliery whilst the tracks in the foreground are the westbound departure tracks from Wath Yard. (**M. Rhodes**)

Below:- Although the Woodhead route had been closed for nearly a year when this picture was taken in 1982, Wath Yard is still fairly busy and the signal box on the eastbound hump still operational. The box is located on the horizon above the 16th and 17th wagons on the 6T22, Wath to Hickleton MGR with Class 45 No. 45026 at the head of it. Class 31 No. 31220 shunts 8T61, the morning trip to Healey Mills in the foreground. (**M. Rhodes**)

MIDDLESBROUGH ERIMUS [13] [14] [15]

Opened: 1908
Closed: 1963
Classification tracks: 28 + 20 + 20
Capacity in 24 hours: 6000 wagons

In spite of the massive expansion in freight yards around the UK after the construction of the Edge Hill Gridiron, the majority were still flat-shunted. The "new" hump yard at Wath was regarded as revolutionary and the result of a visit by GC staff to the USA. Indeed some authors suggested that "hump shunting" was an American fad which was to be avoided at all costs. That said, it was recognised that hump and gradient shunting were quicker and more efficient than flat shunting, but with the disadvantage of damage to wagons and cargoes when wagons were not slowed down enough.

A review of the UK yards in 1914 reported that the only railways to embrace the new American-designed hump yard were the Great Central (GC) at Wath; the London North Western Railway (LNW) was said to have hump yards at several locations and certainly there were such yards at Wembley (Sudbury), Nuneaton "up" sidings and Northampton "down" sidings. The most hump yards were, however, on the North Eastern Railway. York Goods Yard (York North), two yards at Hull, two at Gascoigne Wood (minerals) and one at Stockton were all hump yards. In addition to this there was the famous hump yard at Shildon and no less than three manual hump yards at Middlesbrough Erimus.

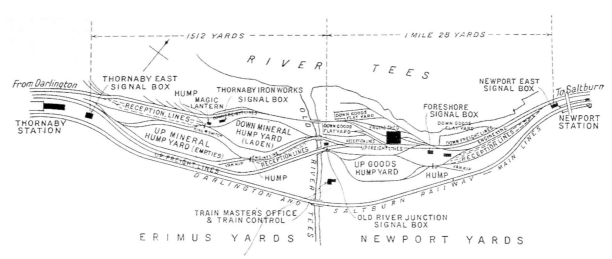

DIAGRAM OF ERIMUS AND NEWPORT YARDS, NORTH EASTERN RAILWAY.

Above:- A schematic diagram of the yards at Middlesbrough Erimus from 1914 clearly shows the three hump yards. It is noticeable how much shorter the trains were, allowing the "up" goods and "up" mineral hump yards to follow on from each other on the southern side of the complex where later just the "up" hump yard fitted.

Left:- Reproduced from the archives at Kew, this faded image gives an idea of the scale of the 28 sorting sidings in the "down" yard at Middlesbrough.

These were all "rider" humps, with the shunters chasing the wagons down the hump and applying the brakes manually. The largest of these was the "down" mineral hump yard with 8 reception sidings and 28 sorting sidings. This was of course the receiving yard for the large volumes of coal from the Durham Coalfield and Shildon Hump Yard. As the accompanying images show, the yards at Erimus were subsumed by the new double hump yard at Tees, parts of which still exist today.

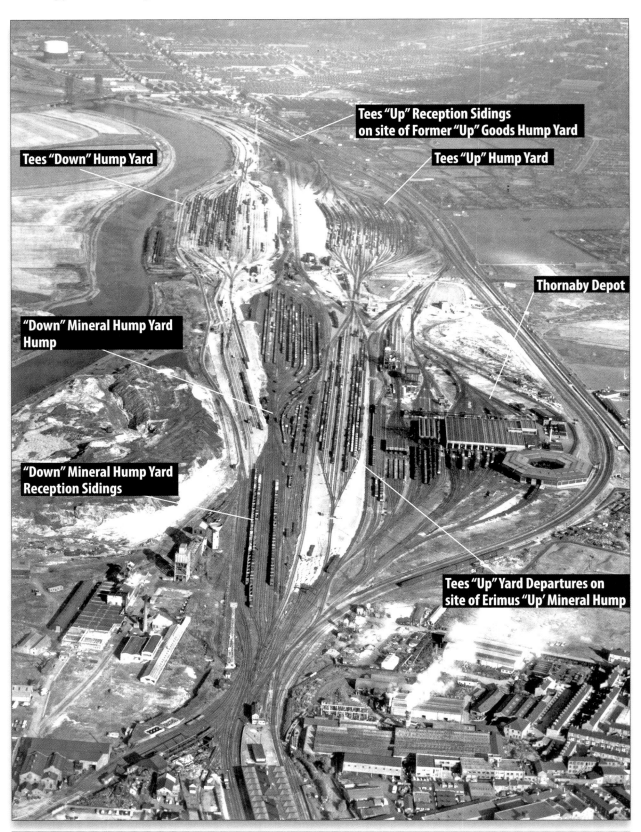

Tees "Up" Reception Sidings on site of Former "Up" Goods Hump Yard

Tees "Down" Hump Yard

Tees "Up" Hump Yard

"Down" Mineral Hump Yard Hump

Thornaby Depot

"Down" Mineral Hump Yard Reception Sidings

Tees "Up" Yard Departures on site of Erimus "Up' Mineral Hump

Above:- This wonderful aerial shot taken by BR (ER) in 1961 shows the new Tees yards taking shape, yet with significant remnants of the old Erimus "down" yard still in use. (BR ER - M. Rhodes collection)

FELTHAM YARD [16]

Opened: 1923
Closed as hump yard: 1969
Classification tracks: 14 + 17
Capacity in 24 hours: 3500 wagons

The London and South Western Railway started planning the yards at Feltham in 1919. Visits were made to notable yards in both Europe and the USA before the two hump yards were finally built. This seems unusual as the yard operated as a "rider" hump and did not have any retarders, even though retarders were in use in both Germany and the USA at this time. The yards at Feltham were provided to marshal all traffic from the London & South Western Railway to and from the metropolis and whilst normal operating through the 1920s and 1930s saw around 2500 wagons sorted daily, they had a capacity to handle as many as 3500 wagons in 24 hours.

One feature of the new yard was space to add extra tracks to both the reception sidings and the classification bowls, should traffic require it. This method of construction is well illustrated in the USA at yards like Selkirk, near Albany and Moorman Yard in Ohio, but was not a feature in any other yards built in the UK. The adjacent table lists all the sidings in the yard with sidings which might be added in the future also shown.

DOWN SIDE. Reception Roads.

No.	Length. Feet.	Wagon Capacity.	No.	Length. Feet.	Wagon Capacity.
1	Not yet provided.	—	6	1,125	56
2	Not yet provided.	—	7	1,056	52
3	1,205	60	8	1,211	60
4	1,169	58			—
5	1,090	54			340

Marshalling Sidings.

No.	Length. Feet.	Wagon Capacity.	Allocation.
1	1,564	78	Southampton Docks.
2	Not yet provided.		
3	1,435	71	Southampton Town.
4	1,435	71	Basingstoke.
5	1,448	72	Portsmouth via Eastleigh.
6	1,448	72	Eastleigh.
7	1,555	77	Dorset line.
8	1,555	77	Andover and Salisbury line.
9	1,639	82	Transfer wagons for Up side.
10	1,635	81	Wimbledon.
11	1,545	77	Chertsey to Surbiton.
12	1,545	77	Woking.
13	1,487	74	Guildford.
14	1,487	74	Reading.
15	1,435	71	Windsor and Reading line.
16	1,435	71	Twickenham, Richmond and Thames Valley.
17	1,435	71	Kingston.
18	Not yet provided.		
19	Not yet provided.		
20	1,435	71	Stock, wait orders and cripple traffic.
	1,267		

UP SIDE. Reception Roads.

No.	Length Feet.	Wagon Copacity.	No.	Length. Feet.	Wagon Capacity.
1	1,376	64	6	1,426	67
2	1,288	60	7	1,375	64
3	1,367	64	8	1,477	70
4	1,350	63			—
5	1,350	63			515

Marshalling Sidings.

No.	Length. Feet.	Wagon Capacity.	Allocation.
1			
2			
3	Not yet provided.		
4			
5	1,600	76	G.C.R.
6	1,600	76	Brentford to Point Pleasant.
7	1,495	70	Common users.
8	1,495	70	Common users.
9	1,725	82	N.L.R.
10	1,662	79	L. & N.W.R.
11	1,547	73	Hounslow.
12	1,493	70	Nine Elms loaded.
13	1,520	72	Nine Elms empties.
14	1,531	72	Nine Elms loaded.
15	1,542	73	G.N.R.
16	1,531	72	Midland Railway.
17	1,481	70	Transfer wagons to Down yard.
18	Not yet provided.		
19	1,331	62	Cripples, stock, &c.
	1,017		

Above:- The listing of the sidings at Feltham shows the destinations served from the yard and also highlights the capacity for extra sidings, should traffic levels increase. (**M. Rhodes collection**)

Table 2
West End Departures—Feltham Marshalling Yard

From 12.01 am to 11.59 pm 17th March 1924

Train		Load
1.45 am	Feltham to Twickenham.	49.
2.45 am	Feltham to Exeter.	61.
3.05 am	Feltham to Woking.	69.
3.50 am	Feltham to Eastleigh.	64.
4.15 am	Feltham to Reading.	44.
5.10 am	Feltham to Reading.	58.
5.40 am	Feltham to Southampton.	67.
6.05 am	Feltham to Windsor.	49.
8.00 am	Feltham to Feltham Station.	59.
9.30 am	Feltham to Woking.	62.
10.00 am	Feltham to Eastleigh.	69.
10.40 am	Feltham to Southampton.	69.
11.00 am	Feltham to Reading.	70.
12 noon	Feltham to Kingston.	45.
12.40 pm	Feltham to Alton.	50.
1.15 pm	Feltham to Staines.	46.
1.30 pm	Feltham to Twickenham.	40.
1.40 pm	Feltham to Southampton.	70.
2.20 pm	Feltham to Bracknell.	36.
3.10 pm	Feltham to Surbiton.	63.
5.40 pm	Feltham to Southampton.	70.
6.40 pm	Feltham to Eastleigh.	61.
7.00 pm	Feltham to Woking.	35.
8.00 pm	Feltham to Surbiton.	41.
9.00 pm	Feltham to Woking.	64.
9.25 pm	Feltham to Wimbledon.	50.
9.33 pm	Feltham to Kingston.	41.
10.25 pm	Feltham to Southampton.	63.
11.05 pm	Feltham to Wimbledon.	62.
11.50 pm	Feltham to Exeter	67.

| 50 trains | | Total | 1694 |

Average 56 wagons per train

Left:- The table on this page shows a typical day during the first full year of operation of Feltham "down" Yard. (**M. Rhodes collection**)

Below:- Wagons roll down the westbound hump in this undated official SR photograph. Interestingly by the time it was taken, all 20 tracks had been installed in the "down" sorting sidings. (**M. Rhodes collection**)

Left:- Like Wath, built nearly 20 years earlier, Feltham Yard benefitted from automatic points to the sorting sidings as seen here in the "down" hump tower. (**M. Rhodes collection**)

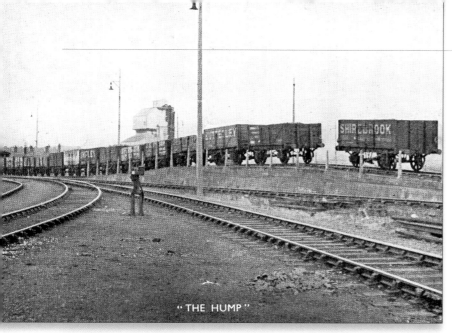

"THE HUMP"

Left:- It is noticeable how small the hump earthworks were at Feltham when compared to other yards built in the first part of the 20th century. Wooden bodied coal wagons roll westward with coal for the South and West. (M. Rhodes collection)

Below:- This view from the era of the airship, shows a steam locomotive on the "down" hump and the impressive locomotive depot at Feltham. (Aerofilms)

Down Marshalling Sidings

Down Hump

Feltham Engine Shed

Down Reception Sidings

Up Marshalling Sidings

Spare land for extra sidings

Right:- By the time this enigmatic view was taken at Feltham, the yard's days were numbered. It closed as a result of the National Freight Train Plan which concentrated London's wagonload traffic on Acton, Willesden and Temple Mills yards. (Paul Bartlett)

On 15 November 1967, Class 31 No. D5505 draws away from the "up" sorting sidings with a cross-London freight bound for Temple Mills. Next to it, an unidentified Class 33 has a Hoo Junction train behind it. (**Paul Bartlett**)

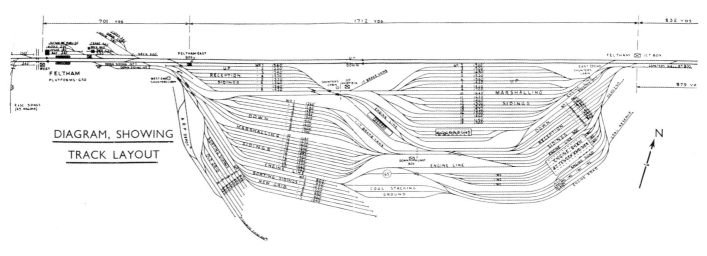

DIAGRAM, SHOWING
TRACK LAYOUT

Above:- The official LSWR plan of Feltham. (**M. Rhodes collection**)

Right:- This wonderful view of SR Urie 4-8-0 tank No. 30493 is clearly taken after nationalisation in 1948 and before this locomotive was withdrawn in December 1959. The locomotive is shunting at the west end of the "down" sorting sidings, putting together a departure for the Southampton direction. (*Ben Brooksbank*)

SEVERN TUNNEL JUNCTION YARD & WALES'S FORGOTTEN HUMP YARDS

SEVERN TUNNEL JUNCTION [17]

Opened: 1931
Closed as hump yard: 1978 & 1982
Classification tracks: 21 + 19
Capacity in 24 hours: 3000 wagons

Severn Tunnel was a favourite spot of mine in my youth; it was a great spot to watch trains and also the entry point for just about all long distance freight to South Wales and the South West. Because of this there was always "foreign" motive power to be found on the depot there. The yards on this site date back to the 1930s when a small "rider" hump was opened on the "up" side of the line. This was built as a result of a 1929 Act of Parliament which allowed the Great Western Railway the opportunity to remodel three of its most important yards at Banbury, Rogerstone and Severn Tunnel Junction. Prior to 1931, sidings at Severn Tunnel dealt with traffic from the Cardiff and Newport districts bound for London and the South West of England. Traffic from Bridgend and places further west was handled at Stoke Gifford Yard on the Bristol side of the tunnel. The expansion of 1931 increased the size of the yard and combined all traffic marshalling on one site. The accommodation increased from 1405 wagons to 2652, nearly doubling the yard's capacity.

It was however, as part of the Modernisation Plan, that significant changes were made to the yard in 1960 and 1962. This is when both the "up" and "down" humps were modernised. Neither received automated retarders and both were operated by the shunter running along with the wagon into the classification tracks and manually pinning down the brakes to slow the wagon down; sometimes riding

on the wagon, hence the term "rider" hump. The "up" yard had eleven reception sidings, known as Undy Yard which led over a hump to 21 sorting sidings. The "down" yard had seven reception roads, leading to 19 sorting sidings.

As the 1960s and 1970s progressed, more and more traffic was channelled through Severn Tunnel Junction and as the Speedlink network expanded, so just about every Speedlink service in the South West and South Wales was routed through the yard. In 1978, the "down" hump closed and the yard was shunted from the west end. The flat-shunted yard became the focus for Speedlink traffic, whilst the Undy Yard and "up" sorting sidings were still used for vacuum and un-braked rolling stock; mostly coal traffic. By 1983, all coal traffic was handled in air-braked wagons and the "up" hump also closed. The 1980s were busy for Severn Tunnel Junction. Records show that during a typical week in 1984, the yard received a total of 3494 air-braked wagons and dispatched a total of 3661 in a total of 529 trains. This made an amazing 100 freight departures per day, making Severn Tunnel Junction one of the busiest yards on the network. All was not well however. Speedlink was in decline and in 1986,

Right:- Class 60 No. 60033 passes Severn Tunnel Junction in 1996 with a Round Oak to Margam empty steel service. The former "up" and "down" sorting sidings lie to either side of the train. (M. Rhodes)

the South Wales Freight Plan was published. In this report it was suggested the Severn Tunnel yards closed completely and this took place in November 1987. Within 3 years the yards had gone from perhaps the busiest Speedlink location in the UK to total closure. I remember hearing news of the changes on Radio 4 and finding the news impossible to believe! The closure of course took place and in 2015 the yards are just derelict land under the approach to the second Severn Crossing.

Top & centre:- Back in June 1984, Class 47 No. 47066 leaves the "up" yard at Severn Tunnel with 6E92, the morning Speedlink service to Ripple Lane. Thirty one years later and the church and the old engine shed act as markers to orientate the 2015 scene. A Swansea to Paddington express passes a Birmingham to Cardiff service. The former railway cottages have now been painted white and sit amongst pleasant trees whilst the approach to the new Severn Crossing is seen in the left background, where once the shunting neck of the "down" sidings lay.

Right:- Interestingly, going back again to the 1980s, the third image, taken in May 1984, shows HST power car No. 43077 heading a Paddington to Swansea service - the HST a constant in a sea of change! To its right is Class 47 No. 47089 with a Llandarcy oil train, whilst Class 56 No. 56033 is in the background with the Robeston to Theale oil train, another service which still runs in 2016. (All M. Rhodes)

Right:- The 1985 image is taken from a lighting mast, level with the railway cottages but south of the main running lines. All the "down" sorting sidings are still in place, but the wagon repair building is long gone. The yard is shunted from the west end and the two yard pilots on 25 January 1985 are Nos. 08354 & 08760. Class 37 No. 37298 is just arriving with a train from the Cardiff direction. **(M. Rhodes)**

Above:- By 1996, when Class 158 No. 158865 is seen passing on a Cardiff to Portsmouth Harbour service, all the tracks have gone. Taken from the road works that became the new M4, the church and railway cottages help to orientate the viewer. Above the multiple unit is the ground where the "down" sorting sidings used to be, whilst the left half of the image shows the waste ground formerly occupied by the "up" sorting sidings. **(M. Rhodes)**

Three images of the modernised "up" hump taken in 1962. The expansion at Severn Tunnel added 12 reception sidings to the "up" yard and a new hump control tower with electric switches to control the points to the sorting sidings. Even so as the lower two images on this page show, the hump was manually operated with shunters controlling the separation and the speed of wagons being sorted. (All BR WR – M. Rhodes collection)

Right:- This Western Region publicity shot shows the eight new arrival lines constructed in 1961 as part of the modernisation upgrade of the yards. Two steam hauled freights are about to cross on the main line and the steam shed in the background is still busy. (BR WR – M. Rhodes collection)

Below:- Notes at the time suggested that building a hump yard at Severn Tunnel would have been prohibitively expensive so the GWR opted for "up" and "down" yards with three reception tracks each. Both were shunted on the "pull back" principle as can be seen from this plan. At this stage the yard was flat-shunted and it was not until the rebuilding of the 1960s that humps were introduced. (M. Rhodes collection)

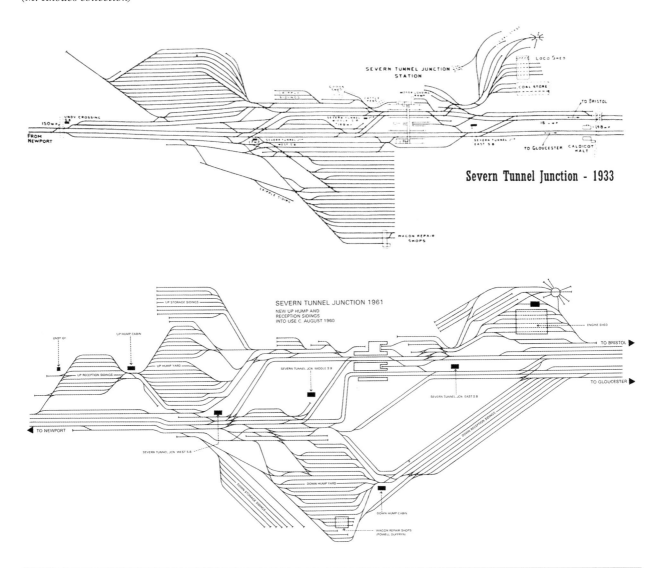

Severn Tunnel Junction - 1933

SEVERN TUNNEL JUNCTION 1961
NEW UP HUMP AND
RECEPTION SIDINGS
INTO USE C. AUGUST 1960

Above:- The 1960s rebuild introduced two new humps and 11 "up" reception sidings as compared to 8 on the "down" side. This plan was drawn for my 1988 book about British yards by a retired Ordnance Survey draftsman. (M. Rhodes)

Left:- By December 1982, when this image was taken, the "up" hump had ceased to operate at Severn Tunnel, but the "up" reception sidings, or Undy yard as it was known, provided the ideal yard for Speedlink traffic. Looking east, the 12 lengthy tracks are shown here. Class 47 No. 47088 has just arrived with 8V37, a Temple Mills to Severn Tunnel freight, whilst Class 46 No. 46045 stands with 6V47, the afternoon arrival from Toton. (**M. Rhodes**)

Right & below:- Taken from similar perspectives these two images show the eastern end of the "up" sorting sidings. In 1962 the yards are full of low capacity coal and general merchandise wagons. By 1985, the fall in traffic is quite stark. Class 47 No 47202 is about to depart with 6E91, the daily Severn Tunnel to Dagenham Dock Speedlink train. Class 08 No. 08848 is the yard pilot. The boarded up windows of the "up" hump tower can be seen in the distance. (**M. Rhodes**)

Right:- This splendid panorama of the "down" hump shows the 19 sorting sidings to good effect. The wagon repair shops are on the left of the yard beyond the bridge whilst the "up" yards can just be seen on the right of the image stretching away to the horizon. *(BR WR – M. Rhodes collection)*

Below:- Taken from the "down" hump, this 1962 publicity picture shows the sorting sidings. As a nice touch the four shunters (or chasers as they were called in the USA) pose with their

shunting poles (used to apply a wagon's brakes). *(BR WR – M. Rhodes collection)*

Right:- Taken in 1978, this is my only image of hump shunting at Severn Tunnel Junction. At the time, there was no inkling that this timeless scene would change so quickly and so completely. The hump closed just months after this image was taken and now the whole area is filled with large birch trees and it is almost impossible to imagine there was ever a railway here. *(M. Rhodes)*

Severn Tunnel Junction 47s

Right:- In January 1982, Class 47 No. 47264 arrives at Severn Tunnel Junction with 7V61, a Bescot to Severn Tunnel mixed freight. The recently closed "down" hump tower is seen behind the train as are the now empty and abandoned "down" reception sidings. (**M. Rhodes**)

Left:- By the summer of 1983, Speedlink traffic was handled mainly in the Undy Yard where Class 47 No. 47090 has just arrived with 7V97, the daily Eastleigh to Severn Tunnel Junction Speedlink service. The 1960-constructed arrivals cabin is just to the left of the locomotive and still in use for train crew and staff in 1983. (**M. Rhodes**)

Right:- The morning was always relatively quiet at Severn Tunnel Junction. Most departures were in the afternoon and evening. There were however, a couple of long distance services scheduled to leave in the morning, including the 6A27 Speedlink to Acton Yard seen here leaving the "up" yard behind Class 47 No. 47358. (**M. Rhodes**)

Wales's Forgotten Hump Yards

Four smaller hump yards in South Wales which are rarely mentioned and which escape most articles are those at Llandeilo Junction, Swansea Burrows, Rogerstone and Pontypool Road. All four dealt mainly with coal traffic and had manual "rider" humps where shunters rode on the wagons, using their shunting poles to slow wagons down as they rolled into the sorting sidings.

Pontypool Road

The yard at Pontypool Road lay south of Pontypool Road station, filling much of the land between there and Panteg Steelworks. In 1960 the sidings here numbered a total of 52 with a fan of 10 sidings called Coedygric and New Sidings, hump shunted from the south. In 1964, when the Vale of Neath Line closed, much of the strategic importance of the yards was lost and when the engine shed closed in 1965 the die was cast. Sidings remained to handle local coal and steel traffic until closure of Hafodyrynys Colliery in 1979. There is now no sign of the yards as the picture taken looking south from Pontypool Road in 1982 shows.

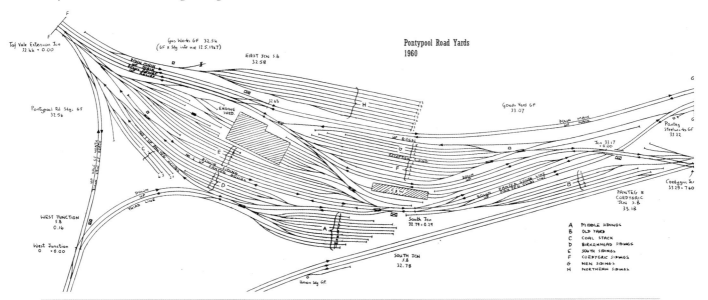

Above:- The yards at Pontypool Road are shown at their most extensive in this 1960 plan drawn by R A Cooke in his excellent series of books of Great Western Railway plans. (**R.A. Cooke**)

Above:- By 1982, the land formerly occupied by the sidings was a new bypass. Looking south, Class 37 No. 37294 rounds the curve from Panteg with 6Z81, an extra steel train from Llanwern to Dee Marsh. The road curving to the right is along the alignment of the Taff Vale extension and the whole triangle of flat land was once filled with the 50 sidings that made up Pontypool Road Yard. (**M. Rhodes**)

Rogerstone

Rogerstone Yard, mentioned here but with a section dedicated to it on page 101, lay north of Newport at the entrance to the Western Valleys, and was also a yard that handled mainly coal traffic. In 1931 the Great Western opened a new 18 track "down" hump yard. This was in addition to 28 "up" sidings arranged with 9 reception roads and 19 dead end sorting sidings, shunted from the north end. Changes here have been just as drastic with the "down" hump yard closed in 1968 and the "up" sidings taken out of use in 1977. Now a single track is all that remains of this once vast yard.

Llandeilo Junction

The third of the yards in South Wales was the hump yard at Llandeilo Junction, east of Llanelli. The hump yard was opened in 1961 and taken out of use in 1982. As can be seen from the 1982 image at the bottom of this page, the yard remained busy with coal and general traffic well into the 1980s. In addition to the hump yard, the sidings between Llanelli and Trostre Steelworks numbered an additional 40 or so tracks in yards situated east from the 1961 hump yard.

*Above:- In June 1982 the yard pilot at Llandeilo Junction was Class 03 No. 03151 which is seen here shunting wagons for the thrice weekly trip to Llandovery. This carried household coal but also MOD supplies for the army ranges near Llandovery. (**M. Rhodes**)*

*Above:- Llandeilo Junction Yard in 1982 showing the derelict hump in the background, above the second and third carriage of the Swansea to Milford Haven passenger service. The 17 sorting sidings were shunted from the east via a single "pull back" track. Class 33 No. 33026 is on the Milford Haven passenger whilst Class 37 No. 37235 waits to enter the yard with the afternoon trip from Cynheidre Colliery. Behind this Class 46 No. 46004 is leaving the yard with the 1350 Llandeilo Junction to Severn Tunnel Junction freight. (**M. Rhodes**)*

Swansea Burrows and Jersey Marine

The final, and much neglected hump yard was at Swansea Burrows[18] (sometimes called Jersey Marine). There is however, historical confusion, as it seems there were two hump yards in the area. But to start at the beginning, the 1931 Great Western project in the area led to the diversion of main line passenger services to Swansea, via Neath, freeing up the land around Jersey Marine for redevelopment as a series of yards for coal export traffic. In addition to this the opportunity was taken to expand the "up" hump sorting sidings at Jersey Marine on the north side of the Vale of Neath Line.

The second hump yard was built in 1931, along with the modernised yards at Severn Tunnel, Banbury and Rogerstone. It was situated on the site of the abandoned Jersey Marine passenger station and contained six reception sidings and 16 sorting sidings. These were unusually named "riddling" sidings and were used to sort coal into its different grades. Once sorted, trainloads were drawn forward to four sets of storage sidings. These were needed because once sorted it was often several days before a consignment of coal was loaded onto a ship and exported. The four sets of sidings contained 11, 13, 15 and 10 tracks respectively. It was the final ten tracks that formed the Swansea Burrows Yard, still in use in 2016. There were six adjacent tracks leading back towards the site of the former Danygraig locomotive depot which also had traffic until the late 1990s. The former Danygraig Freightliner depot, visible in the iimage below, was built on the site of the former sorting or riddling sidings.

Below:- Looking east from the "Jersey Marine", this view shows Swansea Burrows Yard in 1983. Class 08 Nos. 08662, 08400, 08592 and 08660 are stabled for the weekend. Above them are the most westerly of the storage sidings. These 15 roads have become the main yard by this time. Above the final shunting engine is the crane at Danygraig Freightliner depot, situated on the ground formerly occupied by the sorting sidings of the 1931-built hump yard. On the right of the image are a further 6 sorting sidings and behind them the distinctive arches of the former locomotive depot help to orientate the viewer. (**M. Rhodes**)

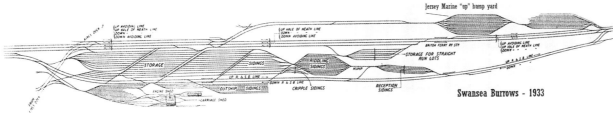

Above:- The extensive yards at Swansea Burrows are shown - the extensions of 1931 expanded their capacity to nearly 3000 wagons (from 1188, a 60% increase). These figures didn't include the capacity already available in the Jersey Marine "up" hump yard at the top of the diagram. (**M. Rhodes collection**)

Left:- This was difficult to find but in 1983 I managed to locate the site of the old "up" hump yard built by the Great Western early in the 20th century. Class 37 No. 37301 is leaving the old sorting sidings (which can be seen once stretched to almost 20 roads), with a Margam to Onllwyn coal train. (**M. Rhodes**)

Left:- In November 1993, the "Jersey Marine" sidings have been rationalised and the signal box has been demolished. Class 08 No. 08790 winds out of the yard with coal from Coedbach, for export to Ireland. The 15 storage sidings are intact but the additional 6 sidings seen in 1983 have gone. Danygraig locomotive depot is still there with blue doors on the distinctive entrances. (**M. Rhodes**)

Right:- By 2015 the view from the "Jersey Marine" is partially obscured by vegetation as the yards at Swansea Burrows do indeed change from "Gridirons to Grassland". Class 66 No. 66084 runs round an empty coal train from Aberthaw Power Station to Onllwyn. The white cabin is approximately where the signal box used to sit, but most of the yard is obscured by trees. (**M. Rhodes**)

ROGERSTONE [19 20 21]

Opened: 1931
Closed: 1968
Classification tracks: 18
Capacity in 24 hours: 1500 wagons

The hump yard at Rogerstone was constructed as a result of tremendous pressure on the existing sidings and thanks to the 1929 Development (Loans Guarantees and Grants) Act. The GWR took full advantage of the Act which was designed to give grants of up to £25 million for public works schemes which would reduce unemployment during the industrial depression. The company submitted 35 schemes worth a total of £8 million, one of which was the construction of a new hump yard at Rogerstone. Railways had come to the Western Valleys as early as 1805 with the Sirhowy Tramroad and by the start of the 20th century rail traffic was booming, thanks mainly to the worldwide demand for Welsh steam coal. In 1900 the railway at the lower end of the Western Valley was widened to four tracks and by the 1920s the facilities at Rogerstone were overwhelmed by the volume of traffic, leading to lengthy delays.

The new hump yard had two reception sidings, each capable of holding 75 coal wagons. The hump, which was ten feet above the sorting sidings, was controlled by a new Hump Signal Box with electrically-operated points leading to the 18 sorting sidings. Total capacity of the sorting sidings was 1120 wagons. The siding allocation in 1931, when the yard opened, is shown in the table on the right alongside the revised allocation around 1960.

Electric floodlighting was also installed and in the 1930s there were four pilot engines permanently on duty around the yards at Rogerstone. The hump pilot (Target R4) worked from 1200 for two shifts until 0400 the next day to cater for the arrival of colliery traffic from up the valley. At the end of this shift, there was time for the engine to return south to Ebbw Junction shed for servicing and a crew change. The hump dealt with a train in an average of 13 minutes with an average of 14 cuts of wagons for each arrival. As well as the four pilot engines allocated to the yard, there were a further 22 "Targets" or trip workings based at Rogerstone, numbered from R6 to R28, serving the Western Valley, Ebbw Vale, the Penar Branch, Abertillery, Aberbeeg, Quakers Yard and finally twice each day to Barry.

Siding	Holding capacity of Siding	Allocation 1931	Allocation 1960
No.1	50	Bristol	Miscellaneous
No.2	58	Reading, Slough, Southall, and Old Oak Common	Swansea & West
No.3	60	To be utilised for train formation	Margam
No.4	67	Taunton and below	Gloucester
No.5	74	Severn Tunnel Junction and Westbury	Yeovil or Honeybourne
No.6	64	East Usk, Lydney, and Gloucester	Taunton and below
No.7	64	Bordesley	Bristol
No.8	81	Swindon	ER via Woodford
No.9	76	Rogerstone	Old Oak Common
No.10	73	Newport	Newport
No.11	69	Alexandra Docks	Penarth & Barry
No.12	72	Cardiff and District	Cardiff and District
No.13	72	Cardiff Docks	Cardiff Docks
No.14	68	Penarth	Severn Tunnel Junction
No.15	76	Barry Dock	East Usk Junction
No.16	76	Barry and District	Uskmouth
No.17	10	Brake Vans and Engines	Brake Vans and Engines
No.18	10	Brake Vans and Engines	Brake Vans and Engines

North of the yard, the CEGB built Rogerstone Power Station in 1954, a big consumer of local coal. There was also the local Alcan aluminium works which survived until the early 1970s, but traffic declined rapidly at Rogerstone in the 1960s. By 1968, when the hump yard closed, most coal was marshalled at Severn Tunnel Junction. The "up" sidings, pointing up the valley, continued in use until 1977 but these too were closed and lifted by 1981 when the Western Valley main line was realigned to its current position. The last tracks to be lifted in 1984 were those at Rogerstone Power Station. The whole area is unrecognisable today with the A467 dual carriageway passing through where once the main line used to lie.

Left:- Class 14 No. D9519 has just arrived in No.1 reception road with a short train from the valleys. This image is taken in 1967, from the cab of the Class 08 on hump duty. To the left of the Class 14 are the freight running lines and the points that allow access to Rogerstone Power Station. To the right are the main passenger running lines. The link to the power station was opened in 1955 and was only disconnected in 1984 when the power station closed. The cooling towers were demolished in 1991 and there are now houses on part of the land formerly occupied by the building. (**Malcolm James**)

Right:- In September 1963, GW 2-8-2 tank No. 4254 leaves Rogerstone "up" yard heading north to Marine Colliery with a rake of empty wagons. The steam from the loco is obscuring the large lighting gantry to the south of the hump. The hump pilot is Class 08 No. 4195. Behind the Class 08 is the Hump Signal Box whilst to the right of the departing freight is Rogerstone Middle Signal Box. (**Malcolm James**)

Left:- The hump at Rogerstone is shown here, before the introduction of diesel shunters in the early 1960s. The "Target R4" pilot is a pannier tank. The eastern half of the sorting sidings is seen beyond the locomotive. (**Malcolm James**)

Left:- By 1982 when this picture was taken, the former four-track main line up the Western Valleys had been reduced to a single track. The only sidings left intact at Rogerstone were those to the power station. Here Class 37 No. 37254 heads south with 6A93, an empty steel train from Waunllwyd to Severn Tunnel Junction on 23 June 1982. (**M. Rhodes**)

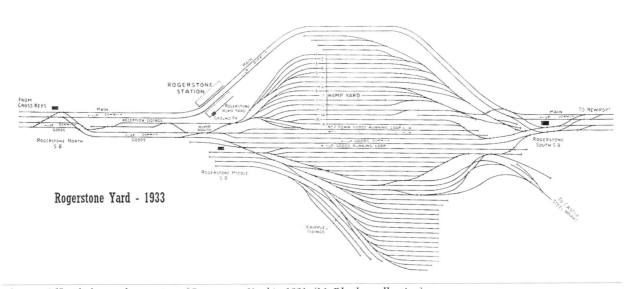

Rogerstone Yard - 1933

Above:- Official plan at the opening of Rogerstone Yard in 1931. (**M. Rhodes collection**)

Left:- Trains from Severn Tunnel Junction did bring "foreign" motive power to Rogerstone and Westerns, Warships and Hymeks were all sighted there, as well as locomotives from further afield. Often arrivals from Toton and Tinsley would deposit their engines on shed at Severn Tunnel where the duty foreman might allocate them to a quick run to Rogerstone and back before they returned north later in the day. Here, on 20 January 1968, Warship No. D826 "JUPITER" arrives from Severn Tunnel with a Saturday "extra" freight which as well as empty coal wagons has open wagons carrying pit props and some general goods in 11-ton vanfits. (**Malcolm James**)

Above:- *This view, taken in May 1971 well illustrates the land occupied by the 18 sorting sidings. The station at Rogerstone had closed in April 1962 when passenger traffic was withdrawn from the Western Valleys. The yard then closed in 1968 and as can be seen all track had been removed by 1971. To the right of the picture is Rogerstone Middle Signal Box and behind it, the "up" sidings, which remained in use until 1978.* (**Malcolm James**)

Above:- *This view taken in the 1980s shows Class 37 No. 37702 heading past the old Rogerstone Yard with steel coil from Llanwern to Ebbw Vale. The area of the sorting sidings to the right of the train is well seen as woodland whilst the site of the former"up" yard is filled with the A467 dual carriageway. Even in 2016, the shape of the former "down" sorting sidings is clearly seen on Google Earth, mostly still covered in trees.* (**Malcolm James**)

BANBURY [22]

Opened: 1933
Closed as hump yard: Early 1970s
Classification tracks: 19
Capacity in 24 hours: 1500 wagons

A new hump yard in Banbury was part of the Great Western Railway's strategy to handle interchange traffic with the LNER via Woodford Halse. The yard, north of Banbury station, had four reception sidings and 19 sorting sidings. It increased the standing capacity for wagons in the yards at Banbury from 500 to 1600. It is interesting in that it was a "chaser" hump but had partial automation of the points to the sorting sidings with electrical plungers fitted along a guide rail along the western and eastern perimeters of the sorting sidings. This unusual way of changing points seems to have been a cheaper solution than the electromechanical signal box installed at Rogerstone at the same time, but nonetheless provided some automation as compared to hand-pulled points. Electric lighting was provided for 24-hour operation and in 1966 the hump yard handled 3774 wagons in the trial

week. The "down" sidings, which were flat-shunted, handled almost as many wagons at 3112, making a total weekly throughput at Banbury of 6886 wagons.

As elsewhere, wagonload traffic fell drastically as our 1969 image overleaf shows, with the sidings virtually empty and nothing in the receiving tracks. The hump closed in the early 1970s and by 1980 the yard was shunted from the south end. It remained busy with Speedlink traffic and boasted two afternoon departures to Bescot in 1982 as well as several trip freights to local sidings. With the collapse of Speedlink in 1990, the yard fell into relative disuse with just a few engineers' wagons using what remained of the sorting sidings. In 2015 the entire yard area is covered with new housing and you would never know there was once a hump yard on the site.

Left:- A Great Western publicity shot taken in 1933 shows the hump area at Banbury. The novel yardside point switches are clearly seen. **(M. Rhodes collection)**

Below:- The hump yard north of Banbury station was strategically located to capture traffic from both the LMS and the LNER as can be seen by this track diagram from 1933. **(M. Rhodes collection)**

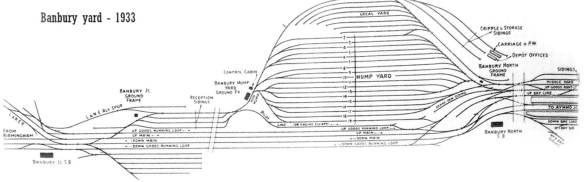

Banbury yard - 1933

Above:- *When this picture was taken in 1982 there was discussion as to whether the yard at Banbury might be reduced to three tracks from the ten seen here. The yard pilot, Class 08 No. 08740 shunts wagons for 9T36, the afternoon trip to Bescot, which will be taken north by Class 20 Nos. 20077 & 20157 seen to the left of the yard. Class 45 No. 45068 is at the head of VDA vans from Fenny Compton and Kineton MOD depot which will depart as 6G55, the evening Speedlink to Bescot. The yard is full of air-braked vans reflecting the high volume of MOD traffic handled here but there are also a couple of fertilizer wagons in the centre of the view, destined for Akeman Street depot, as well as numerous unfitted engineers' vehicles.* (**M. Rhodes**)

Right:- *With the newly modernised Banbury station in the foreground, this 1969 view gives a good impression of the sorting sidings at Banbury towards the end of their life as a hump yard.* (**M. Rhodes collection**)

MOTTRAM [23 24 25]

Opened: 1935
Closed as gravity yard: 1971
Classification tracks: 20
Capacity in 24 hours: 2100–3000 wagons

The Great Central Woodhead Route was a key freight artery linking Yorkshire to Lancashire and Cheshire which closed in July 1981. In the 19th century the main sidings at the western end of the line were to the east of Guide Bridge at Dewsnap. By 1900 there were 3 reception roads and 57 single-ended sorting sidings with capacity to hold just over 2400 wagons. The yard operated by gravity assistance in that wagons pushed into the single-ended sorting sidings rolled down a falling grade of 1 in 77 and were retarded by shunters chasing after them (sometimes called "chasers"). All points within the yard were hand points and without a tannoy system the sidings into which wagons were to be sorted were indicated by hand signals and whistle codes. The yard was inefficient and inadequate for the amount of freight traffic passing along the Woodhead Route in the early 20th century. It was because of this that, between 1900 and 1902, a gravity yard with four reception sidings and 16 sorting sidings was built high in the Pennines at Dunford Bridge. This marshalled only eastbound traffic and eased the pressure on the Dewsnap sidings. With a fall in wagonload traffic, the yard at Dunford Bridge fell into disuse during the 1960s but Dewsnap remained busy, handling 5701 wagons during the week of the 1966 marshalling yard survey.

Just as the yard at Dunford Bridge had eased pressure on eastbound or "up" traffic in 1902, so the new yard at Mottram, opened by the LNER in 1935, took the pressure off the sidings at Dewsnap and Godley Junction by handling the majority of long distance westbound traffic. Eight reception sidings, each holding 80 wagons were built on a continuously falling grade of 1 in 85. These led to 20 sorting sidings, each with the capacity to hold 65 wagons. No hump was built, but the falling grade from the reception sidings meant the yard was "gravity" shunted with shunters chasing the wagons as no retarders were installed either. Indeed there was a short section of track between the reception yard and the sorting sidings which fell abruptly at 1 in 30 and speeded up wagons as they moved in a westerly direction to the sorting sidings.

The yard was equipped with a signal tower controlling all points in the yard via an electro-pneumatic system. Modern electric lighting was installed as well as a system of loudspeakers which allowed the shunter at the top of the 1 in 30 gradient into the sorting sidings to tell the hump tower which siding the wagons were headed for. Then in 1951 the yard was electrified, along with the Woodhead Route from Manchester to Wath, Tinsley and Rotherwood. The yard handled 1000 wagons per shift if these were all unfitted, but the throughput decreased to 700 per shift if vacuum-braked wagons were sorted. The reason for this drop in productivity was because of the need to manually detach the vacuum pipes on fitted wagons and then reconnect them once a completed train was ready for departure.

The 1962 timetable shows over 150 arrivals and departures from Mottram Yard each 24 hours, reflecting its key role on the Woodhead Route[26]. By 1966, the weekly wagon throughput was still 7974, but the dramatic collapse of wagonload freight in the late 1960s led to the cessation of marshalling at the end of 1971 when the sorting sidings were effectively closed. The eight reception sidings continued to be used for stabling and re-crewing MGR coal trains until 1980 when they too became redundant. In 2016 just waste land and trees fill the cutting so expensively excavated for the yard back in 1935.

Above:- In the summer of 1971, the sidings at Mottram are still busy. Road four contains a rake of HAA MGR hoppers which were to take over power station traffic to the newly opened Fiddlers Ferry Power Station near Warrington. Quite a contrast with the black and white view from the same position, taken just months later. (**Ivan Stewart collection**)

Above:- By 1972 the 20 sorting sidings are disused and await the cutter's torch. The main Woodhead Route is seen above the yard and to the right whilst the signal tower is still operational, controlling access to and from the reception sidings which are behind the photographer. (**Ivan Stewart collection**)

Opposite:- By 1976, the majority of coal crossing the Pennines was hauled in MGR wagons and bound for Fiddlers Ferry. Traction from Wath or Rotherwood was usually behind a pair of Class 76 electric locomotives and the old reception sidings at Mottram were used to change engines to diesel traction in the form of Class 47s. Class 47 No. 47342 is seen leaving the reception sidings in 1976 with a Fiddlers Ferry bound MGR. By 1980 the exchange of motive power and crews took place at Godley Junction, a couple of miles west of here. (**Tom Heavyside**)

A Brief Summary of Other Selected Major Hump Yards

It has not been possible to mention every manual hump yard in the UK in detail, but the 1967 report on marshalling yard activity, discussed in Chapter 2, does mention all major yards, both hump and flat-shunted. Some yards, like the sidings at Chaddesden, north of Derby, are places of mystery from where almost no photographs exist, whilst others like the yards at Doncaster became strategically more important in the 1980s and 1990s as freight traffic patterns changed to first Speedlink wagonload trains and then block load freights. For others like Barrow Hill "up", Worksop "up" and Jersey Marine, pictures of the hump shunting there are almost non-existent.

Barrow Hill "up" yard was hump shunted from the west end. Three reception sidings lay alongside the main line and each had the capacity to hold 70 wagons. Arrivals were drawn westward into a head shunt and could be sorted into a total of 12 sidings, 5 double-ended and 7 dead-ended. There was one additional siding for cripples on the southern edge of the yard. The sorting sidings had the capacity to hold 610 wagons and in 1966 the yard marshalled 4593 wagons in the sample week. Barrow Hill also included the Summit Sidings which handled 2437 wagons, Seymour Junction handling 3286 wagons, Old Yard handling 2115 wagons and the "down" sidings, 12 in number and with a capacity for 800 wagons and handling 4742 wagons in a week. Thus the sidings in and around Barrow Hill were some of the busiest in the UK handling a total of 17173 wagons in the 1966 survey.

Worksop "up" yard was a gravitation yard, built on a falling grade. Three "up" reception sidings parallel to the main line and the sorting sidings were shunted by pulling wagons back in an easterly direction into a loop between the yard and Worksop station. Traffic could then be shunted on a falling gradient into 16 sorting sidings which survived well into the 1980s. Back in 1966 the sidings here handled 5527 wagons in a week as compared to 2965 dealt with in the flat-shunted "down" yard on the other side of the main line.

Of course everywhere had a freight yard and according to the 1966 survey there were 20 mechanised hump yards, all covered in detail in this book. On top of that there were 32 non-mechanised hump yards, most of which have been detailed in this chapter along with a summary of the major flat-shunted yards which follows this section.

*Above:- Taken in 1990, this view is from the top of the lighting mast which stood over the entrance to the sorting sidings at Barrow Hill "up" hump yard. The hump was behind the photographer and had been flattened by this stage. On the left there are three rakes of HAA MGR hoppers filling the three reception sidings. Directly ahead, four of the five through sorting sidings are similarly filled with HAA hoppers. All seven single-ended sorting sidings as well as the extra track for crippled wagons are still intact on the right of the picture. Two of the tracks have been re-ballasted to allow access to the Dixons coal disposal point from where coal from smaller collieries was collected and loaded onto rail. (**M. Rhodes**)*

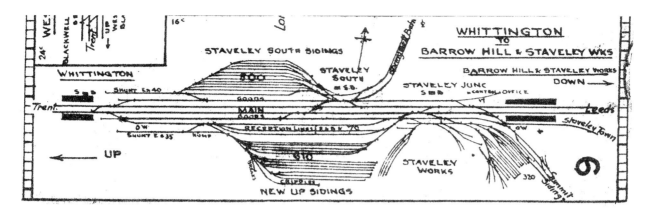

Above:- An official Midland Railway track diagram shows the extensive sidings at Barrow Hill. The layout here remained essentially unchanged until resignalling in 1981.

Below:- All 16 sorting sidings at Worksop "up" yard were still in use in 1986 and indeed were quite busy. The falling gradient into the yard which allowed gravity assisted shunting can just be discerned in this image, taken looking west from the shunting neck. On the left is the yard pilot, Class 08 No. 08824. Next stands Class 56 No. 56087 at the head of 6D66, a loaded MGR from Worksop Yard to Scunthorpe, carrying coal from Dinnington Colliery bound for the Scunthorpe Steelworks Coal Handling Plant. Then comes Class 37 No. 37120 at the head of 9T84, a ballast working from Beighton Sidings, bound for Cottam Power Station. Finally Class 20 Nos. 20098 & 20015 are at the head of a short rake of MGR wagons which will be tripped to Doncaster as the 6T13 working. **(M. Rhodes)**

CHADDESDEN

Chaddesden Sidings, north of Derby, had been designated as the site for a new mechanised hump yard in the original 1955 Modernisation Plan. Here, on the northern avoiding line for Derby, there had been a manual hump of considerable size and importance. Nine reception sidings, with a capacity for 640 wagons led over the hump to 30 sorting sidings which could hold 1760 wagons. There were then seven departure tracks to the east. In addition, the "up" side had an extra eleven short sidings for secondary marshalling which could hold 220 wagons.

On the south side of the line, the "down" sidings were made up of 13 single-ended sorting sidings which held 507 wagons and then 10 long sidings in the storage yard with the capacity to accommodate 980 wagons. In the 1966 yard survey Chaddesden marshalled 8444 wagons in the sample week. It continue to be used during the 1970s, mainly for engineering traffic, but fell into disuse in the 1980s. In 2016, the site of the former sorting sidings has been revitalised as a virtual quarry and sees daily freight trains carrying ballast for the railway.

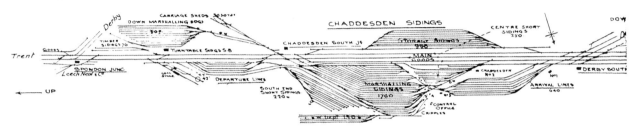

Above:- At one stage during the 1955 Modernisation Plan, it had been envisaged that there would be a new mechanised hump yard at Chaddesden. The extensive sidings and the manual hump yard are well displayed in the official Midland Railway track plan.

Above:- The land formerly occupied by Chaddesden yards is still partly utilised because a virtual quarry has been set up on much of the railway land formerly covered by sidings. Class 56 No. 56312 arrives at the sidings in June 2014 with 6Z56, an empty ballast service from Willesden Brent Yard. (**Paul Robertson**)

DONCASTER

The yards at Doncaster were never considered for mechanisation during the Modernisation of British Railways report which in some ways is quite surprising. The town boasted two hump yards. On the "up" side was Doncaster Bank Yard with six reception sidings leading over a manual hump to 18 sorting sidings. On the "down" side was Doncaster Belmont Yard with four reception roads leading over the hump to 25 sorting sidings. During the 1966 national marshalling yard survey Doncaster Bank handled 5239 wagons as compared to 2901 in Doncaster Belmont Yard. There were also flat yards at Doncaster Decoy and Hexthorpe with a further 60 plus sidings, used mainly for coal traffic.

Rationalisation started in the 1970s with the closure of Bank Yard and the gradual contraction of Hexthorpe Yards (which were used for a time as an electrification depot when the ECML was electrified). The area formerly occupied by Bank Yard is now covered in silver birch trees which fill the exact shape of the old sorting sidings when viewed on Google Earth. As for Hexthorpe Yards, eight tracks remain, used by coal trains. After closure of Bank Yard, all wagonload traffic was transferred to Belmont Yard.

By 1986 the former "down" hump yard at Belmont had been remodelled into an "up" and "down" yard and was busy with Speedlink wagonload traffic. Once Speedlink was abandoned, the yard continued as a focus for engineers' traffic and is still in use in 2016, although the number of sorting sidings has been reduced to 18. The yards at Doncaster Decoy have become somewhat busier with the "down" sidings used by both Freightliner and GB Railfreight traffic and the "up" sidings by intermodal and engineers' services. Decoy "down" yard has nine through sidings whereas on the "up" side there are 15 tracks in the main Decoy Yard with an additional three sidings for intermodal traffic. In addition to this there is a virtual quarry, north-west of the main "down" Decoy Yard and a further 19 sidings for ballast traffic.

Below:- This view looking from the sorting sidings back up to the hump at Doncaster Belmont was taken in 1986. The brick built, hump shunters' cabin is still standing and can also be seen in the wonderful aerial view of Doncaster overleaf, from the English Heritage collection. What is evident in this view is how the yard has been remodelled, such that only the northern half of the sorting sidings remain connected to the hump. The waste ground to the right of the foreground, had been occupied by the other half of the 25 sorting sidings, but these have now been realigned to be shunted from the northern end. Class 08 No. 08876 was the "down" yard pilot on this occasion. (**M. Rhodes**)

Left:- This small sketch from my 1988 marshalling yard book shows the extent of the yards around Doncaster at their peak in 1950. (**M. Rhodes**)

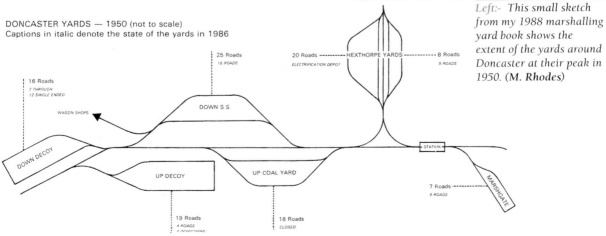

DONCASTER YARDS — 1950 (not to scale)
Captions in italic denote the state of the yards in 1986

25 Roads
16 ROADS

20 Roads --------- HEXTHORPE YARDS --------- 8 Roads
ELECTRIFICATION DEPOT   *5 ROADS*

16 Roads
7 THROUGH
12 SINGLE ENDED

WAGON SHOPS

DOWN S.S.

DOWN DECOY

UP DECOY

UP COAL YARD

STATION

MARSHGATE

7 Roads
5 ROADS

19 Roads
4 ROADS
4 RECEPTIONS

18 Roads
CLOSED

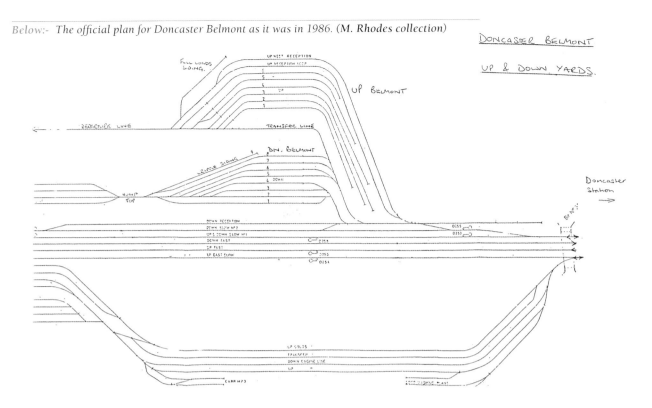

Above:- By 1977 when this view was taken, the Bank Yard was used almost exclusively for MGR traffic, and no longer hump shunted from the north end. The sorting sidings can be seen on the left of this view which shows Class 37 No. 37161 with what is probably a through freight headed from Tyne or Millerhill to Whitemoor Yard. The single ferry wagon suggests it may be heading for East Anglia, where this wagon will return to the continent via the Harwich train ferry. Classes 08, 31 and 40 can be seen on Doncaster Carr locomotive depot in the background. (**Les Nixon**)

Left:- Brand new "out of the box" Class 58 No. 58035 is just days old in this view at Doncaster Decoy "up" yard. The loaded MGR service was being used for crew training on 18 December 1985. **(M. Rhodes)**

Below:- Class 08 No. 08876 approaches the hump crest at Doncaster Belmont Yard. The four reception sidings were built on a twenty foot high embankment with brick retaining walls to allow for appropriate elevation at the hump. **(M. Rhodes)**

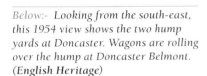

Below:- Looking from the south-east, this 1954 view shows the two hump yards at Doncaster. Wagons are rolling over the hump at Doncaster Belmont. **(English Heritage)**

Doncaster Station

Belmont Down Yard

Doncaster Carr Loco Depot

Doncaster Bank Yard

Signals in Les Nixon image

Shunters' cabin in 1988 image on page 113

NUNEATON [27] [28]

The LNWR yards at Nuneaton were expanded in 1905 to cater for increased stone and coal traffic. The expansion led to the construction of an "up" hump yard with 21 sorting sidings and the capacity to hold 931 wagons. The "down" yard was flat-shunted and had 18 sorting sidings with a capacity of 534 wagons. The "up" yard was bigger because it handled large volumes of coal from local mines, predominantly destined for London and the South. A list of the siding allocations gives an idea of the destinations served: London Goods, Rugby, Watford, Tring, Leicester Line, Oxford, Hawksbury Lane, Coventry and Northampton. Arrivals drew into a loop alongside platform 5 at Nuneaton and once their locomotive had been detached a shunting locomotive would draw them south of the station into a headshunt. From here trains would be propelled back north over the hump.

The hump itself was equipped with a cabin which had a searchlight to illuminate the numbers chalked on the wagons and then a tannoy to shout out the siding for which they were headed. The manual hump was operated by "chasers" who ran alongside the wagons and manually applied their brakes. There is also note in several places of "slippermen" who were shunters employed to place an wrought iron "slipper" on the track to slow wagons down. This device is still widely used, especially in Germany where it is called a "Hemmschuh". The English version is never mentioned in later literature, but was clearly used at Nuneaton from 1905 onwards. The "slipper" was described as a piece of wrought or ductile iron fashioned to match the head of the track and the flange of a standard wagon wheel. If a wagon was running away beyond the capability of the shunter to apply the brakes, it was placed on the track in front of the wagon and friction caused the wagon to slow and stop. Accidents were common and one incident is recorded where a fast moving wagon caused the slipper to ping off the track and through the window of the "up" sidings signal box - goodness knows what would have happened if it had hit a shunter!

In 1966 the "up" yard handled 3736 wagons in the sample week as compared to 3152 in the "down" sidings. Amazingly by 1968 the yards were almost deserted, except for the odd engineers' train and they closed shortly thereafter.

WELLINGBOROUGH

The Midland Railway yards at Wellingborough were built to serve the heavy coal traffic from the Nottinghamshire and Derbyshire pits to the Capital. As such, the "up" sidings were far more extensive, and always busy with coal arriving from Toton, to be sorted for a variety of southern destinations. The "up" yard had six reception sidings located parallel to the main sorting bowl. Hump shunting was undertaken by drawing wagons back to a head shunt, north of Neilson's Sidings Signal Box, from where they were pushed south over the hump in to an array of 19 sorting sidings with the capacity to hold 1230 wagons. During the 1966 yard survey the yard sorted 5276 wagons as compared to the much smaller "down" yard which handled 4780 wagons in its eleven sorting sidings.

The "down" sidings were closed in the late 1960s and are now covered by an industrial estate. The "up" yard continued to be hump shunted until 1980, after which wagonload traffic declined very rapidly. For 3 or 4 years in the early 1980s the yard continued to be used by small volumes of wagonload freight, shunted from the south end as a flat yard. Then much of the land was redeveloped by Network Rail so that it could be used for infrastructure services. In 2015 the "up" yard is still used as a virtual quarry and engineers' yard and is busy with GB Railfreight infrastructure traffic.

Right:- In March 2014, the yards at Wellingborough are still well used. Here Class 66 No. 66714 reverses into the yard with a train of track panels from Washwood Heath, whilst Class 66 No. 66605 passes with a Theale to Hope empty cement train. Class 222 No. 222015 heads to London with an express from Derby. The former "up" sorting sidings can be seen filled with ballast and track trains. **(M. Rhodes)**

*Above:- In this 1968 view, most of the "down" yard at Wellingborough has already been lifted and industrial units are beginning to appear on the site of the former iron works. A rake of wagons is being pulled north from the "up" reception sidings for humping and the "up" sorting sidings are full of 16-ton mineral wagons, loaded with coal. (**M. Rhodes collection**)*

*Below:- The original Midland Railway plan of the yards at Wellingborough. (**M. Rhodes collection**)*

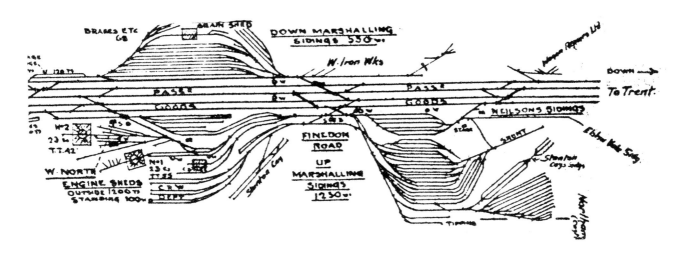

*Above & Below:- What a difference a couple of years makes! In 1979 Class 45 No. 45050 winds out of Wellingborough "up" yard with 8V26, the daily Welligborough to Acton mixed freight. The train is made up almost entirely of household and industrial coal bound for the west side of the Capital, carried in HTV, 21-ton coal hoppers. At this time the yard still had a permanent Class 08 pilot and was hump shunted. By 1983, when Class 31 Nos. 31294 & 31171 are seen passing the same location with a Mountsorrel to Radlett stone train, the yard is deserted, with just a few withdrawn guards vans scattered in the once busy sidings. Class 47 No. 47362 heads north with an empty oil train returning from Colnbrook to Lindsey Oil Refinery, passing Neilson's Siding Signal Box, the site of the former hump. (**Both M. Rhodes**)*

YORK YARDS INCLUDING DRINGHOUSES

Both of the hump yards in York were operated on the pull-back principle, with reception sidings situated alongside the sorting sidings. Trains to be hump shunted were drawn back into a headshunt and then propelled over the hump. The yard at York North was never modernised, whilst the sidings at Dringhouses benefitted from the installation of two retarders in 1961 as part of the 1955 Modernisation Plan.

York North Yard had three reception sidings which could receive freights from both the north and south. Pull-back was into a head shunt to the north of the yard, from whence wagons were propelled south over the hump into 16 sorting sidings. The yard remained in use well into the 1980s and even in 2016 the sidings are still recognisable from the bridge over the railway to the north on Water End, still used by Freightliner to store coal wagons needing attention in their York wagon works.

Dringhouses was a bigger yard with five reception sidings on the "up" side of the London main line. Drawback allowed hump shunting into 18 sorting sidings. Originally this was a manual "rider" hump, but in 1961 it was mechanised as part of the Modernisation Plan. By 1966, the throughput was 6466 wagons in a week and the yard did remain busy into the late 1980s with Speedlink traffic. Just before the end of Speedlink in 1988 the sidings closed and are now covered by a housing estate.

*Left:- A busy scene from 1963, taken by the late Vernon Murphy, shows a Black 5 No. 44954 leaving Dringhouses with a freight south as WD No. 90339 drifts by on the "up" main line. By this stage the hump at Dringhouses had been mechanised and it was the main yard in York. (**V. Murphy - M. Rhodes collection**)*

Right:- In June 1986, the yard at Dringhouses is full of VDA vans from the Rowntrees factory in York. In the centre of the picture, Class 47 No. 47319 arrives with 6O49, the daily Tees Yard to Eastleigh Speedlink service. To the right, behind the lighting mast, is Class 47 No. 47007 which brought 6O44, the daily Tyneside Central Freight Depot to Dover Speedlink into the yard. The two trains will swap portions before departure south. The yard tower in the background is still in use, but only survived another two years after this view. (M. Rhodes)

Above:- This view can be aligned with the 1963 picture by Vernon Murphy using the house on the right of the picture. Class 56 No. 56115 passes Dringhouses Yard with an Easington Colliery to Drax MGR train. Notable in this picture is the use of the hump; a rake of VDA vans can be seen descending from the hump, in the distance, directly above the third MGR wagon and to the left of the Dringhouses control tower. (**M. Rhodes**)

Above:- Class 56 No. 56092 passes York North Yard with 6N70, a York to Tees Yard empty MGR train. The York North Yard fills the left of the background. Its three reception sidings on the far left have two loaded MGR trains and an empty road. An unidentified Class 08 stands on the hump crest. (**M. Rhodes**)

Above:- An aerial view from the late 1960s shows the disused roundhouses of York South shed at the bottom of the image. In the centre right of the upper half of the image is York North Yard with a train being hump shunted from the pull-back siding to the north of the yard. (**M. Rhodes collection**)

OTHER MAJOR FLAT-SHUNTED YARDS

Introduction

At the time of the Beeching report it was estimated that there were over 1000 discreet sets of sidings or yards around the UK. Many were small and received very little traffic. In other cases there was duplication of facilities, like in Carlisle, where the construction of Kingmoor Yard in 1963 allowed closure of nine other significant marshalling yards in and around the city. By 1966, as wagonload traffic was falling, there were still at least 148 flat-shunted yards large enough to handle at least several hundred wagons every day.

On the Southern Region, with just one hump yard at Feltham, there were major yards at Tonbridge, Ashford, Eastleigh, Hoo, Norwood and Hither Green. The original 1955 Modernisation Plan had envisaged new mechanised hump yards in the first three locations, but a fall in traffic led these plans to be aborted at an early stage. Even so, in 1966 wagon throughput was 7367 per week at Eastleigh, 3735 at Ashford ("up" & "down" yards) and 2914 at Tonbridge. Hoo Junction handled 4814 wagons per week, as compared to 4469 in the "up" and "down" yards at Norwood Junction and 7701 in the various yards at Hither Green.

At the other end of the country on the Scottish Region, more hump yards were built as part of the modernisation programme, leaving just one really busy flat-shunted yard at Mossend (featured in detail below). This handled 4433 wagons on the "up" side and 6280 on the "down" side, a total of 10713 in a week. Elsewhere the yards at Ayr (5670 wagons), Grangemouth (4388 wagons) and Polmadie (3771 wagons) remained busy with coal and chemical traffic.

In the Eastern and North Eastern Regions, the busiest flat yards were almost all involved in handling large volumes of coal. The yards at Normanton, Carlton and Cudworth were all within a few miles of each other but together marshalled an amazing 20,613 wagons in the sample week in 1966. Normanton Sidings consisted of 20 northbound classification tracks with a capacity to hold 500 wagons, and 24 southbound tracks holding 722 wagons. It handled 6030 wagons in a single week. Carlton Sidings in contrast consisted of 17 northbound sidings, holding 900 wagons and 13 southbound with the capacity to accommodate 550 wagons. These sidings handled 9784 wagons in the same week. Finally the sidings just a few miles away at Cudworth handled an additional 4799 wagons. Other yards almost exclusively dedicated to coal were to be found at Mansfield Coal Concentration Sidings which handled a total of 8903 wagons in "up" and "down" yards. Even the much smaller neighbouring yard at Warsop Colliery Junction shunted 4374 wagons in a week.

One modernisation scheme which was cancelled in the early 1960s was at Stourton in Leeds. Here the flat yards at Neville Hill, Hunslet and Stourton continued to marshal 10,731 wagons per week in 1966. Other Eastern Region yards which were flat shunted were amazingly busy in the 1960s. Grimsby West and East Marsh Sidings dealt with 2804 and 2289 wagons respectively, much of it fish and sundries traffic related to the docks here. King's Cross Goods Yard handled 3788 wagons a week whereas traffic had fallen at the vast flat-shunted yards in Peterborough to just 5423 wagons per week as traffic was diverted away from the East Coast Main Line down the Joint Line to March Whitemoor Yard.

Yards in East Anglia at Norwich, Ipswich, Kings Lynn and Cambridge handled 2927, 4044, 1849 & 1991 wagons respectively. The busiest flat yard on the Eastern Region was however in Scunthorpe - Trent Eastern Yard[29,30]. Indeed the traffic was so heavy that it was in Scunthorpe that Britain's last new hump yard was opened in 1971 (described in detail in chapter 7). The Trent Yard handled 21,641 wagons in 1966 which would have justified a new hump yard on site here but for the fall in traffic which led to the smaller Scunthorpe West Yard being built.

The Western Region also had many large flat-shunted yards. Acton, which was the busiest of these is featured below. Thereafter the next busiest yards were in South Wales and again used mainly by coal traffic. Radyr handled 6513 wagons per week and Pengam 6608. The yard at Radyr is featured in detail below. General merchandise traffic still flourished with 6645 wagons a week at Stoke Gifford Sidings and 6529 in the sidings at Bristol West Depot. Interestingly the large array of sidings at Westbury was much less busy with just 3316 wagons in a week in 1966. This reflects the fact that the quarries at Merehead and Whatley had not yet fully developed, nor had the national road building programme, which proved such a major customer for Mendip stone.

Finally, the region with the most major flat-shunted marshalling yards was the Midland. Those which handled predominantly coal traffic were the busiest. Starting in London, the vast array of sidings at Brent, north of Cricklewood handled 14,637 wagons a week in 1966, fed by trains from Toton and Wellingborough, as well as traffic from Acton and South Wales. Flat yards at Burton and Nottingham handled 9110 and 7741 wagons a week respectively, whilst the yards in Wigan and Northwich, which were mainly coal and chemicals respectively, handled 5929 and 7010 wagons. The yards at Warrington, which became much more important

Above:- There were hundreds of marshalling yards all over the country until the 1960s and it is hard to picture the sheer volume of wagonload freight that ran on Britain's railway network. The goods yard at Derby St. Mary's is seen here in 1984, still boasting a couple of daily trains and most of the thirty plus sidings which had held over 1000 wagons during the yard's heyday. In 1966 the yard sorted 3284 wagons in the week of the national yard survey, more than many hump yards were classifying by the 1980s. Here Class 45 No. 45043 passes St. Mary's with a train of scrap metal in MXV, vacuum-braked 16-ton mineral wagons, bound for Tinsley. (**M. Rhodes**)

Above right:- Scunthorpe Trent Yard, also known as Entrance C to Scunthorpe Steelworks is seen here in 1992. By this time much of the yard was used for storage of wagons, although Class 08 No. 08632 is about to pick up a train of steel bars bound for Allied Steel and Wire in Cardiff and take it to Scunthorpe West Yard. Behind the shunting locomotive the stored locomotives include a large number of former "top link" Class 47s, surplus after the electrification of the East Coast Main Line (Nos. 47406, 407, 411, 417 & 418). In addition Class 47 No. 47115 is present along with Class 31 Nos. 31108, 31156 & 31249 and Class 20 No. 20205. (**M. Rhodes**)

when wagonload freight was withdrawn from Crewe Basford Hall in 1972, are featured separately below. Other major yards included Coton Hill in Shrewsbury. A 48-track mechanised hump yard here had been envisaged in 1955, but quickly discounted because of a fall in traffic. By 1966 only 3496 wagons were sorted here each week. Busier by some margin were the yards at Mold Junction, east of Chester, handling a total of 6219 wagons. These disappeared by 1981 and are now wasteland. One final busy yard worthy of note is Northampton. Here the "down" yard was a manual hump which handled 5571 wagons in a week as compared to the flat-shunted "up" yard which handled 3444. The hump was still in use in 1982 but closed shortly thereafter; the land is now occupied by a depot for electric multiple units.

Table 2 Large Non-Hump Yards - Summary of Major Yards

Yard	Tracks	Wagon throughput in October 1966	Status
Cardiff Tidal Sidings	Pre-1945 - >100 1970 - 43	6608 wagons (with Pengam)	18 tracks still used in 2016 by steel traffic
Radyr	64 sorting and engineers	6513 wagons	In 2016 all closed and covered in a new housing estate
Margam Knuckle	18 sorting	Not separately recorded	In use 2016
Arpley & Walton, Warrington	20 & 13 sorting	Arpley - 4125 wagons Walton - 1075 wagons	In use 2016
Dewsnap, Manchester	57 sorting	5701 wagons	Closed 1981
Brent, London	"up" - 36 sorting "down" - 94 sorting	14,637 wagons	Closed 1970s and now covered in industrial units
Acton, London	40 plus sorting	9930 wagons	West London stone terminal with 9 residual tracks
Rowsley	"up" - 12 sorting "down" - 21 sorting	Not recorded	Closed 1967, returned to woodland
Hunslet & Stourton, Leeds	"up" - combined - 31 "down" - combined - 33	10,731 wagons	In 2016 site of freightliner depot and Midland Road sidings for Freightliner.
Normanton	"up" - 6 reception, 23 sorting "down" - 7 reception, 18 sorting	6030 wagons	Closed 1970, returned to woodland
Immingham Reception Sidings	Pre 1960 - >100 1980 - 45	Not recorded	In 2016 there are still 15 sidings but most land is taken up with coal storage
Scunthorpe Trent	23 sorting	21,641 wagons (all yards in Scunthorpe)	In 2016 still in use as main yard in Scunthorpe
Westbury	"up" - 17 sorting "down" - 13 sorting	3316 wagons	In 2016 most sidings still in use for stone traffic
Mossend	"up" - 24 sorting "down" - 46 sorting	10,723 wagons	In 2016, "up" yard is Euroterminal and 20 sidings in use on "down" side.
Woodford Halse	"up" - 3 reception, 11 sorting "down" - 4 reception, 8 sorting	Not recorded	Closed 1965
Annesley	"up" - 4 reception, 18 sorting "down" - 3 reception, 18 dead end sorting	Capacity to hold 2976 wagons until closure	Closed 1965
Ferme Park Yards, Hornsey	"up" - 48 sorting "down" - 26 sorting	3788 wagons	Closed 1968, now "up" yard is site of Hornsey electric depot and "down" yard Network Rail yard.
Masboro Sidings, Canklow, Rotherham	"up" 20 sorting "down" - 10	Not recorded	Closed 1968, now site of Rotherham Steel terminal
New England Yard, Peterborough	Over 60 sidings in 5 separate yards	5423 wagons	Gradually closed and scaled down from 1968 to present when parts are covered in Post Office buildings and GBRf depot whilst others are derelict land.
Brent Yard, Willesden	26 sorting	5881 wagons	Closed as main Speedlink yard for London in 1993 when Wembley Yard opened, now disused sidings.

ACTON [31] [32]

Dating back to 1877 when the Great Western opened the first yard at Acton, the freight yards here have seen varied fortunes through the years. The biggest changes came in 1931, when the Great Western invested heavily in a range of infrastructure projects (including the building of yards at Banbury, Rogerstone, Severn Tunnel and Swansea Burrows). The expansion of Acton in 1931 tripled its capacity and led to a major yard with 28 miles of track being built on the site. This was flat-shunted and made up of three distinct yards. No. 1 yard had 14 tracks and was predominantly for westbound traffic. No. 2 yard had 13 tracks and was bi-directional whilst No. 3 yard (closest to Acton Main Line station) had 13 tracks and was mainly for eastbound traffic.

It was as a result of the 1967 National Freight Train Plan that Acton became responsible for marshalling most of the coal destined for London and South East England. At this time the yard was handling 9930 wagons per week, making it the third busiest on the Western Region after Margam and Severn Tunnel. Acton's importance in the freight network was further enhanced as the yards at Feltham, Hither Green and Norwood were either closed or downsized in the late 1960s. Thus at the start of the 1970s the key services were two train pairs from Toton and Wellingborough each day and then two train pairs each from Radyr,

Margam and Severn Tunnel Junction. The South Wales traffic was slightly different from the Nottinghamshire services in that three trains of empties returned to East Usk Yard in Newport for further distribution to the collieries, and two more to Severn Tunnel Junction. Whilst general goods traffic was carried on these trains, the majority of traffic was coal in vacuum-braked and un-braked wagons.

Other important traffics were scrap metal from London merchants, using the same MCO coal wagons that had come from South Wales and the Midlands. Conveniently the major steelworks taking scrap metal were in South Wales and the Midlands providing revenue earning traffic in both directions for many trains from Acton. On top of scrap and coal the late 1970s still saw a daily freight to and from St. Erth carrying milk, as well as several trains to cater for the Park Royal Guiness traffic.

Coal carriage in unfitted wagons ended in 1983/84 and the sidings at Acton stopped handling general freight from May 1984 when all general goods traffic was transferred to the air-braked network and marshalled at Willesden Brent Sidings. The site at Acton was then used for the staging of aggregate trains and this work continues in 2015 using half a dozen sidings.

Above:- In 1981, Acton was still a very busy yard as this view at the east end of the sidings shows. With trips to other London yards at Willesden, Temple Mills and Norwood at least twice a day, as well as long distance trains to the Midlands there was always plenty of action passing Acton Main Line station. Here, on 27 February 1981, Class 31 No. 31414 prepares to leave light engine, whilst behind it Class 25 No. 25050 waits with 8M85, the afternoon trip to Willesden Yard. (**M. Rhodes**)

Above:- This wonderful 1982 view, taken from the west end of Acton Yard, shows, from left to right; a Class 31 peeping out from sidings 5–14 in No. 1 yard. Further back in No. 1 yard are a Class 03 and a Class 25. Below them is a rake of wagons being drawn from siding 2 in No. 1 yard by Class 08 No. 08798 (out of shot). In the centre of the image, Class 47 No. 47082 "ATLAS" leaves No. 3 yard with empty Tilbury Roadstone hoppers, a sign of the future for the sidings here. Behind the rake of empty stone hoppers are the 13 sidings of No. 2 yard with their Class 08 pilot and beyond them No. 3 yard. (**Paul Shannon**)

Above:- By 1991 when this view was taken from the west end of Acton Yard, most of the sorting sidings had been lifted. Class 59 No. 59102 shunts empty stone wagons which will make up the afternoon Acton to Merehead Quarry freight. (**M. Rhodes**)

Mossend [33]

The yards at Mossend grew up to cater for traffic from the surrounding iron and steel industry and by the 1930s the sidings here handled 2000–3000 wagons daily. When the new steelworks at Ravenscraig opened in 1956, there was a further increase in traffic and by 1966 the yard was the second most busy in Scotland. The busiest yard was Millerhill, but Mossend came a close second and took over as Scotland's busiest yard in 1969 when the Waverley route closed and traffic volumes at Millerhill dropped significantly. The 46 single-ended sidings on the "down" side of the yard handled 6280 wagons per week in 1966 as compared to 4433 wagons dealt with in the 24-track "up" yard. With the development of an air-braked Speedlink network, Mossend became the focal point for almost all traffic in Scotland and in addition sent out 34 local trip freights every day (these are shown in the table below).

Between 1980 and 1990 the "down" yard was significantly reduced in size from 46 to 18 sidings. The land freed up by the track removal was used for a freight terminal handling general goods and aggregates now called the Hattonrigg Industrial Estate. The smaller 18 track "down" yard was initially used just by engineers' traffic with all revenue earning freight concentrated in the "up" yard. Just as elsewhere around the country the abolition of the Speedlink network in 1991 led to a drastic reduction in traffic in the "up" yard. Redevelopment led to a reversal of fortune for the "down" yard which now still has 18 sidings and handles all freight traffic whilst the "up" side of the complex has been rebuilt as a 5 track intermodal and Stobart Logistics yard handling cars and containers.

Mossend Trip Freights - 1983

Headcode	Locomotive	Destinations
T22	Class 37 (dual brake)	Work to control orders
T24	Class 27 (dual brake)	Ravenscraig No. 1
T25	Class 37 (dual brake)	Lanark, Carstairs, Law Junction
T26	Class 20 x 2	Polkemmet Colliery
T28	Class 27	Paisley Canal, Elderslie, Greenock Ladyburn
T29	Class 37 (dual brake)	Gartcosh Russels, St. Rollox, Deanside
T30	Class 47 (dual brake)	Bishopton, Paisley St. James
T31	Class 20 (dual brake)	Sheildmuir, Coltness
T32	Class 37/27/20 (dual brake)	Engineers' route train (Kilmarnock, Perth, Millerhill etc)
T33	Class 27 (dual brake)	Ravenscraig No. 3
T34	Class 27 (dual brake)	AFC instructions to Dalzell North
T36	Class 27 (dual brake)	Clydesdale, Calder Imperial Works
T37	Class 27 (dual brake)	Clydesdale, Calder Imperial Works
T38	Class 27/20 (dual brake)	Motherwell LWR depot
T39	Class 47/20/27 (dual brake)	Ravenscraig No. 4
T40	Class 47/20 (dual brake)	Ravenscraig No. 4

Headcode	Locomotive	Destinations
T41	Class 37 (dual brake)	Ravenscraig No. 4
T42	Class 27 (dual brake)	Ravenscraig No. 2
T43	Class 37 (dual brake)	Salkeld Street, Shields depot, Corkerhill
T44	Class 27 (dual brake)	Ravenscraig No. 3, Gartcosh
T45	Class 27 (dual brake)	Ravenscraig No. 3, Gartcosh
T47	Class 27 (dual brake)	Hamilton, Clydesdale, Sheildmuir, Ross Coup
T48	Class 08	Sheildmuir, Motherwell
T51	Class 27 (dual brake)	Sheildmuir, Coltness
T52	Class 27 (dual brake)	Ravenscraig No. 1 & No. 3
T55	Class 08	Mossend "Down" Yard
T56	Class 08	Mossend "Up" Yard (north end)
T59	Class 08	Mossend "Down" Yard
T60	Class 08	Ravenscraig No. 2
T62	Class 08	Motherwell wagon repairs
T63	Class 20	Whifflet Basin
T64	Class 26	Ravenscraig No. 2, Polkemmet Colliery
T71	Class 37 (dual brake)	Bishopton, Giffen
T77	Class 20 (dual brake)	Newton, Westburn Steel Works

Above:- *This view of Mossend can be dated as taken in 1972 as the new office block adjacent to the "up" sidings has just been constructed. A Class 24 approaches on the "up" main line whilst both "up" and "down" yards are packed with low capacity unfitted wagons. (BR - M. Rhodes collection)*

Above:- *Taken in July 1989, this view from the north end of the "up" yard shows Class 37 No. 37242 leaving with the 6T19 trip to Lugton, hauling two vans of fertiliser from Ince and Elton. The yard is busy with air-braked Speedlink traffic as well as steel from Ravenscraig. (M. Rhodes)*

Left:- In June 1980, Class 40 No. 40061 arrives at Mossend with 4D48, the afternoon Speedlink from Millerhill to Mossend. The train has picked up a dozen carflats laden with British Leyland trucks manufactured in Bathgate. Several Class 85 and Class 81 electrics are stabled in the "up" yard whilst the large "down" yard is still intact with 46 tracks, filled with traffic. (M. Rhodes)

Right:- Class 20 Nos. 20171 & 20175 accelerate away from the "up" yard in a northerly direction with 7N23, the morning Speedlink to Grangemouth. The first wagon conveys a CO2 tank returning empty to Cameron Bridge and routed in 1986 when this was taken, via Grangemouth. To the right of the train is the "down" yard pilot which has just been shunting some containerised coal wagons seen in a now largely empty "down" yard. (M. Rhodes)

Right:- By the late 1980s Mossend effectively collected all Speedlink traffic in Scotland. Here Class 26 No. 26008 arrives with 6D20, the afternoon trip from Ayr. The train is made up of five empty OTA timber wagons which had delivered logs to the paper factory at Irvine. The consist will set back into the "up" yard behind the train where the wagons will be sorted and attached to the evening Speedlink departures from Mossend. (M. Rhodes)

Above:- By 1992, when this shot was taken, Ravenscraig Steelworks had closed and the Speedlink network had ceased to operate. Both led to a drastic reduction in traffic at Mossend. The accommodation block on the right serves as a marker for comparison with the 1972 and 1989 views. The yard was soon to be replaced by an intermodal terminal and logistics park for the delivery of new cars. (**M. Rhodes**)

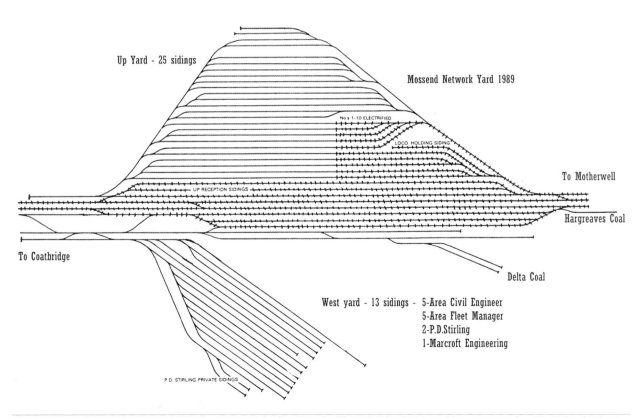

Above:- Since this track plan in 1989, the number of sidings on the "down" side of Mossend has increased to 18 whilst the "up" yard has all but disappeared. Just five tracks remain on the "up" side in the intermodal depot and three long loops beside the main line with four locomotive holding sidings kept at the south end of the yard. (**M. Rhodes**)

WARRINGTON ARPLEY [34]

The town of Warrington grew enormously in the 1970s, the population going from 72,400 to 168,000 within the decade. During the same decade the freight yards at Arpley and Walton also became much more important as the yards at Crewe, Edge Hill, Wigan, Mold Junction and Preston closed or were downsized. In 1966 the town had five discreet sets of sidings at Arpley Junction, Arpley Old Side, Froghall, Warrington South East and Walton - together they handled 8877 wagons. The yards at Dallam, Froghall and Warrington South East closed in the early 1970s leaving the sidings at Arpley and Walton as the remaining marshalling sites in the town. Back in 1966, Arpley had been the busiest yard in Warrington dealing with 3710 wagons in a week as compared to just 1075 being handled in Walton Old Junction Yard.

As wagonload traffic was concentrated on fewer and fewer yards, Warrington became the focal point for all wagonload services in the North West and North Wales, particularly as the air-braked Speedlink network became established. By 1986, rather than handling far fewer wagons than in the 1966 survey, the yard saw a weekly throughput of 4250 wagons, almost as many as back in the 1960s, but with the added complication of large volumes of coal traffic to and from Fiddlers Ferry Power Station passing the yard day and night. Trip freights connected Warrington to the Cumbrian Coast, Speke Junction in Liverpool and industries around Ellesmere Port. There were three out and back trips to North Wales destinations each day as well as five daily trips linking Manchester to Warrington. With 51 daily arrivals and 45 departures, 40 of which were classified as Speedlink trunk services, Warrington was one of the busiest yards in the country during the mid-1980s. With the abolition of Speedlink[35] in July 1991, the traffic levels at Warrington dropped drastically. Some wagonload traffic remained as part of the Enterprise network which tried to retain some Anglo-Scottish wagonload flows, but essentially the yard was given over to engineering traffic and stored wagons. In 2016 there are rarely more than ten revenue earning freights passing through Arpley Yard each day and often no trains at all from the sidings at Walton Old Junction.

Above:- *British Railways Standard Class 9F No. 92160 passes Walton Old Junction Signal Box as it arrives from Stanlow with with a train of fuel oil. The train is made up of a variety of 4-wheeled, short wheelbase tank wagons. Just visible at the rear of the train are several of the then "new" 45-ton tank wagons. The entire cargo would fit easily into half a dozen 100-ton bogie oil tankers today. The track leading out of view on the right is the entrance to Walton Old Junction Sidings.* (**D. Lennon**)

Above:- This overall view of Arpley Yard in the 1960s shows 9F No. 92102 leaving with a special freight - headcoded "4Z17". The 9F was allocated to Birkenhead shed, so it is likely the freight is heading for Ellesmere Port or the Wirral. By 1966, the yard used diesel shunting locomotives, but steam was still rostered for many freights as can be seen by the two further locomotives waiting to leave the yard. (**A. Chester**)

Above:- Taken in 2015 from a Flybe flight from Exeter to Manchester, good fortune gave us a flight path right over Warrington Arpley Yard on a perfect summer's day! A pair of Voyager units speed northwards as a Class 66 arrives from the south with a short container service carrying chemicals. The new white buildings in the extension sidings are a wagon repair shop on the left and locomotive servicing shed to the right. One DBS Class 66 can be seen sticking out of the north end of the locomotive depot. The main sorting sidings are mainly full of ballast and coal wagons, the coal wagons in store because of a drastic reduction in coal traffic following the changes to taxation of power station coal in April 2015. (**M. Rhodes**)

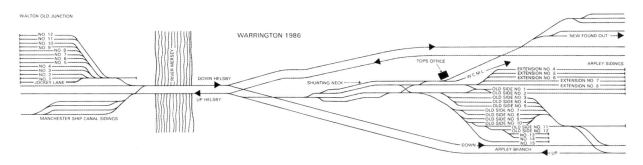

Above:- The track layout of Warrington Arpley as it was in 1986 - the trackwork remains largely unchanged in 2015, although there is much less traffic. (**M. Rhodes**)

Right:- In June 1986, in the midst of the heyday at Arpley Yard, Class 08 No. 08916 shunts the recently arrived Speedlink feeder service from Blackburn. Running as 6F84, the train was made up of 3 PCA cement tanks from Clitheroe to Bescot, 5 ILB ferry vans from Blackburn to Warrington where they were to "await orders", 3 HEA coal hoppers returning empty from Blackburn to Healey Mills Yard, a single ILB ferry van returning empty to Exeter and finally another two ILB ferry vans destined for Bescot and Harwich respectively. The train had arrived behind Class 47 No. 47105 at 1455 and this image was taken at 1521, by which time Class 87 No. 87034 had arrived with the 6V93 Speedlink from Mossend to Severn Tunnel Junction. Whilst the Class 08 shunts the wagons from Blackburn as quickly as possible, access into the yard for 6V93 is blocked. Once 08916 clears the shunting neck, then the Class 87 will shunt its own train. The first two tank wagons were booked through to Wales, but the next 12 wagons needed detaching at Warrington leaving the last 16 to run through to Severn Tunnel with the two tankers reattached on the front of the train. The Speedlink would eventually depart at 1649 that day. (**M. Rhodes**)

Left:- Passing Walton Old Junction in 1986 is Class 86 No. 86422 with 6F86, the Mondays-only Speedlink service from Bescot. To the right of the train is Walton Old Junction Yard and peeping out from behind the Class 08 yard pilot is Class 47 No. 47279, which has just arrived with the 6T78 trip from Stanlow, conveying fuel oil for locomotive depots around the North East of England. (**M. Rhodes**)

RADYR [36]

The yards at Radyr dated back to 1865, when the Taff Vale Railway built a yard to handle coal from up the Taff Valley. At their largest the sidings here had 15 tracks on the west side, which handled traffic headed up the valley, and 26 tracks on the east side for traffic headed south. Much coal from the Taff and Rhymney valleys headed directly for the ports at Cardiff, Barry and Penarth, but Radyr Yard handled traffic destined for elsewhere in the UK and was a crucial marshalling centre. In the 1966 marshalling yard survey the sidings handled 6513 wagons in a week and became much busier in the 1970s when the direct routes to the docks in Cardiff and Barry closed. With the connection between Aber in the Rhymney Valley and Taffs Well in the Taff Valley, the yard handled coal from 30 collieries in the 1970s from the Rhymney, Taff, Cynon and Rhondda valleys. Often in the mid-1970s there would be eight or nine coal trains filling the permissive block between Taffs Well and Radyr Junction, all waiting for access to the yard.

The "Big Hill" connecting Aber to Walnut Tree Junction closed in the mid-1980s, removing all Rhymney Valley services from Radyr. With pit closures in the late 1980s it looked like the end for Radyr. Then in January 1989 Network Coal arrived with 21 new services based on Radyr Yard. The upturn in traffic was however short lived as all Network Coal services were transferred to East Usk Yard in 1991 when the Speedlink wagonload network was abolished. By 1992 an entire eight hour shift could pass without a single train and the yard closed at the end of 1992. In 2015, much of the well-graded and drained land is covered with a new housing estate and is unrecognisable as one of the busiest flat-shunted yards in the country.

Left:- During the "Indian Summer" at Radyr Yard, Railfreight Distribution Class 47 No. 47188 leaves the yard with 6B39, the afternoon trip to East Usk Yard. The large number of HEA air-braked hoppers filled with coal is striking as at this stage in 1989 the yard was the concentration point for all Network Coal traffic in South Wales. **(M. Rhodes)**

Below:- A plan of Radyr in 1960 when the yard was at its largest. **(R.A. Cooke)**

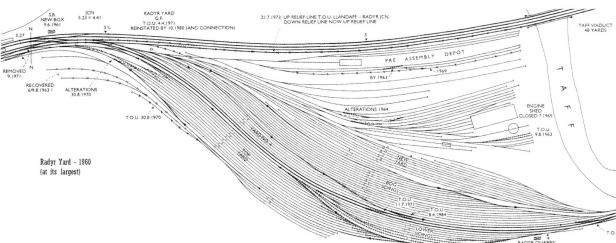

Radyr Yard - 1960
(at its largest)

Above:- Class 08 No. 08352 winds across the main line at Radyr Quarry Junction. It is working as "E86" the yard pilot and is bringing wagons from the "Top Yard" to the "New Sidings", from where they will be tripped to Cathays wagon workshops for repair. (**M. Rhodes**)

Above:- Radyr Quarry Junction serves as a useful "anchor" in this view taken on 20 June 1993. The last train left the yard at Radyr the day before on the 19th with the last remaining wagons which were taken for scrap. The entire vista is now filled with new houses with just the running lines to Cardiff on the left still in situ. (**M. Rhodes**)

REFERENCES

1   Findlay G. The Working and Management of an English Railway. Whittacker & Co. London 1889; 170–181.

2   Appleby KC. Shildon–Newport in Retrospect. RCTS 1990.

3   Editorial. Remodelling of Basford Hall Yard, Crewe. Modern Railways, September 1962; 189–190.

4   Cooke BWC. Basford Hall Marshalling Yard electrification and modernisation. The Railway Magazine, October 1962; 673–676.

5   Shannon P. Freightliner. Ian Allan 2013.

6   Henshaw A. The Great Northern Railway in the East Midlands. RCTS 1999.

7   Waite PB. A History of the Great Northern Railway's Colwick Motive Power Depot and Marshalling Yard. Booklaw Publications 2004.

8   British Railways Board. A Study of Marshalling Yard Costs Capacity and Utilisation. BRB August 1967. (Closed to public until 1998).

9   Rhodes M. Wembley: Britain's Busiest Yard. Rail Express. 1998.

10 Lawrence JT. The Great Central Railway's New Concentration Sidings at Wath. The Railway Magazine, March 1908; 177–186.

11 Christensen M. Wath "A" Hump - Great Central Railway. Signalling Record Society, 1981.

12 Burtt P. The Principal Factors in Freight Train Operating. George Allen & Unwin, London 1923.

13 Lawrence WF. Freight Marshalling Yards. Railway Magazine, February 1914; 101–111.

14 Appleby KC. Shildon–Newport in Retrospect. RCTS 1990.

15 Semmens PWB. Newport Marshalling Yards N.E.R. Trains Illustrated, February 1952; 64–68.

16 Hawkins C. Feltham Yard and Shed. British Railways llustrated, 1994; 4 (1); 18–30.

17 Modern Marshalling Yards - At Banbury, Severn Tunnel, Rogerstone and Swansea. Supplement to the Railway Gazette, December 8, 1933; 56–60.

18 Editorial. Modern Marshalling Yards. The Railway Gazette, December 8 1933.

19 Great Western Railway Notice No.1958. Introduction of "Hump" Yard for Gravitation Shunting at North End, Down Side, Rogerstone. GWR, 1931.

20 Editorial. Modern Marshalling Yards. The Railway Gazette, December 8 1933.

21 Viney R. Rogerstone Marshalling Yard. The Journal Monmouthshire Railway Society. September 2014 No.62.

22 Editorial. The Railway Gazette, December 8 1933; 57–58.

23 Parkes G R. The Hazards of Shunting. Trains Annual 1966 p74-82.

24 Johnson EM. The Woodhead - Part 1. Foxline 1996.

25 Johnson EM. The Woodhead - Part 2. Foxline 1997.

26 Johnson EM. Woodhead - The Electric Railway. Foxline 1997.

27 http://www.nuneatonhistory.com/on-london--north-western-railway-lines.html

28 Lee P. Railway Serendipity. Shunters, Slipper-Men & Fat Boxes. http://nnwfhs.org.uk/files/Journals_pdf_files/2008_04_apr.pdf

29 Rhodes M. 100 Years of Steel - Scunthorpe. Rail, 119; 5–18 April, 1990.

30 Rhodes M. Railfreight Steel Scunthorpe - All Change for the Future. Rail 121, 3–16 May 1990.

31 Ringer B. Acton Twilight of a Marshalling Yard. Backtrack, 2013; 27: 139–145.

32 Ringer B. Acton Twilight of a Marshalling Yard Part Two. Backtrack, 2013; 27: 296–301.

33 Rhodes M. This is Mossend. Rail 108, 2–15 November 1989.

34 Shannon P. Speedlink. pages 40–59. Ian Allan, 2014.

35 Rhodes M. Speedlink's Final Trip. Rail, 139; 9–22 January 1991.

36 Rhodes M. Radyr Yard to Close. Rail, 187: 11–24 November 1992.

CHAPTER 5

BRITAIN'S FIRST MECHANISED HUMP YARDS

1928–1955

MARCH WHITEMOOR [1] [2]

Opened: 1928/1933
Closed as hump yard: 1974/1980
Classification tracks: 2 x 43
Capacity in 24 hours: 8000 wagons

Whilst many UK yards used gravity after the revolutionary Gridiron in Edge Hill and hump yards were first built on a major scale at Wath in South Yorkshire, Whitemoor was the first mechanised hump yard in the UK. Its design and equipment was influenced by a visit of LNER staff to Germany and it became the first mechanised hump yard in the UK when it opened in 1928. Much of the hump equipment was of German origin and indeed the Frölich retarders which LNER engineers had seen in operation at Hamm and Oberhausen Osterfeld Süd yards remained in use on the "up" hump until it closed in October 1980.

The yards at March ended up in that part of the fens largely by accident! Back in the 1860s, the Great Eastern was looking for somewhere to build freight sidings and Wisbech would have liked to host them. The problem: Wisbech Parish Council would not allow shunting on Sundays. In the end March, at the junction of the Great Eastern from Peterborough and the GN & GE Joint Line from Lincoln, provided the ideal location. By the 1920s there were more sidings at March than anywhere else on the GE and it was a busy gateway to both East Anglia and the East End of London. Like most yards in the UK, growth of the sidings had been haphazard and there were major delays at March. Major surgery was needed.

An economic analysis revealed the massive losses that delays in March were incurring and the decision was made to build the all new "up" hump yard at March in 1926. The LNER southern area manager was a guest of the German State Railways in 1927 and as a result of a visit to the marshalling yards at Hamm, Frölich retarders were selected

for the new yard. It was made up of 10 reception sidings, each capable of holding 80 standard wagons. There were 43 sorting sidings, all capable of holding at least 80 wagons. The yard handled 3000–4000 wagons each 24 hours. Such was the improvement in traffic flow that the rebuilding of the March "down" yards became a priority.

The "down" yard was designed with 10 reception sidings and 40 sorting sidings (with 3 extra sidings for cripples). Initially it had been felt that retarders would not be necessary as most wagons flowing north were empty, heading back to the Nottinghamshire coalfields. In the end retarders were installed, but just two of them. It is interesting to note that the Westinghouse design, called the "Eddy Current Brake" was chosen after engineers had visited the test site in Chippenham, and also seen the brake in action in Dresden. Thus the March "down" yard project was completed in 1933. The combined "up" and "down" yards were by far the largest in the UK with the capacity to handle 8000 wagons per day over two humps and standage for 10,500 wagons. This capacity was put under severe pressure during the Second World War and led to the addition of ten new "up" departure sidings, increasing the capacity of this amazing yard yet further. To confuse the crews of German bomber aircraft in the war, hundreds of yard lighting poles were erected in fields a few miles away as a form of "decoy" which looked just like the real yard. Locals recall Whitemoor itself was never hit badly during the war, probably as a result of this ingenious strategy.

Preservation of a busy wagonload yard at March, owed much to the diversion of all freight away from the

East Coast Main Line. In the late 1970s, there were still 4 or 5 train pairs linking March to Temple Mills in East London. The "down" hump closed in 1974 and the "up" hump followed in 1980. The yard remained busy however as a crucial collection point for Speedlink traffic. Once the wagonload network closed and virtually all East Anglian freight disappeared in 1990, the yard's days were numbered. A category B prison stands where once the "up" hump operated. Much of the "down" yard and old "up" departure sidings is however a large infrastructure yard, busy, especially at weekends.

Plans from 1920 to the Present Day

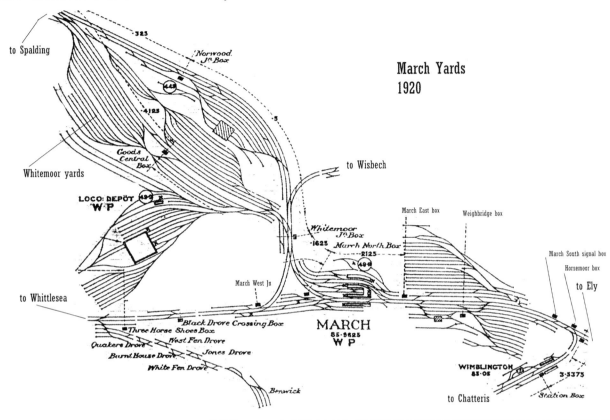

Above:- Prior to the construction of the "up" hump yard in 1927/28, there were almost as many sidings at March East as at Whitemoor. The sidings at Whitemoor, were woefully inadequate for the traffic handled, as this plan shows. The remnants of these sidings, after both hump yards were built, became what was known as Norwood Yard. (M. Rhodes collection)

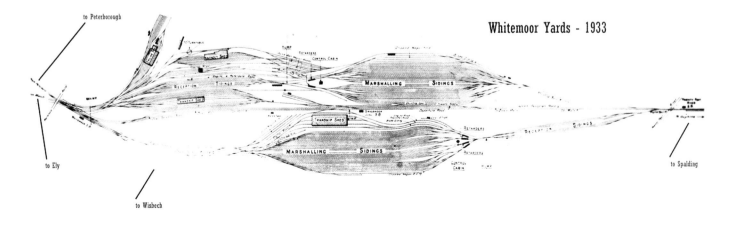

Above:- This official LNER plan shows the Whitemoor Yards in 1933, once the modernisation of the "down" side had been completed. Ten departure sidings were added in the 1940s and these were just above the arrow to the Wisbech branch line on the plan. (BR ER - M. Rhodes collection)

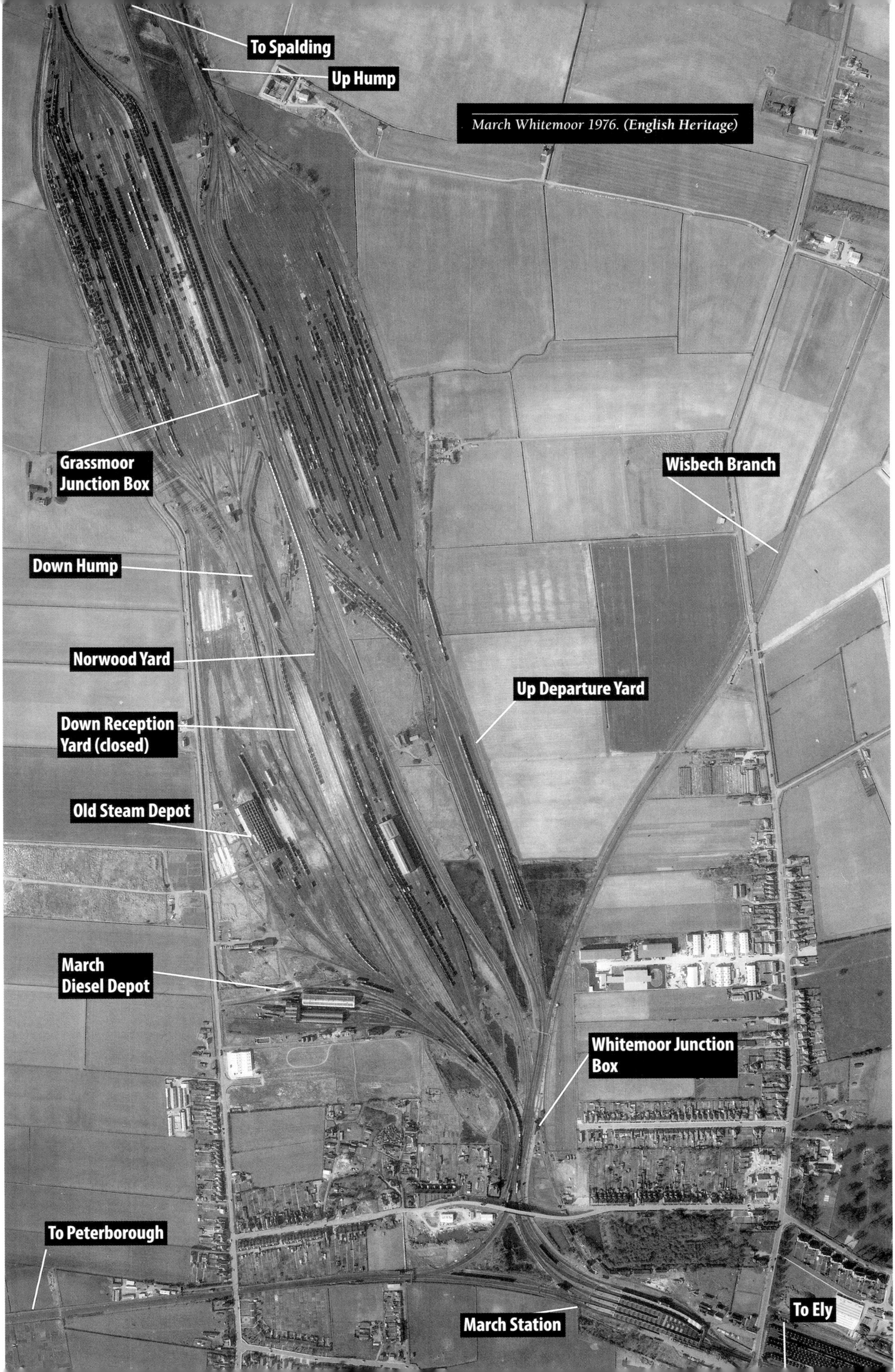

March Whitemoor 1976. (English Heritage)

To Spalding

Up Hump

Wisbech Branch

Grassmoor Junction Box

Down Hump

Norwood Yard

Up Departure Yard

Down Reception Yard (closed)

Old Steam Depot

March Diesel Depot

Whitemoor Junction Box

To Peterborough

March Station

To Ely

Above:- In this LNER publicity shot, wagons are seen rolling down the hump in the "up" yard. The four Frölich retarders are clearly seen as wagons of coal bound for East Anglia and the London Gas Works roll down the hump. (BR ER - M. Rhodes collection)

Above:- The Frölich railbrakes are in the raised position in this 1929 publicity photograph, grasping the wheels of this wooden bodied mineral wagon. (BR ER - M. Rhodes collection)

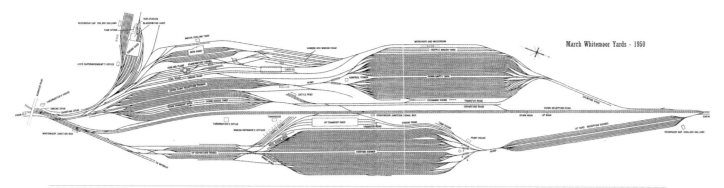

March Whitemoor Yards - 1950

Above:- With the increased traffic during the Second World War, new "up" departure sidings were added to Whitemoor as shown in this plan which dates from the 1950s. (**Origin unknown** - **M. Rhodes collection**)

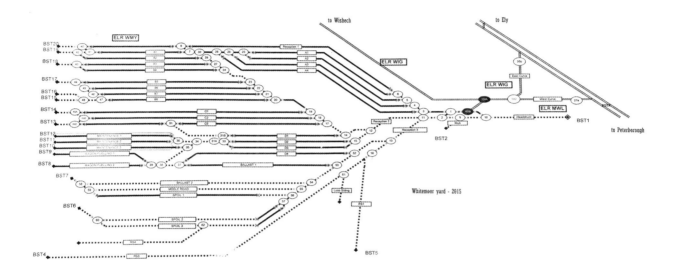

Whitemoor yard - 2015

Above:- This plan from 2015 shows that much of the "up" side of the old hump yards has been used for an infrastructure yard whilst to the west, over parts of the old locomotive depot and down sidings, there are sidings for ballast cleaning and land used for ballast and track storage. (**M. Rhodes**)

Left:- This wonderful LNER poster was released to celebrate the opening of the "up" yard at Whitemoor. Unusually for a graphic artist, the designer of this image has accurately reflected each siding in the new yard and the careful observer will see each sorting siding faithfully reproduced. (**M. Rhodes collection**)

MARCH WHITEMOOR DEPARTURES – SUMMER 1969

Southbound and Eastbound Departures

7J51	0010	Temple Mills	7F19	1016	Parkeston
8L17	0045	Cambridge	8K17	1056	Ipswich
8J35	0055	Temple Mills	8L32	1104	Kings Lynn
8H01	0110	Stratford Old Yard	8N10	1112	Wensum
8J11	0121	Temple Mills	8L35	1218	Bury St Edmunds
8F01	0125	Colchester	8J91	1222	Temple Mills
8J71	0142	Temple Mills	8B40	1240	Hitchin
8K13	0154	Ipswich	8L23	1258	Cambridge
8J75	0233	Temple Mills	8J68	1430	Wisbech East
8P13	0254	Tottenham Hale	8L34	1500	Kings Lynn
7K10	0315	Lowestoft Central	8H99	1550	Stratford Market
8B15	0325	Chelmsford	8J93	1558	Temple Mills
8B19	0332	Lowestoft Central	8J95	1638	Temple Mills
8H95	0350	Leyton Depot or Hitchin	8P17	1709	Broxbourne CEGB
7K15	0405	Ipswich	8L36	1845	Kings Lynn
7N12	0420	Norwich Thorpe	8N14	2020	Wensum
8N02	0430	Norwich Victoria	7J97	2038	Temple Mills
7F15	0456	Parkeston	7F23	2046	Parkeston
8J66	0510	Wisbech East	8N25	2118	Claydon
8L25	0515	Stansted	8P21	2126	Brimsdown
8L28	0530	Kings Lynn	8F51	2130	Colchester
8L30	0626	Kings Lynn	8J85	2138	Temple Mills
8P15	0634	Angel Road	8J23	2155	Temple Mills
8L01	0642	Bury St Edmunds	8B41	2205	Hitchin
8N04	0658	Wensum	8H11	2225	Stratford Old Yard
6L32	0755	Kings Lynn	4E30	2242	Kings Norton–Felixstowe (cars)
8H03	0800	Bow Depot	8P23	2247	Broxbourne
8N06	0818	Thetford	8N16	2302	Wensum
8B39	0824	Hitchin	9N64	2310	Wymondham
8L55	0856	Foxton	8F13	2350	Manningtree
8P29	0952	Broxbourne CEGB			

Northbound and Westbound Departures

8N81	0007	Tees Yard	8J82	0615	Warsop Junction
8M04	0020	Colwick Yard	8D19	0655	Scunthorpe
8J98	0035	Ollerton Colliery	8D22	0705	Worksop
8D09	0045	Carlton Colliery	8D85	0730	Doncaster Decoy
6S68	0140	Millerhill	8M29	0742	Colwick Yard
7D03	0200	Grimsby East Marsh	8D86	0754	Doncaster Decoy
6D51	0230	Branston	8J83	0806	Mansfield Concentration
8L00	0327	Healey Mills	8D28	0828	Scunthorpe
8D84	0406	Doncaster Decoy	8D41	0849	Scunthorpe/Santon
8M01	0430	Colwick Yard	8M23	0900	Colwick Yard
8J81	0440	Thoresby Colliery	8J80	1019	Warsop Junction
8D08	0524	Boston Goods	8D68	1103	Worksop

8D67	1115	Bentley Colliery	8J37	1835	Broughton Lane
8J29	1425	Tinsley	8J48	2023	Mansfield Concentration
8D67	1437	Worksop	7M35	2105	Mottram
8N89	1450	Tees Yard	6N65	2217	Tyne Yard
8J89	1510	Mansfield Concentration	7N28	2227	Tees Yard
8S44	1521	Kirkcaldy	8D81	2232	Normanby Park
8J94	1555	Mansfield Concentration	7M66	2254	Nottingham New Sidings
8M73	1609	Colwick	7J67	2304	Tinsley
8D73	1619	Santon	7D12	2338	Worksop
8L24	1716	York	7J73	2348	Thoresby Colliery
8D21	1750	Boston	6L63	2358	Healey Mills
8H32	1835	Doncaster			

Above:- With eleven train pairs every 24 hours linking March Whitemoor and Temple Mills Yard, as well as several trains to Bow, Stratford and Broxbourne, it is clear that the majority of traffic being handled at March was coal for the fires and gas works of East London. Traffic the other way not only linked Whitemoor to the main general freight marshalling yards at Doncaster, York, Tees, Tyne, Millerhill, Healey Mills and Mottram, but crucially to four key locations where thousands of tons of coal were collected each day: Mansfield Coal Concentration Sidings, Worksop, Colwick Yard and Warsop Junction. On top of that regular daily flows also linked the yard directly with collieries like Thoresby, Bentley and Carlton. As for general goods, Whitemoor dispatched and collected freight from every corner of East Anglia, as the list of southbound and eastbound departures attests.

*Above:- This view of the locomotive depot shows the usual array of motive power, with Eastern Region Class 37s and 31s in the majority along with a visiting Class 45 and Class 25 from the London Midland Region. My old notebook records the following locomotives on the depot on Saturday 6 October 1979. (**M. Rhodes**)*

Class 08	Class 25	Class 31	Class 37	Class 40	Class 45	Class 47
08026	25132	31179	37039	40071	45003	47217
08094	25136	31194	37047	40169	45035	
08095		31239	37055		45050	
08096		31240	37090			
08097		31255	37092			
08100		31260	37125			
08139		31297	37136			
08209		31315	37289			
08258						
08549						
08713						
08889						

Above:- *Although the "down" hump yard closed in 1974, the sidings were still used to store wagons awaiting the cutter's torch. Remarkably, five years later in 1979, the tower and retarder pits are still intact. The western side of the yard is filled with unfitted wagons which carried grain, cement, coal and steel, but are all now withdrawn.* (**M. Rhodes**)

Above:- *The sorting sidings at Oberhausen are still controlled by a hump tower which bears a striking resemblance to the towers at March "up" and "down" yards. Even the position of the building between the two central groups of tracks and the design of the sorting sidings in four groups is copied at March from this German yard.* (**M. Rhodes**)

Above:- The yards at Whitemoor were controlled by five signal boxes. Along the main line were, from north to south, Twenty Feet River, Grassmoor Junction, and the largest of the boxes, Whitemoor Junction. Then of course there were the two control towers at the "up" and "down" humps. Here, well known railway author Paul Shannon puts a lever back, in January 1981. (M. Rhodes)

Above & left:- Taken in January 1981, just three months after the "up" hump closed, this shows the original control panel, installed in the "up" tower back in 1928. Beyond the window the array of sorting sidings spreads out, full of wagons, several of which have derailed as a result of shunting the yard from the south end. As a comparison, the second image shows the east to west hump at Oberhausen Osterfeld Süd in 1985 with a switch panel which looks remarkably similar to the one from March "up" yard, testament to the origins of Britain's first hump yard. (Both M. Rhodes)

Above:- The view from Grassmoor Junction Signal Box shows the old "down" hump and tower, which by 1981 were still standing, but with all tracks removed. Class 31 No. 31227 winds out of the Norwood Yard with 7J46, a Whitemoor to Mansfield Coal Concentration Sidings freight. The train is made up entirely of empty coal hoppers and will be routed via Spalding, Lincoln and High Marnham. (**M. Rhodes**)

Above:- By 1986, when this view was taken, just the south end of the "up" sorting sidings remained. From left to right in the background here are the old "down" sorting sidings, Grassmoor Junction Signal Box (partially obscured by a lighting mast), the old "up" hump and the north end of the "up" sorting sidings. Whilst Speedlink traffic continued to be marshalled at Whitemoor until 1990, most of the shunting was done in the old "up" departure sidings behind the photographer. (**M. Rhodes**)

Whitemoor Junction Shunters' Cabin

In my 1988 book, The Illustrated History of British Marshalling Yards, on page 247 there is a marvellous image taken by John Baker, at the same spot as these three images. The wooden shunters' cabin, on the right of the view is looking a bit worse for wear in 1960 (having presumably been installed back in the 1920s when Whitemoor was modernised). Made of sleepers which are exceptionally durable, the cabin acted as a "constant" as everything around it changed from the first image here in 1979, to the last taken from the same spot in 2005.

Above:- On 8 June 1979, Class 08 No. 08889 shunts VDA vans which have arrived from Wisbech (the branch to which is in the background). The vans were used to carry both Metal Box traffic and also pet food from the Spillers factory at Wisbech.

Left:- On 13 June 1991, Class 20 Nos. 20133 & 20147 arrive light engine at Whitemoor, passing the same hut. Housing fills the land behind the old Whitemoor Junction Signal Box and the trackwork has been greatly simplified. The locomotives are heading for March Traction Maintenance Depot to refuel after working a coal train from Kings Lynn Docks to Foxton Cement Works.

Right:- By 7 May 2005, the housing has greatly expanded and Network Rail has built sound barriers and an embankment to protect householders from "rail noise". Class 66 No. 66705 departs the new Whitemoor with a train of ballast for weekend engineering work on the Ely to Norwich line. The shunters' cabin still survives; some comic has even tried to erect a "for sale" sign outside it! (*All M. Rhodes*)

Below:- A ballast reprocessing plant and a large yard to handle infrastructure services have been constructed on the remains of the Norwood Yards, the "up" departure sidings and some of the "down" sorting sidings. In this view, taken from the new control tower, Class 09 No. 09002 shunts open wagons containing sleepers and pieces of track recovered from work undertaken at Peterborough station. The sidings on the far right are exactly where the "up" departure sidings (added in the second world war) had stood. (**M. Rhodes**)

Below:- The new yards at Whitemoor are working to capacity, with several new services introduced in the last few years. Here the daily Hoo Junction to Whitemoor infrastructure service passes March East behind Class 70 No. 70806 in March 2016. The former March East Yards behind the signal box, which are now full of birch trees, are to be re-opened to cope with the large number of infrastructure services using Whitemoor. (**M. Rhodes**)

TOTON SIDINGS [345]

Opened: 1939/1950
Closed as hump yard: 1978/1984
Classification tracks: 37 + 35
Capacity in 24 hours: 7000–8000 wagons

Perhaps the most startling statistic about Toton Yard is that between 1939 and 1951 there was never a year when less than 2 million wagons were handled over its two humps! The sidings at Toton have been central to freight traffic in the Midlands since the 1870s. The yards were originally flat-shunted with all shunting undertaken by horses. In 1899, 70 animals were employed to shunt wagons at Toton[6]. Then in 1900 and 1901 the sidings were converted to a gravitation yard with a hump. Control of wagons descending into the sorting sidings was by shunters or brakesmen who chased the wagons down the incline and manually applied the hand brake to bring them to a stop. It was not until 1939 that the "down" sidings were automated with Frölich-type rail brakes and electro-mechanical points. After the interruption of World War II, the "up" yard received similar treatment. This time, in 1950, ten purpose built reception roads led to 37 sorting sidings, entrance to which was controlled by four Frölich retarders. Both "up" and "down" sidings at Toton dispatched trains straight onto the main line without separate departure sidings.

Toton was to become part of the London Midland Region in the 1948 nationalisation, as were most of the routes to the collieries of the Nottinghamshire coalfield. This led to a gradual increase in traffic as trains to Colwick were gradually diverted to Toton during the 1960s. Indeed, whilst many yards saw a fall in wagon throughput during the 1960s, it actually increased at Toton so that in the 1967 marshalling yard survey, throughput in the "up" yard was 22,975 wagons per week, as compared to 18,270 in the "down" yard. This made Toton by far and away the busiest yard in the country with an amazing annual throughput of 2,129,140 wagons. Added to this figure was the through traffic to Radcliffe Power Station, as well as other cross-country freights that paused at Toton for a crew change. An idea of the amazing volume and variety of traffic at the yards here is given by the table listing all scheduled departures in 1973. The table constructed from the 1973 working timetable shows an amazing 160 departures

from the yards during an average 24 hour period. This may not be the busiest year, but the range and scale of traffic can be well judged from the table.

It is not certain which was the busiest post-war year at Toton. It seems likely it was some time between 1966 and 1973. The locomotive allocation to Toton depot peaked at 356 in 1971 and the yards remained exceptionally busy until the widespread introduction of MGR coal services in the early 1970s. From 1973 onwards, the rise of MGR services, combined with the introduction of North Sea Gas (leading to the closure of dozens of gasworks), led to a rapid fall in wagonload coal traffic which needed marshalling over the hump. Thus in 1978, the "down" hump closed. This was followed by closure of the "up" hump in 1984. It is highly likely that this closure was precipitated by the 1984 miners' dispute. Illustrated in this section is an original audit sheet given to the author during a visit to Toton in 1985, which clearly shows the catastrophic effect the miners' strike had on traffic levels.

During the 1980s, parts of the "up" and "down" yards were retained to handle Speedlink wagonload traffic and Speedlink Coal services, not to mention the stabling of MGR wagon sets, both between shifts and at the weekend. The end of Speedlink and Speedlink Coal networks spelt the end for most of the sidings at Toton and it is now mainly an engineers yard used for Network Rail traffic and also a storage facility for dozens of DB Cargo Class 60 locomotives. Toton remains crucial as a freight centre in 2016, but only because DB Cargo has its main depot there. Add to the end of wagonload coal services the fact that there are now no deep coal mines left in England and it is easy to understand why the sidings at Toton are filled either with trees or derelict locomotives and wagons! That said, the land where the yards once stood has been earmarked for a potential East Midlands Parkway station on the proposed HS2, high speed rail route from Birmingham to Leeds - perhaps many years in the future, but a fitting transformation for what was once Britain's busiest hump yard.

Toton Departures – Summer 1973

Headcode	Time	From	To
8M79	0002	Stanton Gate	Boston
8E13	0005	North Yard	Worksop
8E61	0015	North Yard	Mansfield Concentration
8D95	0035	North Yard	Bentinck Colliery
8E35	0045	Meadow Yard	Seymour Junction
8M28	0050	Radyr	Stanton Gate
8F51	0050	East Yard	Corby Lloyds Sidings
8P16	0052	West Yard	Burton
8O64	0115	Thoresby Colliery	Southfleet APCM
8D82	0115	North Yard	Rufford or Clipstone
8E87	0125	North Yard	Worksop
7B80	0148	West Yard	Northampton
8F53	0155	East Yard	Winsford
6O59	0155	Welbeck (MGR)	Northfleet APCM
6D46	0203	Blackwell (MGR)	Radcliffe CEGB
9P01	0225	West Yard	Willington CEGB
8E33	0235	Meadow Yard	Seymour Junction
8G34	0247	East Yard	Three Spires
8A24	0255	East Yard	Willesden Sudbury
6D49	0300	Pinxton (MGR)	Radcliffe CEGB
8V92	0303	West Yard	Reading
8F32	0310	East Yard	Wellingborough
8E05	0310	Meadow Yard	Tees Yard
8D15	0312	Blackwell	Drakelow CEGB
8G79	0324	West Yard	Bescot
8E89	0325	North Yard	Dinnington
9B07	0400	East Yard	Rugby
8E37	0400	Meadow Yard	Tinsley
6D31	0407	Ratcliffe CEGB	Blackwell Sidings
8G61	0413	West Yard	Aston
8E36	0415	North Yard	Manvers Main
6E41	0425	Northfleet APCM	Welbeck Colliery
6D56	0426	Pinxton	Radcliffe CEGB
8F36	0440	East Yard	Corby
9M22	0440	Meadow Yard	Ashburys
6D55	0442	Ratcliffe CEGB	Bentinck Colliery
8E34	0500	North Yard	Scunthorpe
8D43	0510	North Yard	Clipstone Colliery
8D40	0520	North Yard	Rufford Colliery
7M15	0550	Beighton CCE	Narborough
8F12	0605	East Yard	Knighton South Junction
8P36	0607	West Yard	Chaddesden
6D57	0607	Ratcliffe CEGB	Bentinck Colliery
8D72	0615	Willington CEGB	Blackwell Sidings
8M85	0630	Meadow Yard	Edge Hill
8P05	0633	West Yard	Drakelow CEGB
8D72	0642	Drakelow CEGB	Blackwell Sidings
8V62	0655	West Yard	Severn Tunnel Junction
8G06	0711	West Yard	Bescot
8A26	0715	East Yard	Watford
8O73	0725	Thoresby	Southfleet APCM
9D09	0725	North Yard	Riddings Junction
7M40	0746	York	Loughborough
8E65	0753	Meadow Yard	Tinsley
8F40	0815	East Yard	Ashwell
8G55	0839	West Yard	Aston
8F27	0840	East Yard	Lloyds Sidings
8K83	0918	West Yard	Stoke Yard
7M70	0929	Wakefield	Croft CCE
8D81	0938	North Yard	Clipstone Colliery
8E97	0939	Narborough	Beighton CCE
8V12	0950	West Yard	Reading
8E73	0950	North Yard	Dinnington Colliery
8P54	0955	West Yard	Chaddesden
9D05	0955	North Yard	Langley Mill
6D40	1005	Pinxton	Radcliffe CEGB
8E50	1010	North Yard	Mansfield Concentration
8E80	1035	North Yard	Tinsley
8F33	1045	West Yard	Wellingborough
9P68	1047	Stanton Gate	Willington CEGB
8D50	1055	North Yard	Bentinck Colliery
8D51	1130	North Yard	Tibshelf Sidings
7M41	1140	York	Loughborough
8E34	1145	Loughborough	York CCE
8D65	1145	North Yard	Rufford Colliery
6D41	1152	Ratcliffe CEGB	Bentinck Colliery
6O85	1210	Thoresby	Northfleet APCM
8E81	1210	Meadow Yard	Seymour Junction
6D32	1211	Langley Mill	Radcliffe CEGB
8E04	1225	Meadow Yard	York North Yard
8E74	1240	North Yard	Dinnington Colliery
9M14	1245	Belvoir Junction	Stanton Gate
9D14	1300	North Yard	Clipstone Colliery
8E57	1310	Ashwell	Scunthorpe
8E50	1315	North Yard	Parkgate
6D48	1317	Riddings Junction	Radcliffe CEGB
7M71	1325	Wakefield	Nuneaton CCE
6E43	1325	Northfleet APCM	Welbeck Colliery
8D46	1330	North Yard	Blackwell Sidings
8D60	1340	North Yard	Blackwell Sidings
8F01	1400	East Yard	Ashwell
8P44	1410	East Yard	Castle Donnington CEGB
8D72	1430	North Yard	Sherwood Colliery
6D58	1433	Pinxton	Ratcliffe CEGB
8D35	1441	Cockshute	Stanton Gate
6D50	1442	Ratcliffe CEGB	Langley Mill
8F06	1445	East Yard	Corby
8P20	1455	West Yard	Coalville
8P55	1503	East Yard	Chaddesden
6D39	1507	Ratcliffe CEGB	Riddings Junction
8E51	1525	Meadow Yard	Mansfield Concentration
8E85	1540	Meadow Yard	Scunthorpe
8E77	1548	North Yard	Shirebrook Sidings
8E41	1555	Loughborough	York CCE
6D42	1558	Pinxton	Ratcliffe CEGB
8E38	1605	Meadow Yard	Seymour Junction
8F39	1615	West Yard	Wellingborough
8M88	1615	Meadow Yard	Edge Hill
9D30	1620	North Yard	Riddings Junction
6D59	1622	Ratcliffe CEGB	Bentinck Colliery
8E25	1625	North Yard	Mansfield Concentration
8D39	1645	North Yard	Rufford Colliery
8E42	1655	Croft	Wakefield CCE
9D23	1711	Corby	Stanton Gate
8V54	1712	East Yard	Westbury
6D50	1752	Ratcliffe CEGB	Bentinck Colliery
8F48	1800	East Yard	Wellingborough
9D37	1810	West Yard	Castle Donnington CEGB
8D61	1810	North Yard	Tibshelf Sidings
8E55	1820	North Yard	Worksop
8E32	1835	Ashwell	Scunthorpe
8F22	1840	East Yard	Wellingborough
8F29	1915	East Yard	Wellingborough
8D07	1915	North Yard	Langley Mill
8G37	1925	West Yard	Three Spires
9M07	1934	Belvoir Junction	Stanton Gate
6O33	1945	Welbeck Colliery	Northfleet APCM
6E37	2000	Northfleet APCM	Welbeck Colliery
8D68	2005	North Yard	Tibshelf Sidings
6E50	2017	Long Eaton	Port Clarence
8V49	2024	West Yard	Severn Tunnel Junction
8D69	2025	North Yard	Tibshelf Sidings
6D52	2028	Pinxton	Ratcliffe CEGB
8E53	2030	Nuneaton	Wakefield CCE
8P10	2048	West Yard	Derby St Marys
8A32	2050	East Yard	Wellingborough
8D85	2100	North Yard	Clipstone Colliery
8P19	2110	West Yard	Willington CEGB
8F40	2110	East Yard	Lloyds Sidings
6D32	2115	Riddings Junction	Ratcliffe CEGB
8G57	2120	West Yard	Aston
8E88	2120	North Yard	Shirebrook Sidings
8B88	2140	East Yard	Northampton
8E98	2145	North Yard	Worksop
6D34	2148	Langley Mill	Ratcliffe CEGB
8O47	2200	East Yard	Southfleet APCM
8E40	2205	Meadow Yard	Tinsley

Headcode	Time	From	To
9M50	2220	Meadow Yard	Garston
6D51	2222	Ratcliffe CEGB	Bentinck Colliery
8P09	2225	West Yard	Overseal Sidings
9M21	2227	Meadow Yard	Glazebrook
8V22	2235	West Yard	West Drayton
8E66	2238	Meadow Yard	Barrow Hill
8F10	2250	East Yard	Lloyds Sidings
6D30	2302	Ratcliffe CEGB	Riddings Junction

Headcode	Time	From	To
8E49	2310	Meadow Yard	Scunthorpe
8B17	2315	East Yard	Northampton
8E63	2325	North Yard	Shirebrook Sidings
6D38	2327	Ratcliffe CEGB	Langley Mill
8D10	2332	Meadow Yard	Tibshelf Sidings
8D62	2345	North Yard	Tibshelf Sidings
9D68	2348	Kegworth	Stanton Gate

Plan of Toton

Below:- This plan shows the yards at Toton when they were at their most extensive, between the 1948 modernisation of the "up" hump in 1948 and the closure of the "down" hump in 1978. (**M. Rhodes collection**)

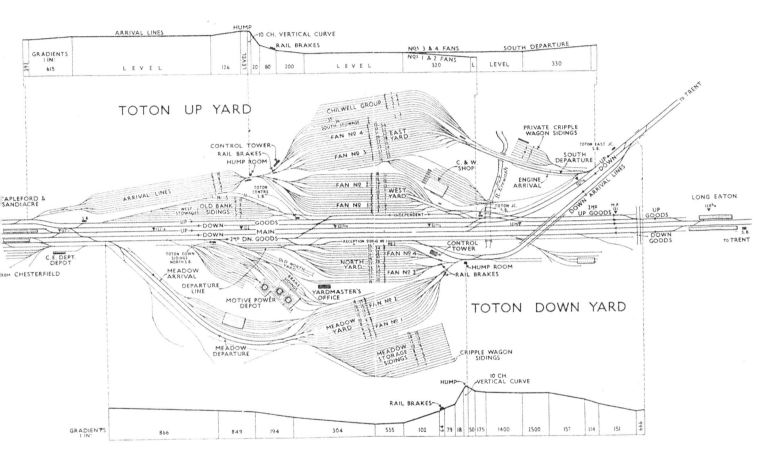

Locomotive Depot

Down hump

Up Reception Sidings

Up Hump

Left:- This 1951 Aerofilms image captures the sheer scale of the yards at Toton extremely well. (English Heritage)

Above:- Toton Traction Maintenance Depot visit - 8th January 1977 (day of Derby Works open day - 79 Locos on Derby Works that day). Total 95 locos. (**M. Rhodes**)

Class 08	Class 20		Class 25	Class 31	Class 44 (Peaks)	Class 45	Class 47
08021	20006	20154	25120	31138	44002	45004	47186
08045	20013	20157	25124	31243	44004	45008	47188
08181	20030	20158	25126		44005	45033	47205
08270	20037	20159	25132		44006	45037	47306
08275	20040	20163	25188		44007	45057	47324
08292	20041	20164	25218		44008	45065	47326
08320	20045	20168	25267		44009	45069	47327
08332	20047	20169			44010	45070	47330
08399	20048	20170				45103	47331
08685	20050	20171				45131	47366
08741	20070	20173				45133	47514
08757	20073	20175				45136	
08829	20077	20178				45141	
08858	20081	20180				45144	
	20088	20185				45145	
	20135	20188				45148	
	20136	20189					
	20140	20190					
	20150						

Right:- Three images taken over a 30 year period show the one constant feature at Toton, the diesel maintenance depot. In 1980, Class 20s predominate with the Class 44 "Peaks" still all on shed for the weekend. By 1987, newer railfreight liveries predominate with Class 58 and Class 56 making up the majority of the residents. By 2010 the depot is packed with dozens of stored Class 60 locomotives and a degree of uniformity has descended with almost all operational locomotives being GM Class 66 engines. (**All M. Rhodes**)

Toton in Transition

These 7 images, all taken from the A52, well illustrate the transition from 1980 to 2010.

Left:- Looking at the variety of traffic and the time of day, this view, taken in March 1980, shows Class 25 No. 25209 arriving from the south with what is almost certainly 8D43, the 1327 freight from Corby to Toton. The "up" reception sidings are full of unfitted and vacuum-fitted arrivals, most consisting of coal wagons, but also including quite a bit of mixed freight.

Middle:- Within 18 months, the scene has changed radically with unfitted wagons almost eliminated and more evidence of MGR air-braked trains. Here Class 20 Nos. 20196 & 20016 arrive with coal from Hucknall Colliery which will cross over to the east and then reverse into the "up" reception sidings.

Below:- By 1985, the "up" hump had closed and the former Old Bank Sidings (seen above Class 31 No. 31130) were used to marshall Speedlink traffic. The former "up" reception sidings (New Bank) are being used to stage block loads of coal as seen here with a Class 56 pausing with HEA hoppers. The former "down" yard is filled with MGR sets and HEA air-braked hoppers used for the short-lived Speedlink Coal Network which was centred on Toton. The train is 7D09, the afternoon trip from Burton to Toton and is bringing MGR wagons which have been repaired in the wagon works at Burton.

Left:- By 1988 the abolition of non-air-braked stock is all but complete. The sidings are increasingly filled with just HAA MGR hoppers and HEA air-braked, Speedlink Coal hoppers. Here Class 37 No. 37235 arrives with 6D50, the daily Washwood Heath to Toton Speedlink Coal working.

Below left:- Class 20 Nos. 20053 & 20094 arrive at Toton on 1 August 1990 with an MGR from Cotgrave Colliery. The Old Bank sidings are now full of HEA Speedlink Coal wagons as other Speedlink traffic had been diverted away from Toton by this date.

Below:- By 2006, 32.5 ton MGR hoppers had made way for 100 ton wagons, several rakes of which are seen in the old "up" reception yard, which by this time only had six surviving tracks. The "relaxed" policy about weed control is evident and much of the yard is beginning to disappear under birch trees. The Old Bank sidings above Class 60 No. 60008, are filled with engineers' traffic. The train is the Saturdays-only empty stone service returning from Bletchley to Peak Forest.

Below:- Just four years later and the old reception sidings are now out of use. The Old Bank Yard has several sidings filled with stored Class 60 locomotives and redundant parcels stock. Class 66 Nos. 66119 & 66165 are leaving Toton depot after maintenance. (**All M. Rhodes**)

Toton "up" hump

Left:- *The New Bank Yard or "up" reception sidings are seen here at the time of the yard opening in 1950.* (*BR LMR - M. Rhodes collection*)

Right:- *In 1950, 24-ton coke hoppers were considered the revolutionary high-capacity wagons of the day. It is not surprising therefore that the LMR photographer has chosen to record six of them descending the hump of the newly modernised "up" yard in 1950.* (*BR LMR - M. Rhodes collection*)

Left:- *Looking south from the hump in 1950, this official LMR photograph shows the hump control tower on the left, whilst Toton Middle Signal Box is on the extreme right. An 8F is heading south on the engine release road for servicing in Toton depot.* (*BR LMR - M. Rhodes collection*)

D1

WAGONS HANDLED PER MAN SHIFT: TOTON YARD

1984		NUMBER OF WAGONS			SHUNTERS			DRIVERS			C & W		
		US	OB	DS	US	OB	DS	US	OB	DS	US	OB	DS
January	7	2502	842	1620	12	28	27	50	—	108	45	56	108
	14	3572	1314	2441	17	44	41	71	—	163	65	88	163
	21	3337	1288	2025	16	43	34	67	—	135	61	86	135
	28	3060	1532	2321	15	51	39	61	—	155	56	102	155
February	4	3511	1204	2458	17	40	41	70	—	164	64	80	164
	11	3490	1403	2617	17	47	44	70	—	174	63	93	174
	18	3652	1338	2684	17	45	45	73	—	179	66	89	179
	25	3485	1719	2855	17	57	48	70	—	190	63	115	190
March	3	3597	1462	2375	17	49	40	72	—	158	65	97	158
	10	3544	2062	2871	17	69	48	71	—	191	64	137	191
	17	3355	1364	2589	16	45	43	67	—	173	61	91	173
	24	3446	1430	2036	16	48	34	69	—	136	63	95	138
	31	3733	1486	2595	18	50	43	75	—	173	68	99	173
April	7	3278	329	1304	16	11	22	66	—	87	60	22	87
	14	2713	170	1269	13	6	21	54	—	85	49	11	85
	21	2412	268	1456	11	9	24	48	—	97	44	18	97
EASTER	28	1397	120	864	11	7	24	47	—	96	42	13	96
May	5	2387	365	2517	11	12	42	48	—	168	43	24	168
	12	2484	215	1659	14	9	35	62	—	138	56	18	138
	19	1954	389	1906	9	13	32	39	—	127	36	26	127
	26	2564	669	1459	12	22	24	51	—	97	47	45	97
June B/Hol	2	1345	242	912	6	8	15	27	—	61	24	16	61
	9	1467	518	1478	7	17	25	29	—	99	27	35	99
	16	2179	542	1409	10	18	23	44	—	94	40	36	94
	23	1709	311	1013	8	10	17	34	—	67	31	21	67
	30	1175	422	1001	6	14	17	24	—	67	21	28	67
July	7	1428	463	1296	7	15	22	29	—	86	26	31	86
	14	1151	532	1119	5	17	19	23	—	75	21	35	75
	21	1061	440	1196	5	15	20	21	—	80	19	29	80
	28	1053	340	854	5	11	14	21	—	60	19	23	60
August	4	746	327	721	4	11	12	15	—	48	14	22	48
	11	1187	193	690	6	6	12	24	—	46	22	25	46
	18	1112	374	851	5	12	14	22	—	57	20	25	57
	25	987	415	1018	5	14	17	20	—	68	18	28	68
September	1	913	369	869	4	12	14	18	—	60	17	25	58
	8	1156	343	951	5	11	16	23	—	63	21	23	63
	15	1103	292	939	5	10	16	22	—	63	20	19	63
	22	1039	369	959	5	12	16	21	—	64	19	25	64
	29	1214	415	1160	6	14	19	24	—	77	22	28	77
October	6	1174	645	944	6	21	16	23	—	63	21	43	63
	13	1491	621	1000	7	21	17	30	—	67	27	41	67
	20	1264	436	1070	6	15	18	25	—	71	23	29	71
	27	1554	645	985	7	21	16	31	—	66	28	43	66
November	3	1546	498	904	7	17	15	31	—	60	28	33	60
	10	1466	462	1112	7	15	19	29	—	74	27	31	74
	17	1589	338	894	8	11	15	32	—	60	29	23	60
	24	1015	472	936	5	16	16	20	—	62	18	31	62
December	1	1343	343	1133	6	11	19	27	—	76	24	23	75
	8	1348	563	880	6	19	15	27	—	59	24	37	59
	15	1535	605	846	7	20	14	31	—	56	28	40	56
	22	1890	873	1562	9	29	26	38	—	104	34	58	104
	29		CLOSED PERIOD							CLOSED PERIOD			
No of turns per group:					210	30	60	50	—	15	55	15	15

NCB DISPUTE
NCB DISPUTE

Above:- This document, released to me at the time of an official visit to Toton in 1985, shows the virtual collapse of wagonload traffic precipitated by the miners' strike of 1984. It is a graphic display of the dependence of Toton on the British coal industry and showed why the "up" hump finally closed in 1984. **(M. Rhodes collection)**

Left & below:- *The main control tower at Toton "up" yard had two sections. The northern half contained the retarder operator and his controls. Frölich retarders were used at Toton and these were applied to the wagons by levers as shown here. The system is remarkably similar to that used at the same time at Oberhausen, where the levers were not encased as at Toton, but mechanically almost identical in their mode of operation. (**Both M. Rhodes**)

Above:- Paul Shannon discusses the operation of the hump at Toton, in March 1980, with the yard manager. A guards van drifts past the picture windows as the hump signaller finishes off his paperwork for the train that has just finished humping. (**M. Rhodes**)

Below:- Also in 1980, looking from the yard control tower towards the north, empty HTO & HTV hoppers roll into the "up" sorting sidings. A group of Cambridge students stand to the west of the hump to observe proceedings. (**M. Rhodes**)

Right:- During an official visit by the Cambridge University Railway Club in 1980, access was granted to both the "up" hump and the control tower. Here Class 20 Nos. 20022 & 20096 pass over the hump, having arrived with a coal train from Barrow Hill Yard. The author's trusty bicycle is visible, propped against the hump signal cabin! (**M. Rhodes**)

Right:- With the closure of the "up" hump in 1984, the former reception sidings became the main marshalling area for freight as this 1989 view shows. From left to right are: Class 20 Nos. 20177 & 20142 with an up MGR, Class 56 No. 56017, again with an MGR, stabled before dispatch to Ratcliffe Power Station, Class 58 No. 58046 light engine, awaiting work, Class 08 No. 08263, the yard pilot and finally Class 20 Nos. 20214 & 20170 with a rake of HEA coal hoppers. Study of the wagon labels revealed the following traffic in the HEA wagons: coal from Bolsover to Hull, coal from Gedling to Gobowen and Llandovery, as well as 8 HEAs from Gedling to Marshgate Sidings at Bow in London. A reminder of the "old days" is given by the pole-mounted loudspeakers, still standing and used when hump shunting took place to relay instructions from the hump cabin to the shunters. (**M. Rhodes**)

Above:- With the collapse of both wagonload freight and wagonload coal in 1990/91, the need for marshalling at Toton all but disappeared. Six of the reception sidings have been removed and the other six are used to stable MGR traffic. Class 60 No. 60088 and Class 58 No. 58024 are at the head of two rakes of empty wagons in this 1996 view. (**M. Rhodes**)

*Left:- Even eight years after the "down" hump at Toton closed, much of the infrastructure was still in situ. The concrete control tower (built to withstand bombing) was still standing and the four Frölich retarders were still on the ground. Two of the former sorting siding fans were still in daily use, as can be seen from this view taken from up one of the hump lighting masts. The south end of Toton diesel depot can be seen on the left in the background (**M. Rhodes**)*

*Above:- By 1981, there were not many non-air-braked services still running south to London on the Midland Main Line, as most traffic had been diverted via Whitemoor and Temple Mills yards. There were still however a couple of vacuum fitted, 45 mph freights south to Wellingborough and on to Brent Yards in London and one of these is seen leaving Toton behind Class 45 No. 45064 in June 1981. Note how trains left Toton directly from the sorting sidings as no departure yard was ever built here. (**M. Rhodes**)*

*Above:- This panorama of the "up" reception sidings shows Class 31 No. 31161, which has just arrived with one of several daily services from March Whitemoor. By February 1986 when this image was taken, most of these trains were air-braked Speedlink services, but this arrival was the 9M40 daily unfitted freight (running on this occasion as 7M40 because of being completely vacuum braked). (**M. Rhodes**)*

Above:- Class 08 No. 08757 shunts the south end of the "up" yard in 1985. With the closure of the hump a year earlier all marshalling was done from the south and the yard was still busy with Speedlink air-braked traffic as this view shows. (**M. Rhodes**)

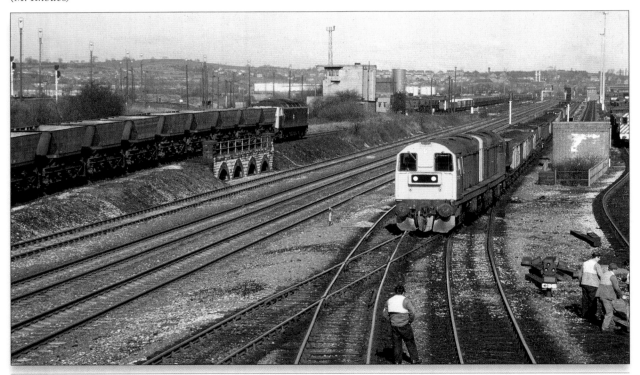

Above:- Old and new at Toton in March 1980. Class 47 No. 47327 heads north with an empty MGR coal service from Ratcliffe Power Station. Behind the train is the old "down" hump tower, watching over a now closed "down" hump. As can be seen to the right of the hump tower the "down" yard is full of MGR coal trains by this time. On the right Class 20 Nos. 20152 & 20156 head south, past the "up" sorting sidings with the old style coal train, made up of assorted unfitted low capacity wagons. (**M. Rhodes**)

HULL INWARD YARD [78]

Opened: 1935
Closed as hump yard: 1977
Classification tracks: 30
Capacity in 24 hours: 2500 wagons

The LNER marshalling yard in Hull opened in December 1935 and was the second (after March Whitemoor) to employ mechanical retarders. Four retarders were installed, all controlled by a single operator. The German design, by Frölich, was the most widespread of the day and employed a hydraulic mechanism, which in the case of Hull Inward Yard had glycerine added to the water to avoid freezing in winter ("it's grim up north!"). Hump shunting was performed by ex-North Eastern, 3-cylinder 4-8-0 tank engines originally designed to work at Erimus hump yard on Teeside and dating from 1909. These engines were also used at Whitemoor. The capacity of the yard was 2500 wagons per 24 hours, although up to 3000 were sorted on occasion. With six reception sidings and 30 classification tracks, the yard was also one of the first to benefit from electric floodlighting, which was said to illuminate the hump area "brilliantly". The yard remained busy, as the list of main line departures from 1957 shows.

The yard was not only the first to utilise floodlights, but also the first large hump yard in the world to use the now industry-standard Dowty retarders. A British Railways Research Department Report from 1962[9] reveals that in 1961 and early 1962 the Dowty retarder was used on tracks 29 and 30 of the sorting sidings at Hull Inward. The retarders performed faultlessly, except when asked to handle 26-ton loaded tippler wagons (GLW 35 tons) which entered the retarding area at a speed above 15 feet per second. This was the sternest test as these were the heaviest wagons hump shunted and arrived at the retarders faster than the advised maximum speed. Nevertheless, it was reported that siding 30 worked from December 1961 to February 1962 without problems. The hydraulic power pack only overheated once, requiring a short shut down, and 12 of the small "dash pot" retarders sustained damage. This was even though wagons were supposed to arrive from the primary retarders in the siding with a speed between 3 and 8 mph, yet some arrived as fast as 13.5 mph. The suggested solution to the imprecision of arrival was to use Dowty retarders throughout the yard as was the case when Tinsley was opened just three years later.

Decline came in the 1960s, as both Beeching cuts to sidings and goods depots, and inflexibility in the Port of Hull led to a seismic fall in traffic. Hump shunting finished over Christmas 1977. Calvin Hope, a shunter at the yard from 1974, remembers that year on year when he worked at Inward Yard, the number of wagons being hump shunted decreased. When he started in 1974 the yard had two pilots; one was the hump pilot, the other the yard pilot and they worked from 0600 Monday until 2200 Saturday. When Calvin left the yard there was only one yard pilot that worked 0600 Monday until 2200 Saturday. The number of wagons being hump shunted in the final year could be as few as 50 or 60 per shift.

During the late 1970s trunk trains were made up for places like Doncaster Belmont, Dover (train ferry traffic), Healey Mills, Dringhouses, Toton and trips to Melton Lane (Capper Pass Rio Tinto Smelting Works & Earles Cement Sidings), Thurcroft and Maltby Collieries, Goole and Selby, Hull Sweet Dews Sidings (scrap in and out), Springhead and Sculcoates CCDs and roofing tiles and bricks for Sculcoates along with the coal traffic, crippled wagons to Dairycoates WRD and also perishable traffic to Hull Neptune Street and Hull Central Freight Depots (this line was abandoned in 1982). The Hull to Bridlington line had a daily trip; this saw chalk traffic from Beverley and house coal to Beverley, grain & other agricultural traffic to and from Driffield and the same to Bridlington.

From 1978 the yard was flat-shunted, but from the summer of 1978 more and more sidings became spiked out of use pending removal and by 1980 only 20 sidings remained in daily use.

Hull Outward Yard closed in 1972; much of its site is the Tarmac northern depot that sees a daily train of limestone from Rylstone Quarry. Some of the sidings did see further use but for non-revenue earning traffic. The Civil Engineer used these remaining sidings to make up engineers' traffic for mid-week & weekend engineers' possession trains. The yard was shunted by the Dairycoates C&W Shops pilot loco and the site of the sidings is now occupied by the A63 trunk road.

The DCE had these sidings until 1984 when they closed, along with Dairycoates WRD and Dairycoates West & Hessle Haven signal boxes, and all marshalling of traffic was carried out in the new six siding Speedlink Yard. This was never busy with just one train in and out each day to Doncaster during the 1990s. In 2016 the sidings lie derelict as freight traffic moves directly in and out of Hull Docks as block loads.

Hull Outward Yard

Inward Mineral Yard

Above:- Hull Yards in 1958 taken as part of a UK wide aerial survey. The "modern" Hull Inward hump yard at the bottom of the image is dwarfed by the larger flat-shunted yards which handled the millions of tons of mineral traffic which used to be exported through Hull Docks. (**English Heritage**)

Hull Timetable

The 1957–58 timetable for Hull yards shows the departures over 24 hours. Notably, there are more long distance departures from the flat-shunted Hull Outward Yards (OY). The Inward Yard only has departures to the east and only the long distance services are listed, like that to Beverley. The table of course omits the many trip workings to Hull Docks and the myriad private sidings and goods depots in the Hull area.

2
DEPARTURE OF FREIGHT TRAINS FROM
HULL
WEEKDAYS

W.T.T. No.	Time	Days Run	Class	From	To	Worked by Locomotive	Worked by Trainmen
907	12 35 a.m.	MX	H	Hull O.Y.	Stainforth and Mexboro' Top Yard	DY.31	DY.31
935	12 55 a.m.	MX	H	Hull O.P.	Ickles	E.R.1	DY.116
2157	1 0 a.m.	MX	H	Hull O.Y.	Selby	SL.18	SL.18
905	1 50 a.m.	MX	H	Hull O.Y.	Stainforth	DY.28	DY.28
2207	2 5 a.m.	MX	H	Hull O.Y.	Goole	DY.29	DY.29
2106	2 20 a.m.	MX	H	Hull O.Y.	Croft	DY.60	DY.60
2108	2 40 a.m.	MX	H	Hull O.Y.	York Down Yard	DY.33	DY.33
—	3 15 a.m.	EWD	—	Hull	ANYWHERE	DY.65	DY.65
2179 {	3 30 a.m. MO / 3 25 a.m. MX	MO MX	C	Hull E.M. / Hull O.Y.	Milford	DY.38	DY.38
—	3 55 a.m.	EWD	—	Hull E.M./O.P.	ANYWHERE	DY.25	DY.25
D.1	4 5 a.m.	EWD	E	Hull E.M.	Markham/Firbeck	DY.41	DY.41
2224	4 15 a.m.	EWD	E Bkd.	Hull I.Y.	Scarborough	DY.1	DY.101
2297	4 15 a.m.	EWD	H	Hull E.M. MO / Hull O.Y. MX	Neville Hill	DY.35	DY.35
2226	4 25 a.m.	EWD	H	Hull I.Y.	Bridlington	DY.2	DY.102
563	4 30 a.m.	EWD	H	Hull O.Y.	Colwick	DY.7	DY.107
905	4 45 a.m.	MO	H	Hull E.M.	Stainforth	DY.40	DY.40
2163	4 50 a.m.	MX	H	Hull O.Y.	Gascoigne Wood	DY.40	DY.40
D.4	5 10 a.m.	EWD	E	Hull E.M.	ANYWHERE	DY.48	DY.48
D.5	5 45 a.m.	EWD	H	Hull I.Y.	Bridlington	WD.23 MO / WD.21 TThSO / WD.22 WFO	DY.108
D.2	6 5 a.m.	EWD	H	Hull I.Y.	Beverley	DY.3	DY.103
909	6 25 a.m.	EWD	H	Hull O.Y.	Crewe G.L.	DY.6	DY.106
2258	7 5 a.m.	MWFO	K	Hull I.Y.	Withernsea	DY.39	DY.39
537	7 10 a.m.	EWD	F	Hull O.Y.	Colwick	DY.49	DY.49
2260	7 30 a.m.	TThSO	K	Hull I.Y.	Hornsea Bridge	DY.39	DY.39
D.14	7 40 a.m.	EWD	E	Hull E.M.	Thorne Colliery/Maltby	DY.30	DY.30
557	8 35 a.m.	EWD	H	Hull O.Y.	Decoy	E.R.11 MO / DY.34 MX	E.R.11 MO / E.R.34 E'men MX / E.R.48 Guard MX
2185	8 50 a.m.	MWFO	K	Hull O.Y.	Selby	BD.11	DY.125
D.9	9 38 a.m.	EWD	E	Hull E.M.	So. Yorks. line/ Rossington	DY.57	DY.57
2104	9 40 a.m.	MX	F	Hull O.Y.	York Down Yard	DY.52	DY.52
2195	9 45 a.m.	MO	E	Hull E.M.	York S.N.S.	DY.52	DY.52
527	9 55 a.m.	EWD	H	Hull O.Y.	Whitemoor	DY.55	DY.55 E'men / E.R.50 Guard / DY.56
—	10 25 a.m.	EWD	—	Hull E.M./O.P.	ANYWHERE	DY.56	DY.56
2110	11 0 a.m.	EWD	E	Hull E.M.	York S.N.S.	DY.58	DY.58
931	11 20 a.m.	EWD	E	Hull E.M.	Markham Main	E.R.26	E.R.26
D.11	11 35 a.m.	EWD	E	Hull E.M.	Thorne Colliery/Maltby	DY.28	DY.28
2165	12 40 p.m.	MX	H	Hull O.Y.	Carlton North Sdgs.	RN.29	RN.29
D.12 {	12 0 noon SX / 12 45 p.m. SO	SX SO	E	Hull E.M.	Thorne Colliery/ So. Yorks. line	DY.29	DY.29
601	12 50 p.m.	SX	C	Hull F.S.	Banbury	DY.60	DY.60
2279	12 55 p.m.	SO	H	Hull O.Y.	Goole	GL.18	GL.18
2209	1 15 p.m.	SX	C	Hull F.S.	Leeds City	DY.31	DY.31
603	1 25 p.m.	SO	H	Hull O.Y.	Decoy	DY.60	DY.60

3
DEPARTURE OF FREIGHT TRAINS FROM
HULL—continued
WEEKDAYS—continued

W.T.T. No.	Time	Days Run	Class	From	To	Worked by Locomotive	Worked by Trainmen
2279	1 25 p.m.	SX	H	Hull O.Y.	Goole, L.M.R.	GL.18	GL.18
D.13	1 50 p.m.	EWD	E	Hull E.M.	Thorne Colliery/Firbeck	DY.41	DY.41
—	2 10 p.m.	EWD	—	Hull E.M./O.P.	ANYWHERE	DY.33	DY.33
581	3 32 p.m.	EWD	C	Hull F.S.	East Goods	DY.62 MO / ER.21 TThSO / ER.22 WFO	DY.62 MO / ER.21 TThSO / ER.22 WFO
2291	5 30 p.m.	SO	H	Hull O.Y.	Goole	GL.18	GL.18
585	5 38 p.m.	SO	C	Hull F.S.	Guide Bridge	DY.38	DY.38
2239	6 20 p.m.	EWD	C	Hull O.Y.	Manchester Ex. SX / Leeds SO	DY.35	DY.35
587	6 45 p.m.	EWD	C	Hull F.S.	Banbury	DY.38 SX / DY.40 SO	DY.38 SX / DY.40 SO
589	6 55 p.m.	EWD	C	Hull F.S.	King's Cross	DY.40 SX / DY.49 SO	DY.40 SX / DY.49 SO
2201	7 0 p.m.	EWD	C	Hull	Dringhouses	DY.42	DY.42
915	7 15 p.m.	SOQ	H	Hull O.P.	Ickles	E.R.3	DY.114
2291	7 35 p.m.	SX	H	Hull O.Y.	Goole	GL.18	GL.18
2249	7 35 p.m.	SO	C	Hull O.Y.	Normanton	DY.61	DY.61
585	7 42 p.m.	SX	C	Hull O.Y.	Guide Bridge	DY.49	DY.49
915	7 50 p.m.	SXQ	H	Hull O.P.	Ickles	E.R.1 MO / E.R.3 MSX	DY.114
2295	7 50 p.m.	SO	H	Hull O.Y.	Wakefield T.L.	WD.21	DY.126
332	8 0 p.m.	EWD	C	Hull O.Y.	Niddrie	DY.63	DY.63
917	8 30 p.m.	SO	H	Hull O.Y.	Annesley	DY10.	DY.110
525	8 40 p.m.	EWD	D	Hull O.Y.	Whitemoor	DY.34	DY.34 E'men / E.R.54 Guard
2249	8 50 p.m.	SX	C	Hull O.Y.	Normanton	DY.56	DY.56
921	8 55 p.m.	SO	E Bkd.	Hull O.Y.	Mottram	DY.58	DY.58
2295	9 10 p.m.	SX	H	Hull O.Y.	Wakefield T.L.	WD.23 MO / WD.21 TThO / WD.22 WFO	DY.126
591	9 45 p.m.	SX	C	Hull O.Y.	East Goods	DY.55	DY.55
591	9 45 p.m.	SO	C	Hull O.Y.	Selby (East Goods load)	DY.66	DY.66
917	9 55 p.m.	FSX	H	Hull O.Y.	Annesley	DY.10	DY.110 E'men / E.R.24 Guard / DY.109
595	10 5 p.m.	EWD	D	Hull O.Y.	Burton SX / Colwick SO	DY.9	DY.9
2263	10 15 p.m.	EWD	E Bkd.	Hull O.Y.	Neville Hill	DY.57	DY.57
2102	10 20 p.m.	SO	H	Hull O.Y.	Croft	DY.64	DY.64
2221	10 25 p.m.	SX	E	Hull E.M.	Gascoigne Wood	DY.30	DY.30
921	10 40 p.m.	SX	E Bkd.	Hull O.Y.	Mottram	DY.58	DY.58
901	10 50 p.m.	SX	H	Hull O.Y.	Sheffield	DY.5	DY.105
593	11 0 p.m.	EWD	H	Hull O.Y.	Decoy	DY.52 SX / E.R.14 SO	DY.52 E'men SX / E.R.14 E'men SO / DY.111 Guard SX / E.R.24 Guard SO
775	11 15 p.m.	EWD	H	Hull O.Y.	Bradford	8D.11	DY.122
2104	11 50 p.m.	SO	F	Hull O.Y./E.M. or O.P.	York S.N.S.	DY.47	DY.47

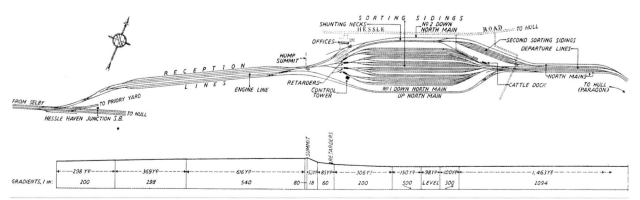

Above:- The track layout at Hull, as it was when the yard was opened in 1935. (**M. Rhodes collection**)

168

Above:- On a dull day in February 1962, a rake of mineral wagons descends the hump at Hull Inward Yard. They are headed to the northern fan of sorting sidings, which include sidings 29 and 30 which were used in 1961 and 1962 to trial the new Dowty retarder. The retarders were in use at the time of this image. (**BR ER - M. Rhodes collection**)

Above:- This view from the Mick Nicholson collection shows the newly constructed hump and the four primary retarders all pristine before any wear and tear from the thousands of wagons handled here once the yard was opened. (**M. Nicholson collection**)

REFERENCES

1   Farquarson N. Whitemoor. British Railways Illustrated, April 1994; 356–369.

2   Editorial. Whitemoor Marshalling Yard, London and North Eastern Railway. The Railway Magazine, December 1929; 425–440.

3   Editorial. The Mechanisation of a Marshalling Yard. Toton Down Sidings LM & S Railway. The Railway Gazette, August 18th, 1939.

4   Editorial. Modernised Up Marshalling Yard at Toton. The Railway Gazette Nov-Dec 1951.

5   Copeland D.M. Toton Yards and the Erewash Valley - A Brief Railway History. Published 1998.

6   Snell. Engineers Works Inspection at Toton. 8th August 1939.

7   Nock OS. New Marshalling Yard at Hull LNER. The Railway Magazine, March 1936; 186–191.

8   Rose P. Hull Inward Yard. British Railways Illustrated, May 1995; 428–435.

9   Dowty Tests Hull (4th February 1962). British Railways Research Department Engineering Division - Report No.394B.

Below:- Looking towards Hull in this 1986 view, the "new" Hull Speedlink Yard is seen with its six sidings. Class 08 No. 08499 shunts the wagons for the evening Speedlink service (6L91) to York Dringhouses Yard. The cargo will be acetic acid tanks from the Saltend Chemical Works and empty coal wagons which had delivered household coal to the depot at Sculcoates. The Class 31 (No. 31464) has just arrived from Saltend and is running light engine to Hull Botanic Gardens for refuelling and a crew change. The expanse of land behind the yard was formerly the sorting sidings of Hull Inward Yard, now taken up with retail developments. **(M. Rhodes)**

CHAPTER 6

THE 1955 MODERNISATION PLAN YARDS

1955–1963

THORNTON YARD

Opened: 1956
Closed as hump yard: Early 1970s
Classification tracks: 35
Capacity in 24 hours: 3000 wagons

The Scottish Region was the first to complete a "Modernisation Plan" yard and this was at Thornton. Opened in 1956, the yard was built on a green-field site and was designed to concentrate the marshalling of all the Fife coal traffic on a single site. It was also the first yard in the UK to utilise radar to measure the speed of wagons descending from the hump and thereby judge how much pressure to put on the retarder or rail brake to slow the wagon down. Along with the much smaller yard at Alloa, Thornton was successful in streamlining the handling of coal in Fife. It never handled as many wagons as it was designed to and in 1958 the weekly throughput averaged 10,150 (rather than a capacity of 15,000 based on a 5 day

week). The flood in the neighbouring Rothes colliery led to lower than expected traffic levels. Another problem was identified almost as soon as it opened in 1956; uncoupling vacuum fitted wagons was time consuming and in the absence of automatic couplings this wagon separation, followed by labour intensive reconnection before departure, slowed operation at the yard down considerably. This problem perhaps highlights more than any other the lack of "joined-up" thinking in the Modernisation Plan. Had the modernisation of the wagon fleet incorporated automatic couplers, then the many new hump yards

Right:- An official Scottish Region publicity photograph shows a pristine Thornton Yard in 1956. A Class 08 shunting locomotive is testing the retarders with loaded and empty coal wagons. The brand new Rothes colliery is seen in the background. (BR ScR - M. Rhodes collection)

may have been much more efficient, as their German and American contemporaries were.

With the closure of much of the Fife coalfield in the 1970s, the hump was closed. The yard continued to be busy, shunted as a flat yard from the east end. It handled both coal traffic and Speedlink trips from the many Fife branch lines[1]. With the abolition of Speedlink in 1991, traffic levels fell significantly. In the first part of this century, much of the yard was covered by a coal collection point, where opencast coal was collected from around Fife and loaded into HAA hoppers for transport to Longannet Power Station. Today the yard is completely closed and derelict.

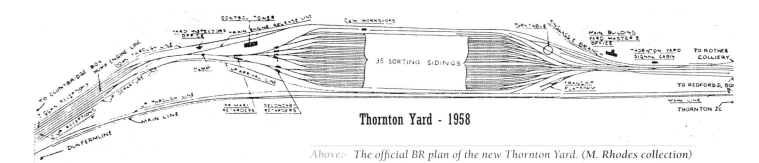

Thornton Yard - 1958

Above:- The official BR plan of the new Thornton Yard. (M. Rhodes collection)

Right:- A sunrise shot from 1986 and the winding gear from the long abandoned Rothes colliery defines the view. The control tower still stands, but half the sorting sidings have been disconnected whilst the southern half remain active with Speedlink and MGR traffic. The southern-most sidings are used to store MDV mineral wagons which had been used on coal trains from Westfield to Methil Power Station. (M. Rhodes)

Left:- Class 56 No. 56106 awaits departure from Thornton Yard on 17 August 1990 with an MGR from Thornton Yard to Millerhill. The train conveys coal from Westfield opencast collection point to Cockenzie Power Station. By 1990 the yard at Thornton had lost all its Speedlink traffic and handled just these MGR workings, no longer requiring the extensive sidings here. The long disused diesel depot is seen behind the train, whilst to the left are a variety of diesel multiple units displaced from Edinburgh suburban services. (M. Rhodes)

With Speedlink still flourishing in 1986, Class 47 No. 47337 arrives with 6B66, the daily wagonload service from Perth to Millerhill. Two empty china clay wagons were attached before the train headed south. The winding gear of the flooded colliery at Rothes acts as a constant in all the views of Thornton Yard, which had trip freights to Markinch, Auchmuty, Methil, Cameron Bridge, Crombie and Rosyth Docks at this time. (**M. Rhodes**)

Right:- Now preserved, Class 20 No. 20227 backs into the sorting sidings at Thornton Yard in May 1986 with the afternoon trip from RNAD Crombie. To the right Class 26 No. 26027 stands in front of the depot, a prefabricated building installed at Thornton Yard in the 1980s, when neighbouring Dunfermline Townhill depot closed. (**M. Rhodes**)

MARGAM YARD [2] [3] [4]

Opened: 1960
Closed as hump yard: 1980
Classification tracks: 50
Capacity in 24 hours: 4500 wagons

Margam Yard opened in 1960 and was one of three projected Western Region hump yards. As the years from the 1955 Modernisation Plan passed, it became clear that the other two (in Gloucester and Shrewsbury) were not needed. Indeed a feature of Margam was its high capacity, which was never fully utilised. Even in the mid-1960s, when the yard was at its busiest, it usually handled only 2500 wagons per 24 hours as compared to a capacity of 4500. The location for Margam was chosen because of its proximity to the Steel Company of Wales works at Port Talbot and because of its suitability as a collection point for freight from the West of Wales. Traffic to and from the neighbouring steelworks was always well over 50% of the work at Margam. Indeed the original 1961 siding allocation for the 50 sorting sidings has 15 roads specifically for traffic to and from the Steel Company of Wales, with a further 10 for traffic linked to the steel plant.

The 178 acre site contained 33 miles of track and 240 sets of points. At the east end of the complex 12 reception sidings, accessible from both the "up" and the "down" main lines, led to a fully automated hump.

The classification bowl contained 50 sorting sidings. By 1975 throughput at the yard had fallen from its peak of 2500 wagons each day to 1800 and by 1978 it was down to less than 1000 wagons per 24 hours. In 1980 the hump at Margam closed and rationalisation of the site began in earnest.

By 1985 the yard had been reduced to just 32 sorting sidings, shunted from the west end of the complex. Complete closure as a freight marshalling yard came in 1987, when the rebuilt Margam Knuckle Yard took all freight marshalling in the area. This was an 18 track, flat-shunted yard, designed primarily for receiving and dispatching block loads of steel and raw materials and it remains active in 2016. As for the site of the old hump yard, most of this has returned to nature. The diesel servicing depot has been demolished, as have most other buildings associated with the 1960 yard. Just half a dozen sidings remain on the northern edge of the old classification bowl and these are used for wagon storage. The wagon repair shops at the western end of the old yard continue to maintain the large fleet of steel carriers owned by DB Cargo, but evidence of the once extensive hump yard is disappearing fast.

Above:- An official Western Region publicity photograph has been taken from up a lighting mast in 1960, shortly before the yard at Margam opened. The last short sections between the "king" point and the two primary retarders have yet to be laid and the roof isn't yet in place over the signal room at the front of the control tower. **(BR WR - M. Rhodes collection)**

Top:- Standing on the hump crest in 1978 shows the yard is full of traffic and although only just under 1000 wagons were sorted on the day of my visit, the yard seemed busy. (**M. Rhodes**)

Centre:- With the hump closing back in 1980, it's surprising how much track is still in place by the summer of 1985. Notably the control tower containing NX and IFS panels, opened in March 1960, is still manned because the signal box here controlled access to the former reception sidings at Water Street Junction, on the South Wales Main Line to the east. The box finally closed in November 1987 when control was transferred to Port Talbot panel. (**M. Rhodes**)

Above:- Another decade has passed and the control tower has been demolished, all the tracks have gone and ballast is being salvaged for re-use. (**M. Rhodes**)

Top:- Margam Knuckle Yard[5] was opened in November 1987 at a cost of just £1.3 million. It had been decided to concentrate all freight traffic in and out of the Port Talbot complex on a single set of sidings which would need access directly into the works and also directly out onto the South Wales Main Line. Two possibilities were identified in the form of the BSC-owned Abbey Yard and the old BR-owned Knuckle Yard where the tracks had been lifted back in 1983. The Knuckle Yard was chosen because access in and out of the yard was on ready-drained and ballasted land, whereas to lay new access to the Abbey Yard would have involved putting tracks over unprepared land which was deemed too risky. Here in 1988, shortly after the opening, Class 37 No. 37278 winds out of the 18-track yard with 6B75, the 1310 service to Ebbw Vale. Standing in the yard are Class 37 No. 37802 with an MGR train of coal, loaded in the new coal dock in Port Talbot and bound for Llanwern steelworks, and also Class 37 No. 37197, just visible in the centre of the yard, with 8 BBA steel wagons bound for Dee Marsh. The Ebbw Vale train is passing Margam Abbey Works East Signal Box which was built in 1949 to the "austerity" brick design and had 37 levers. It closed when the new Knuckle Yard opened at the end of 1987. (**M. Rhodes**)

Above:- Margam Sorting Sidings Signal Box controlled the western exit from Margam hump yard. Built in 1959 and closed in 1987 it contained 89 levers. A Class 37 winds out of the yard in June 1982 with 9B88, the afternoon trip from Margam to Tondu. In the background are two other freights, both hauled by Class 47s. On the left one Class 47 has just arrived with a trip freight from Velindre tin plate works, whilst the 47 facing the camera has just arrived with 6C22, the 0700 Severn Tunnel Junction to Margam Speedlink working. Class 08 No. 08361 shunts the wagon repair sidings, on the right of the arrivals. (**M. Rhodes**)

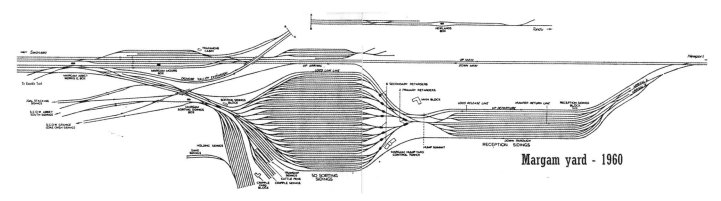

Margam yard - 1960

Above:- Official plan of Margam Yard at the time it opened in 1960. (**M. Rhodes collection**)

Right:- Margam Traction Maintenance Depot was opened in 1960 as part of the new hump yard complex and eventually closed in April 2009 when locomotive refuelling activity was transferred to Knuckle Yard. Here in July 1983 the front of each line of locomotives is as follows, looking left to right: 47066, 45064, 37247, 47246, 08361 & 47087. (**M. Rhodes**)

Left:- In May 1983, Class 37 No. 37020 heads east past the old reception sidings at Margam, with a Margam to Severn Tunnel Junction freight. Even though it is three years since the hump closed, half the reception sidings are still in situ. (**M. Rhodes**)

Right:- It's 10 July 1987 and a perfect sunny evening is a rare opportunity to catch the 6M66, Margam to Tunstead empty limestone working, on this occasion hauled by Class 47 No. 47291 and seen crossing over the western exit to Margam hump yard. The train will then run alongside the old sorting sidings before joining the South Wales Main Line a couple of miles further east. (**M. Rhodes**)

Right:- Taken from the flyover connecting Margam Knuckle Yard and the Tondu branch, this view is looking east towards where the old Margam sorting sidings used to be. By 1987 the area above the rear of this Ellesmere Port to Coed Bach Cawoods container train is already heavily covered in trees. Class 37 No. 37704 heads the train, which had the headcode 6Z07 as it only ran for a short period. (**M. Rhodes**)

Below:- Long after the hump had closed at Margam, the hump control tower continued to function, as it controlled small portions of the main

line and tracks giving access to the remains of Margam sidings to the west end of the old hump yard, which remained in use until November 1987 when the new Knuckle Yard took over. In 1985, the signaller has a chat with the yard staff. Behind him, one of the retarders can be seen clearly through the box window, untouched and unused for half a decade. (**M. Rhodes**)

PERTH YARD [6]

Opened: 1962
Closed as hump yard: 1970s
Classification tracks: 30
Capacity in 24 hours: 1500 wagons

Opened in 1962, Perth Yard had six reception sidings alongside a 30 track automated classification bowl. It operated on a "pull-back" technique with trains pulled north out of the reception sidings into a long head shunt, from where they were propelled over the automated hump. Four local yards were closed when the hump yard opened and freight to and from the Highlands was greatly speeded up. The yard at Perth was hit harder than almost any other yard by the Beeching closures. It was a collection point for general goods from Perthshire and beyond. Most of the lines from which it collected or dispatched its 112 arrivals and departures were either closed after Beeching or lost their goods services. The hump was rendered redundant in the 1970s and whilst the remnant of the yard was still used for engineers' traffic in this century, the site of the yard is now woodland.

Above:- On a quiet evening in the summer of 1990, I had the opportunity to climb the lighting mast to the south of Perth Yard. Twenty or so of the sorting sidings remain on the left of this view and are filled with civil engineers' wagons. The old hump tower still stands in the distance but the hump itself has been razed to the ground. On the right Class 47 No. 47233 awaits departure with 6N64, an empty fuel working to Grangemouth, which at this time ran only once a week and ceased shortly after this picture was taken. The train is standing in the most easterly of the six reception sidings, all of which were still intact. (**M. Rhodes**)

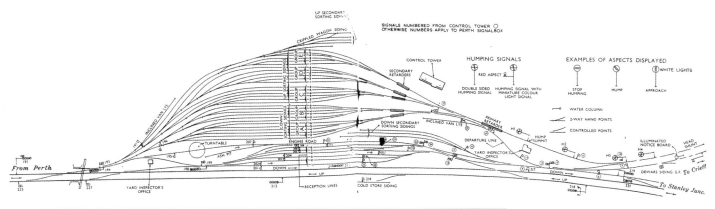

Above:- The track diagram of Perth Yard at the time of opening in 1962. (**M. Rhodes collection**)

Above:- Taken in 1962 as the yard nears completion, this view is taken from the lighting mast directly over the hump crest. The primary retarder is at the bottom right of the image with the five secondary retarders stretching across the middle of the picture. (BR ScR - M. Rhodes collection)

Top:- Looking from the same lighting mast as my 1990 view, but with a less wide angle lens, this 1963 view shows the sorting sidings on the left and the arrival sidings on the right. The lighting mast to the right of the control tower is a useful landmark to compare the two images. The sidings are full of vanfits which were used to carry potatoes from Perthshire and then dozens of 16-ton mineral wagons with domestic and industrial coal. (**BR ScR - M. Rhodes collection**)

Above:- Just before opening to traffic, this view is taken as the retarders are tested. Behind the central lighting mast a shunter and some wagons can just be made out. The wagons are being sent one at a time down into the sorting sidings to test the retarders and adjust their settings. (**BR ScR - M. Rhodes collection**)

MILLERHILL YARD [7]

Opened: 1963
Closed as hump yard: 1970 & 1983
Classification tracks: 40 + 40
Capacity in 24 hours: 4000 wagons

Millerhill was Scotland's largest yard. This double-hump yard lay either side of the fabled Waverley Route and was opened early in 1963. Its twin humps handled 4000 wagons each day and during the seed potato season this rose to nearer 5000. The yard was positioned on the Waverley Route which closed in 1970. This, along with a decline in wagonload traffic led all hump shunting to be concentrated on the "down" yard from 1970. In 1975 this still handled 1500 wagons over the hump each day with 26 departures. In 1983 however, the "down" yard closed completely and all freight was concentrated on the remnants of the "up" classification sidings and here it remains in 2016 with some 30 of the original sorting sidings still used for engineers' traffic and block trains re-manning in the Edinburgh area. Of course in 2015, the new Borders Line reopened along the route of the former "Waverley", but the tracks pass a couple of miles to the west of the former Millerhill Yard.

As for the rest of Scotland the humps at Thornton and Perth had already closed when the "down" hump at Millerhill was shut. There had been plans to build hump yards at both Cadder and Mossend, but these never came to fruition. Both yards continued to operate as large flat-shunted facilities, with the sidings at Cadder closing gradually in the 1980s, so that there is almost nothing but weeds left at this location in 2016. The changes at Mossend have been equally dramatic (see Chapter 4). Where once there was a 46 track "down" yard, there is now a distribution depot and a small remnant of 19 sidings with buffers at their south end. On the "up" side, the once busy yard with over 20 through sidings has largely been replaced by a container depot and just three passing loops remain on the site of what was Scotland's busiest wagonload yard in 1991. Millerhill was therefore Scotland's last operational hump yard when it closed in 1983.

Left, top & above:- Three images taken from the Whitehall Road bridge to the north of Millerhill Yards in 1963, 1981 and 1986 show very eloquently the decline of the "down" sorting sidings at Millerhill. In 1963 a V2 2-6-2 No. 60931 departs northwards with an express freight for Aberdeen. Fast forward nearly two decades and the scene remains much the same in 1981. Class 26 No. 26003 departs northwards with J41, the morning trip to Leith South. The winding gear of Monktonhall Colliery acts as an "anchor" to place the images. In the background another Class 26, No. 26040 shunts wagons for J25, the morning trip to Bathgate and Ratho coal depot. The trip also carried four members of the Cambridge University Railway Club on an official brake van trip; something still possible as late as 1981. Just five years later in April 1986 and the "down" sorting sidings have completely disappeared. A pair of Class 26s Nos. 26041 and 26004 leave the depot on their way to handle coal trains to Cockenzie Power Station. (**Stuart Sellar, M. Rhodes & M. Rhodes**)

*Top & above:- Two images taken from the Old Craighall Road, looking north, show changing motive power, but very little difference in the track work between 1963 and 1978. A J38 0-6-0, No. 65915 leaves the "up" sorting sidings with a short trip for the Dalkeith area. Looking the same way in 1978, Class 37 No. 37154 departs with an engineers' service heading towards the Dalkeith branch, where some track recovery is taking place. (**Stuart Sellar & M. Rhodes**)*

Right & below:- Looking south from Old Craighall Road over the decades shows the changes in both traffic and layout that occurred as a result of the closure of the Waverley route. The first image in 1964 shows Class 40 No. D359 arriving with a Carlisle Kingmoor to Millerhill freight. The headcode lives on in 2016 as the code for the daily Daventry to Coatbridge intermodal service. A second image in the days of the Waverley Route shows Clayton No. D8570, winding across into the "down" reception sidings with coal from the Dalkeith area, whilst Class 40 No. D271 has just been released from another "down" arrival and will cross over to head to the locomotive servicing depot on the "up" side of the main line. (A.A. Vickers - M. Rhodes collection & Cyril Loftus)

Opposite page above & below:- *By 1978, the Waverley route had been closed nearly a decade and track lifting along the section to Dalkeith had almost been completed. Class 26 No. 26015 winds off the Bilston Glen branch with empty ballast wagons on 10 July 1978. The lower image, looking south from Old Craighall Road, shows Class 20 No. 20203 throwing out considerable exhaust as it accelerates away from the loops south of Millerhill, with a Monktonhall Colliery to Cockenzie Power Station MGR service. The derelict track bed of the Waverley route is seen on the left of the train. (**Both M. Rhodes**)*

Top & above:- Taken from adjacent lighting masts at the south end of the "up" sorting sidings, these two images show the changes over a quarter of a century. In an official BR view, taken just after opening, the 40 sorting sidings contain a variety of traffic and a J38 winds out with a rake of empties for the collieries south of Edinburgh. By 1989, the "up" sorting sidings had been through mixed fortunes with the "up" hump closing in 1970 when the Waverley route ceased as a through route to Carlisle. All hump shunting was transferred to the "down" yard, which continued to be hump shunted until 1983. During this 13 year spell the "up" yard handled mainly engineers' traffic and was also used to store wagons used for seasonal traffic like grain and seed potatoes. Then in 1984 all traffic was transferred back to the "up" sorting sidings and the "down" yard lifted completely. In 1989, Class 47 No. 47288 winds past the departure tower (unchanged since the 1963 view) with 6E96, the daily Aberdeen to Scunthorpe Speedlink service. To handle the remaining wagonload traffic four reception sidings were built on the west of the yard and three of the original fans of sorting sidings were retained. The derelict land formerly occupied by the "down" yard can be seen on the left of this image. (**BR ScR - M. Rhodes collection & M. Rhodes**)

Left:- Two of the six retarders at Millerhill "up" yard are seen here. Things didn't always run smoothly on the complex track work! Above and to the right of the derailed 16 ton mineral wagon are the "down" hump tower and then to its right the winding gear of Monktonhall Colliery. (*BR ScR - M. Rhodes collection*)

Below:- The "up" hump tower is seen in action in this wonderful night shot taken at the time of the official opening of Millerhill Yard in 1963. (*BR ScR - M. Rhodes collection*)

Below:- The winding gear for Monktonhall Colliery is being erected in this 1963 view, taken from the "up" hump crest at Millerhill. The photographer is standing on the engine release line, which allowed locomotives released from their arrivals to run back along the arrival tracks and then on to the servicing depot. In some of the 1955 Modernisation Plan yards the vertical curvature at the hump was so much that large diesels like the Class 40s and the Class 45 "Peaks" could not safely negotiate the hump and in these yards a hump avoiding line was constructed. This was not the case at Millerhill. (*BR ScR - M. Rhodes collection*)

EASTERN REGION YARDS

The Eastern Region completed the first English yard of the Modernisation Plan at Temple Mills in East London. The rest of the region received relatively little of the investment provided for yards. Sidings at Peterborough New England were refurbished, but basically remained as they had been since the days of the Great Northern. The extensive yards at Doncaster remained largely unchanged and both Hull and March had already benefited from modernisation. Plans were laid for a new yard in Sheffield at Tinsley, but the only other major project was the remarkable yard at Ripple Lane. It holds the crown for the shortest lived of all Britain's ill-fated hump marshalling yards.

TEMPLE MILLS YARD

Opened: 1958
Closed as hump yard: 1982
Classification tracks: 47
Capacity in 24 hours: 4500 wagons

The haphazard development of freight facilities during the 19th Century meant that in 1900 there were ten separate yards at Temple Mills. The site in the Lea Valley was an ideal focus for traffic to and from London docks and the east of London. In 1954, £3 million was allocated for a new hump yard on the site and in September 1958 Temple Mills opened. After Thornton Yard in Scotland, Temple Mills was the second fully automated hump yard in the UK. Twelve reception sidings led to 47 classification tracks over a modern hump with two primary retarders and eight secondary or group retarders. There were smaller yards to the west and east of the main sorting sidings for local traffic. There were criticisms of the yard at the time because the shunters had to use chalk to identify where the cuts of wagons were headed - this out-dated practice was needed because the card reader could not cope with the complex permutations of the 47 track sorting sidings[8].

Temple Mills survived better than any other London yard in that the 1960s National Freight Train Plan saw all freight diverted off the East Coast Main Line and through March Whitemoor. This kept a large flow of unfitted and vacuum-braked freight directed to Temple Mills, as this author can attest having spent three years in Cambridge trying to catch the March to Temple Mills Class 8 freights, which ran four times a day in the late 1970s! By 1980 however it was clear that Temple Mills' days were numbered. From 4000 wagons each day in 1970, throughput fell to just 600 in 1980. It wasn't just the fall in unfitted traffic, but the collapse of coal to London's gas works because of natural gas, and the closure of 95% of goods sidings along the Lea Valley and in London Docks. The yard remained, shunted from the south end and dealing with Speedlink traffic which amounted to no more than 250 wagons each day. By 1988 it closed completely as a Speedlink hub with work transferred to Willesden. Fast forward to 2013 and the site is unrecognisable. The former wagon works and local yard is the site of the new Spitalfield Market, whilst the sorting sidings now house a Eurostar depot. The old reception sidings have 14 tracks for EMU and carriage stabling and there is no trace of the former hump yard.

Right:- The official plan of Temple Mills as included in the booklet produced when the yard was opened in 1957. (M. Rhodes collection)

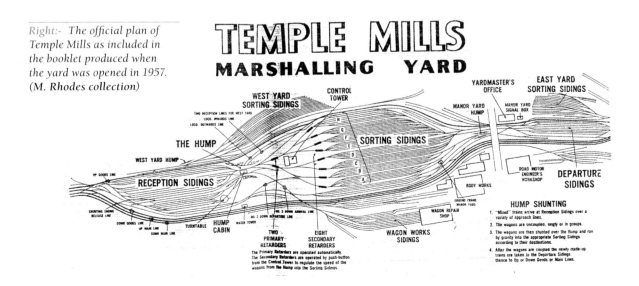

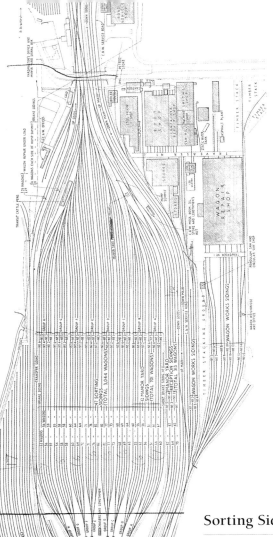

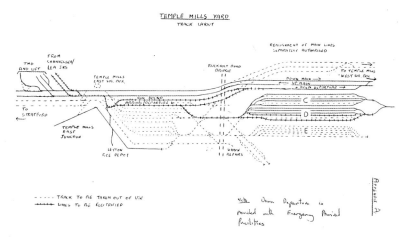

Sorting Sidings

Below & opposite top:- These two views, taken looking north from the Ruckholt Road, are just over five years apart and illustrate the rapid changes to yards like Temple Mills in the 1970s and '80s. The first picture, taken in December 1980, shows a yard full of unfitted and vacuum braked wagons, still served by four daily freights from March Whitemoor and responsible for a couple of dozen daily trip workings to local sidings. By the second image in February 1986, all the sorting sidings except the C and D fans are disused and in the process of being lifted. Class 08 No. 08414 shunts a varied rake of wagons, whilst two Class 47s await departure in the background. Class 47 No. 47356 heads 6C80, a trip to Stratford International Freight Terminal, whilst No. 47276 heads 6R92, a trip to Shoeburyness. (**Both M. Rhodes**)

Below:- Finally in 1989, overhead wires have arrived at Temple Mills. With the derelict hump control tower still standing in the distance, just two fans of the former sorting sidings were in use in 1989, Fans C & D. Class 37 No. 37893 awaits departure with 6C83, the Temple Mills to Bow trip freight. Wagonload traffic from local sidings at Gidea Park and along the Bow branch was collected in the remnants of the yard and tripped to Willesden Brent Sidings where it joined the trunk Speedlink network. **(Paul Shannon)**

Reception Sidings

Top & above:- Another pair of images show the complete transformation of the reception sidings between 1980 and early 1986. In the first image, during an official Cambridge University Railway Club visit, members of the society (including Jeremy Hunns and Rod Nelson), explore the approaches to the hump. The steep gradient of the reception sidings is evident in this view and explains why a pair of Class 08 shunters was invariably used for humping at Temple Mills. The former diesel servicing shed, used for wagon repairs in 1980, is a useful marker to compare the two views. By February 1986 the whole area is derelict, soon to be completely remodelled and eventually to become Orient Way EMU sidings. (**Both M. Rhodes**)

Left:- The yard controller watches a rake of VVV vans carrying seed potatoes as they descend into fan D at Temple Mills. The image, taken in 1972, was part of a series of publicity photos taken by BR ER. (**M. Rhodes collection**)

Below:- The yard control tower and the western half of the yard are seen in this 1961 view taken looking north towards the hump. (**Ivan Stewart collection**)

The Hump

Above & right:- Taken from the same lighting mast in 1972 and 1986, these two images graphically illustrate the devastation that befell many of the UK's yards during those two decades. In 1972 a pair of Class 08 locomotives finish humping an un-fitted freight with a vanfit, a grain wagon and an empty mineral wagon. The yard stretches as far as the eye can see. By 1986, with the hump closing four years earlier in 1982, the scene is one of dereliction. All the windows in the hump tower and yard control tower are broken and weeds and decay have taken over at the hump. (**M. Rhodes collection & M. Rhodes**)

193

Left:- A third view of the hump shows a view from the foot of the hump control tower. By December 1980, the eastern half of the sorting sidings were out of use and utilised largely as a storage area for withdrawn wagons. The shiny tracks leading to the right in this view indicate that hump shunting is still taking place into the western half of the yard. The hump pilots were Class 08 Nos. 08233 & 08494 and are stabled between shunting moves. (M. Rhodes)

Right:- A fourth view of the hump shows seven MXV mineral wagons carrying scrap from Stratford Market, bound for Sheerness Steelworks via Acton and Hoo Junction; a journey of a couple of days to cover just 50 miles! Fully laden and with a cut of seven wagons the retarders will need their maximum setting to slow these wagons down. (M. Rhodes)

Ripple Lane [9] [10]

Opened: 1958/1961
Closed as hump yard: 1968
Classification tracks: 41
Capacity in 24 hours: 2500 wagons

Prior to 1940, the land upon which the Ripple Lane hump yard stood was marshland. By 1940, freight traffic on the London, Tilbury and Southend lines had increased to such a degree that the small yards at Ilford and Plaidstow became overwhelmed. The LMS therefore drew up plans for a £100,000 investment in new sidings at Ripple Lane. An "up" and a "down" yard were constructed, both flat-shunted and both with dead-end sidings, shunted from a single track neck. The "down" side had eight sorting sidings, whilst the "up" had seven (later enlarged to 14 around 1950).

When the BRB reviewed the LT&S electrification they identified the need for a new yard and the separation of burgeoning freight traffic on the LT&S from the busy commuter passenger service. This led to the diversion of the passenger lines so that "up" and "down" lines were diverted either side of the new Ripple Lane hump yard in 1957. The yard was heralded as the first in which both "up" and "down" traffic used a single set of sorting sidings and a single hump. Previous hump

yards at Whitemoor, Hull and Toton had used two yards, one for "up" and one for "down" traffic. It opened partially in 1958, shunted as a flat yard from the east end and then fully in March 1961 when the reception sidings and hump were finally opened.

After closure of the hump yard, Ripple Lane was simplified and remodelled such that two new sets of sidings were opened in 1971. This comprised of six west sidings and six east sidings, on the site of the former approaches to the old hump. Ripple Lane is a record breaker in that opened in 1958, it then closed just ten years later in 1968. Its rapid demise was a result of the introduction of block trains for all the oil from the Thames Haven refinery, as well as the introduction of block workings to Ford's Dagenham plant. It was the UK's shortest lived hump yard. The site remained as a railfreight locomotive depot, staging sidings and container facility and although in 2016 the locomotive facility has gone, the sidings for block trains and containers remain.

Above:- In November 1989 Class 08 No. 08740 leaves the west sidings for refuelling in Ripple Lane depot. Behind it, another Class 08 No. 08531 shunts Speedlink traffic. (**M. Rhodes**)

Above:- *The administration buildings, formerly just to the north of the hump are clearly seen in this 1989 view of the East Sidings at Ripple Lane. The Freightliner terminal stands on the former sorting sidings. Class 37 Nos. 37228 and 37077 pass on the main line, diverted to accommodate the former hump yard, hauling 4M74, a Tilbury to Garston Freightliner service.* **(M. Rhodes)**

Above:- *A wonderful picture of the former hump at Ripple Lane, "anchored" by the administration block seen in the top picture of Class 37s on a Freightliner service. Taken in 1970, much of the track has been lifted, but the two southerly fans of sorting sidings are still in use as a flat yard. Later in 1971 the new Freightliner depot and East and West Sidings were built.* **(Ivan Stewart collection)**

Above:- Taken in the 1960s when Ripple Lane was at its busiest, this view shows Renwick Road at the bottom left hand corner. The diesel depot and administration buildings are seen to the left of the hump and the yard is packed with unfitted wagons, soon to be replaced by high capacity block trains. (**English Heritage**)

REFERENCES

1   Rhodes M. Branchlines and Byways Scotland. www.blurb.co.uk/b/1785421-branchlines-byways-scotland

2   Taylor JFM, District Traffic Superintendent Swansea. Margam Hump Marshalling Yard. British Transport Commission, February 1960.

3   Freeman Allen G. Margam Yard - The Most Modern in Europe. Trains Illustrated, July 1960; 404–411.

4   Freeman Allen G. Margam Yard Revisited. Trains Illustrated, September 1961; 537.

5   Rhodes M. South Wales Steel: The Tide Has Turned. Rail 88, January 1989; 26–32.

6   Freeman Allen G. The New Look in Scotland's Northern Division - II. Modern Railways, October 1962; 267–274.

7   Freeman Allen G. Millerhill Marshalling Yard of the Scottish Region. Modern Railways, November 1963; 332–335.

8   Rhodes M. The Illustrated History of British Marshalling Yards. OPC/Haynes, 1988; 24–34.

9   Kay P. The Brief Lives of Ripple Lane. British Railways Illustrated, 1997; Vol.6 No.8: 360–373.

10   Editorial. Partial Opening of Ripple Lane Marshalling Yard, The Railway Gazette, June 1958: 723.

CHAPTER 7

THE LAST OF BRITAIN'S HUMP YARDS

1963-1970

CARLISLE KINGMOOR [1] [2]

Opened: 1963
"Down" hump closed: 1971
"Up" hump closed: 1981
Classification tracks: 48 & 37
Capacity in 24 hours: 5000 wagons

Kingmoor Yard cost £4.5 million (1960 prices) and was one of the most ambitious projects of the British Railways modernisation programme. Not surprising when one considers the railway melting pot that was Carlisle. With the main lines from Newcastle, Leeds, Preston and Workington converging from the south and then main lines north to Edinburgh (Waverley route) and Glasgow (GSW & Caledonian), not to mention the branch to Silloth, it was one of the busiest rail centres in the UK. The new double hump yard

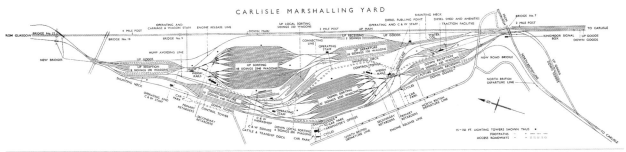

Above:- *The official plan provided with the booklet which the London Midland published to celebrate the opening of Kingmoor Yard* (**M. Rhodes collection**)

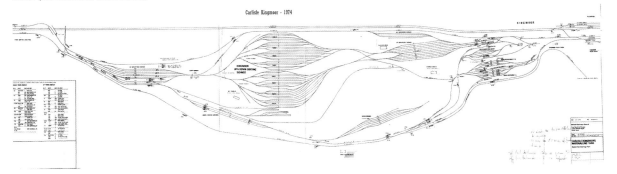

Above:- *With the closure of the Waverley Route in 1969 and the subsequent closure of the "down" yard at Kingmoor, the official plan was redrawn. This official plan dates from 1974 and was produced because, as part of the electrification of the line to Glasgow, a new listing for the placement of signals in and around the yard was needed.* (**M. Rhodes collection**)

Above:- Two images taken from the "down" hump in 1964 and 1985 show the drastic changes brought about by the closure of the "down" hump in 1971. In 1964, vacuum-fitted wagons roll through two primary and six secondary retarders into an array of 37 sorting sidings. Closure and subsequent track remodelling connected with electrification took place between 1971 and 1974, but even in 1985 the "down" control tower was still standing and the space occupied by the former sorting sidings can clearly be seen, mostly still wasteland. (**M. Rhodes collection and M. Rhodes**)

Above:- Looking north from the former "up" hump, the catenary masts which covered the "up" reception sidings are still in place in 1985. The ten reception sidings were closed and lifted in 1981 when wagonload traffic dropped significantly, linked to uncertainty over the future of the Settle and Carlisle line. (**M. Rhodes**)

Below:- Taken in 1985 from the then closed "up" hump tower, this view shows the eight secondary retarders all still in place even four years after closure of the "up" hump. The southern half of the 48 sorting sidings were still used for marshalling traffic, shunted from the south end of the yard. (**M. Rhodes**)

Above:- The crew of Class 85 No. 85022 change in the "up" departure sidings on a gloomy day in August 1985. 85022 is heading 7V93, a Mossend to Severn Tunnel Junction Speedlink service; the train is well loaded with traffic from all over Scotland to Wales and the South West. In 1985 portion swapping and wagonload marshalling took place in these 10 sidings, all electrified throughout since 1973 and more than adequate for the volume of traffic at this time. (**M. Rhodes**)

was predicted to save 7300 engine hours every day by avoiding inter-yard trip freights. This translated into a saving of more than £1000 per day. The plan of the yard shows the two parallel hump yards (the "down" slightly smaller than the "up"). With reception sidings and departure sidings for both yards it was one of only eight double hump yards in the UK (Feltham, Bescot, Millerhill, Toton, March Whitemoor, Tees and Severn Tunnel Junction being the others). It had the largest number of classification tracks at 85 (closely pipping Tees with 82).

The closure of the Waverley route in 1969 drastically reduced work in the "down" hump yard and this closed in 1971, with all wagonload traffic concentrated on the "up" yard. The reduction in freight traffic along the Settle and Carlisle line (which had carried wagonload freights to Leeds, Healey Mills and Tinsley as well as Warrington, Crewe and Severn Tunnel Junction in the 1970s), led to the

closure of the "up" hump in 1981. The remaining air-braked wagonload traffic was handled in the old "up" departure sidings. These ten lines had a capacity for 730 wagons and provided more than enough space for the Speedlink traffic of the 1980s. After Speedlink's withdrawal in 1990, there was still a wagonload service through Kingmoor run by Enterprise, but this hardly justified the extensive yard layout.

In the 21st Century the boom in Ayrshire coal traffic makes up a significant portion of freight through the yard and this traffic still uses the "up" departure sidings. The area occupied by the former "down" hump yard is now industrial units, whilst parts of the old "up" sorting sidings survive. Nineteen roads have been kept for engineers' traffic and much of the rest of the land is used as a virtual quarry by Network Rail. Two sidings on the western extremity of the former sorting sidings are used to load timber traffic from the borders.

Above:- Looking south-east across the remains of Carlisle Yard in 1986. The large area of ballast in the foreground is the former "down" departure yard. Behind this the red and grey vans are in the southern half of the "up" sorting sidings, used for some local sorting of traffic from the MOD sidings at Brunthill, or local traffic from Eastriggs and Dumfries. Most of the wagons filling the remains of the "up" yard are however engineers' traffic or stored vehicles awaiting the cutter's torch. (**M. Rhodes**)

Above:- Like many of the larger yards (Temple Mills, Wath, Tinsley), Kingmoor had a diesel refuelling and servicing depot within the yard complex. In July 1984 the typical array of Classes 25, 26 and 27 are to be found, as well as a Class 85 and a solitary Class 37. Above the single-track servicing shed the "up" hump tower can be seen and the tracks from the hump are still in place, although out of use. From left to right the locomotives which were identified were 27066, 37028, 26026 and 25196. (**M. Rhodes**)

Above:- D200/40122 enters Kingmoor Yard on 8 May 1986 with the afternoon trip from Workington, well loaded with empty timber wagons, vans and empty steel carriers. The disused power box is seen on the right and to its left Kingmoor diesel depot. (M. Rhodes)

Above:- Class 40 No. 40107 winds south from Kingmoor Yard with the 0800 Kingmoor to Severn Tunnel Junction freight in 1980. From left to right are, the "down" reception sidings with a rake of lime wagons from Hardendale and a rake of mineral wagons, then the yard stabling point with an array of motive power awaiting work; next come the "up" departure sidings, from whence 40107 has just come, and finally on the right the West Coast Main Line. (M. Rhodes)

TYNE YARD [3] [4]

Opened: 1963
Closed as hump yard: 1983
Classification tracks: 48
Capacity in 24 hours: 4000 wagons

The Tyne Yard at Lamesley, south of Gateshead, opened in 1963, replacing eight smaller yards on Tyneside. With further concentration of freight in the new yard, the sidings at Croft in Darlington were downgraded for local use only, as was the once extensive collection of

tracks at Shildon. The new Tyne Yard had 14 reception sidings at the south of the complex, leading to 48 primary classification tracks. There was also a smaller 21-track secondary classification yard for local traffic to the many private sidings on Tyneside. Once fully

TRAFFIC STATISTICS TYNE YARD

YEAR	TRAINS HUMPED	WAGONS HUMPED	YARD THROUGHOUT	
			TOTAL TRAINS	TOTAL WAGONS
1977	11,480	266,639	22,114	505,731
1978	10,905	273,994	20,055	483,304
1979	9,691	233,327	19,078	426,561
1980	8,597	189,613	19,059	380,334
1981	8,483	187,484	19,301	396,131
1982	5,007	109,375	17,506	341,261
1983	2,701	56,474	16,903	309,240
1984 P.1	–	–	1,103	19,733
Period 2	–	–	1,409	26,361
" 3	–	–	1,312	24,868
" 4	–	–	1,173	20,304
" 5	–	–	1,150	19,597
" 6	–	–	1,030	16,707
" 7	–	–	999	15,142
" 8	–	–	808	11,728
" 9	–	–	901	13,946
" 10	–	–	1,049	15,957
" 11	–	–	1,030	15,225
" 12	–	–	1,030	13,990
" 13	–	–	763	11,131
1985 Period 1	–	–	777	11,404
" 2	–	–	1,067	16,247

Above:- The collapse of wagonload traffic in the final years at Tyne Yard is demonstrated in this 1985 table. In 1977 just over half the wagons arriving in the yard were hump shunted and there were still around 1000 wagons hump shunted per day. By 1983 less than 20% of wagons used the hump and daily throughput had dropped to around 100 wagons. At this level it was impossible to justify the cost of the hump and it closed. Without the hump in 1984 the yard still handled almost 250,000 wagons in the year, or just under a thousand each weekday. This level of Speedlink and general traffic was maintained until 1989 when Speedlink withdrew from the yard. Apart from engineers' traffic the remaining sidings were then largely used to re-crew block freights passing through. **(M. Rhodes collection)**

operational Tyne Yard was the focal point for all freight traffic on Tyneside and Wearside, with its neighbouring yards being Millerhill to the north, Kingmoor to the west and York Dringhouses to the south. It was designed to handle 4000 wagons every 24 hours, but at its busiest in 1966 the weekly throughput was 14,350

wagons, suggesting at best the yard handled just over 2500 wagons every 24 hours.

Between 1970 and 1985 there were major changes in the coal industry in the North East. Improvements in the staithes at Blyth, Dunston and Sunderland led

Above:- Taken just after opening on 4 September 1963, this view shows Tyne Yard from the south. The yard control tower is on the bottom right and the locomotive servicing depot on the top left of the picture. (BR ER - M. Rhodes collection)

to much more direct working from pit to port, thus bypassing Tyne Yard. The shipbuilding industry along the Tyne and the Wear collapsed. The small goods traffic handled at the nearby Tyneside Central Freight Depot all but disappeared and finally, in 1980, Consett Steelworks closed. The statistics speak for themselves. In the 1960s the yard handled up to 3000 wagons per day over the hump. In 1977, 505,731 wagons passed through Tyne Yard, of which 266,039 were hump shunted. This equates to about 1000 wagons per day using the hump. By 1983 this number had dropped to just 56,474 wagons hump shunted all year - a couple of hundred each day - the hump closed.

For a time in the 1980s Tyne Yard remained busy in the evenings, as long-haul Speedlink trains swapped portions, but Speedlink withdrew from the yard in 1989[5]. After this the wagonload traffic that remained on Tyneside was tripped to Tees Yard to connect with long distance services. In 2016 the "up" staging sidings, which were relaid as part of electrification in 1989, are still used to stage block freights, but otherwise the remains of the yard are dwindling away. Twelve of the original primary sorting sidings remain and are used for engineers' traffic, whilst 15 secondary sorting sidings remain in situ but are unused for the most part. The old diesel servicing facility is still used as a wagon repair site.

Above:- Again in 1963, but on 9 July and taken from the top of one of the 150 foot lighting masts, Tyne Yard is seen looking south towards the hump and 14 reception sidings. (BR ER - M. Rhodes collection)

Above:- Taken on 28 May 1963, just before its opening, the engineers put the finishing touches to the two primary retarders at Tyne Yard. (BR ER - M. Rhodes collection)

Above:- An early example of "containerisation"; this flat wagon, with a wooden container which can be lifted on and off the base and placed on a road vehicle, is seen descending the hump at Tyne Yard on 12 June 1963. It is being retarded by the primary retarder. (BR ER - M. Rhodes collection)

Looking from the south, on 28 March 1963, three months before the yard was completed, Tyne Yard contains just engineers' vehicles and ballast wagons. In the top left hand corner of this view the black patch of ground is where the new diesel servicing facilities will eventually be built. (BR ER - M. Rhodes collection)

Above:- A chapter in the history of Tyne Yard which is rarely told is the £1 million rebuilding planned as part of the ECML electrification. Plans were made after the closure of the hump in 1984 and as part of the upcoming electrification of the line from London to Edinburgh, a purpose built Speedlink yard was envisaged. In this view, taken on 25 February 1989, Class 47 No. 47233 is seen winding out from the south end of the new yard with 6M19, the Saturdays Only Jarrow to Stanlow empty oil train. Above the locomotive is the connection to the west of the yard and the locomotive depot, whilst behind the train is the ten-track yard. The new connection to the west of the yard cuts across land which had been occupied by the northern end of the main sorting sidings. These were removed the year before this view was taken. Six of the sidings in the new yard were 100 SWL in length and designed for portion swapping between long distance Speedlink services and also for crew changes on container trains. The four shorter sidings were for local Speedlink traffic to Hexham and the Tyneside area. At the foot of the lighting mast over the new yard the solitary Class 08 yard pilot can be seen, quite a come down from the 1970s when Tyne Yard boasted three Class 08 pilots as well as a Class 03 for shunting in the yard and tripping to the Tyne Valley. The ten new sidings never did get utilised for their intended purpose as Speedlink was withdrawn from the yard in 1989. The tracks are however busy with block loads, especially coal which stages in the yard. (**M. Rhodes**)

Below:- The official plan of the new Tyne Yard as reproduced in the British Railways booklet produced to commemorate the opening of the yard. (**M. Rhodes collection**)

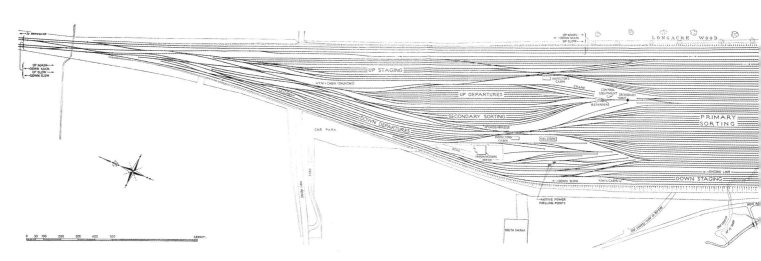

Above:- Class 47 No. 47321 pauses at Tyne Yard with 6S63, the evening Speedlink from Tees Yard to Aberdeen. Alongside it Class 47 No. 47378 has just arrived with 6S66, the Tees to Stranraer Speedlink. Because wagonload traffic was no longer marshalled at Tyne Yard, lime for the fields of Grampian on the Aberdeen service had tripped earlier in the day, south from Thrislington to Tees Yard, only to reverse its route back north with the trunk service from Tees to Aberdeen. In the background the old secondary sorting sidings are full of engineers' traffic and the locomotive servicing point has Class 37s and Class 31s in residence. (**M. Rhodes**)

Right:- A unique use for a disused hump yard! In January 1990 the MOD used the old hump at Tyne Yard to test the winch on one of its tanks. The tank was placed up the gradient of the hump and then its winch was attached to a rake of MXV ballast wagons in the old sorting sidings. In this view, taken on 26 January 1990, a Class 08 is stationed at the other end of the siding containing the MXV wagons. It is not known if it was used to pull against the winch, or if the tank simply pulled the rake of wagons uphill. (**M. Rhodes**)

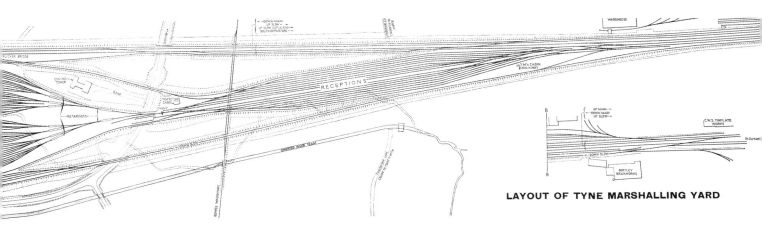

LAYOUT OF TYNE MARSHALLING YARD

Looking from the north in 2003, the 1989 built
"new" yard at Tyne is seen. Class 60 No. 60039
is stabled over the weekend with its Lindsey to
Jarrow oil train. It stands in one of three sidings
that remain from the four tracks originally intended
for local wagonload traffic. The fourth track was
removed in the 1990s to allow electrification of the
six lengthy sidings which were used to stable block
trains, mainly coal, as can be seen in this view.
(M. Rhodes)

TEES YARD [6]

Opened: 1963
Closed as hump yard: 1981 & 1985
Classification tracks: 41 + 41
Capacity in 24 hours: 7500 wagons

Teeside was Britain's largest industrial area, with steel and petrochemical plants on both sides of the river. Back in 1959 nine million tons of railfreight departed from Teeside each year. In this context a yard with inbound and outbound sides, both with semi-automated hump yards, was planned in the late 1950s. The first step in the construction of the yard was the diversion of the Thornaby to Middlesborough main line away from the banks of the Tees. This allowed preparation of the 200 acre site which already contained the four Newport yards. Over a three year period these were incrementally replaced by two parallel hump yards, containing more than 66 miles of track. The yards were designed to handle up to 7500 wagons a day, the most of any British yard. By the time Tees Yard opened freight tonnages from Teeside

had fallen to 5.5 million tons per annum and the peak throughput was therefore not often reached.

The yards were semi-automatic in that the primary retarder was fully automated, but the secondary or group retarders were operated manually by a "brakeman" in the hump tower. This was an imprecise art as the retarder operator had to "eyeball" the speed of the wagon and its weight and judge how much pressure to put on the railbrakes of the retarder. Of course, too little and there was damage when the wagon hit the other vehicles already in the chosen siding. On the other hand too much pressure and the wagon stopped short, often fouling the points into the sorting sidings. This then necessitated a halt to hump shunting and the propulsion of the errant wagon into the sorting sidings, either by the shunter and train on the hump, or on

*Above:- The newly opened "down" hump tower is seen in operation in this BR publicity photograph taken on 20 March 1963. The river Tees is above the head of the nearest controller, who is responsible for the retarders. The second signalman is switching the point into the 41 sorting sidings. (**BR ER - M. Rhodes collection**)*

Top:- This wonderful official view of the yards at Tees was taken on 14 June 1963 from the top of one of the 150 foot lighting masts at the east end of the complex. On the left a Class 08 has almost finished humping its train. In the centre of the view a short trip freight arrives from the east. The right hand side shows the departure end of the "down" sorting sidings.
(BR ER - M. Rhodes collection)

Above:- Looking more like a model railway than real life, the hump area in the "down" yard takes shape as tracks are aligned roughly on the approaches to the retarders. A ballast train hauled by an 0-8-0 rattles past almost unnoticed on 6 June 1962.
(BR ER - M. Rhodes collection)

Above:- *The twelve "up" staging and departure tracks at Tees are where most traffic is staged. In August 2014 Class 66 No. 66013 has backed onto a trainload of steel slabs bound for Skinningrove Steelworks, operating as 6F47. The green area in the left background is where Thornaby locomotive depot once stood and the green hill in the right background is where the old "down" reception sidings used to be.* (**M. Rhodes**)

Above:- Loaded with coal from the Redcar Mineral Terminal, this train, bound for Drax Power Station arrives at Tees Yard in August 2014. Class 66 No. 66101 changes crew here before heading south. In the background above the locomotive are the remains of the "up" sorting sidings and Class 66 No. 66013 can just be seen collecting its trainload of steel for Skinningrove. **(M. Rhodes)**

the "down" hump where there were two tracks and a secondary summit, by a separate shunter.

The Tees Yard of the 1960s did set a record for the UK. During my official visit in 1984 Mr. Noble, the area Supervisor, showed me records from the day when the "down" hump sorted 35 arrivals (containing a total of 2000 wagons) in a single eight hour shift. More realistically however, the 1960s throughput was between 9000 and 10,000 wagons each week handled in the "up" and "down" yards, which is to say 2000 wagons in 24 hours rather than in just eight hours. On the day of the record breaking eight hour shift, the wagons "humped" included many 16-ton mineral wagons from the Durham coalfield, vans with bagged fertilizer from Haverton Hill to goods depots all over the UK and a whole host of wagons with a gross laden weight of less than 15 tons. With the closure of most Durham mines and introduction of MGR coal wagons, this traffic no longer used the yard. Closure of goods depots led to the loss of much wagonload traffic, with chemicals and petroleum especially hard hit. The gradual introduction of air-braked, high capacity wagons for steel also greatly reduced the need for hump shunting at Tees, with most steel services running

Right:- Taken at sunset at the end of November 1984 from the A19 flyover, the hump in the "down" yard is still in operation although it will close within months. **(M. Rhodes)**

Left:- In June 1980 the "up" hump at Tees is seen in operation from the A19 flyover (a judicious cup of water was poured on the hot engine block of a borrowed VW campervan to allow 10 minutes paused on the A66 access road!). Covhops from local chemical works and MCV mineral wagons loaded with coal are seen rolling west. (**M. Rhodes**)

Below:- Again, during a brief "breakdown" on the A19, Class 08 No. 08864 finishes shunting its train on the "up" hump. At its peak the yard at Tees employed five full time Class 08 yard pilots and a sixth locomotive to shunt the carriage and wagon works. (**M. Rhodes**)

Above:- In April 1990 the retrieval of the track in the "down" sorting sidings is almost complete. The site was then redeveloped with much of the land seen here now a country park. The old "down" reception sidings are now occupied by part of the Durham University Queen's Park campus. (**M. Rhodes**)

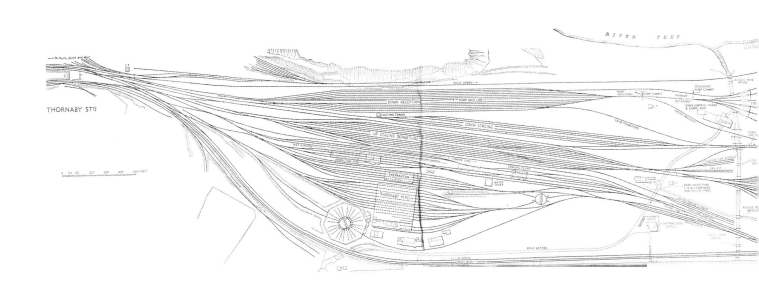

Above:- From the mid-1980s right through to the end of Speedlink wagonload services, Tees "up" yard was busy with this traffic. On 26 March 1986, Class 37 No. 37024 leaves the west end of the "up" sorting sidings with 6F83, the afternoon Tees to Harwich Parkeston Quay Speedlink. Cement and steel at the front of the consist are for domestic customers, whilst chemicals and steel at the rear of the train are destined for the train ferry and continental customers. The train ferry from Harwich ceased operations in 1987, as compared to the Dover freight ferry which lasted longer until 1995. (**M. Rhodes**)

Below:- The official plan of the new yard at Tees as drawn for the official BR launch booklet. (**M. Rhodes collection**)

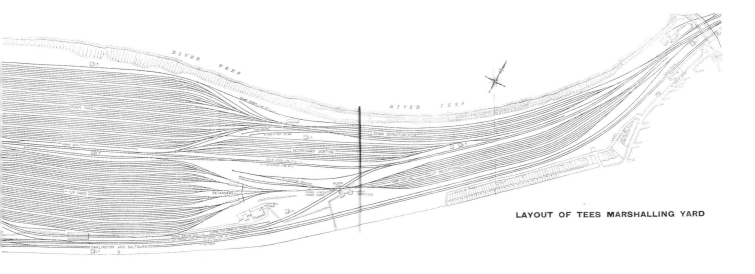

LAYOUT OF TEES MARSHALLING YARD

direct from the yard at Lackenby Steelworks. In 1981, the "up" hump closed; the sorting sidings were shunted from the west end and used for Speedlink traffic. Then in 1985, as there were just three or four trains humped each day, the "down" hump closed.

Since 1990 rationalisation on the site has continued apace[7] [8]. Speedlink wagonload services ceased on 8 July 1991[9]. In March 1993 Tees Yard closed, with the withdrawal of yard pilot duties; that is not to say that freight trains stopped using the yard, but marshalling was stopped and train locomotives were used to rearrange traffic in the sidings that remained. Steel traffic was concentrated on the sidings at Lackenby, whilst most other traffic was concentrated on the 12 "up" staging and departure roads. Since 1993

perhaps the biggest change has been the closure and then demolition of the Thornaby locomotive depot and wagon repair shops, at the south-west end of the complex. In addition the entire "down" side of the yards is now covered by parkland and a retail complex. This leaves just parts of the "up" hump system still in use. The main staging yard for traffic to and from Teeside is the "up" departure yard, which still has its 12 tracks in situ and in regular use. The remains of the "up" sorting sidings are shunted from the west end, just as they have been since 1981. All 41 of these remain and they are mostly filled with stored wagons rendered redundant when Lackenby Steelworks closed in 2009 and again in 2015. To the south of the old sorting sidings are five more tracks used for wagon repairs.

*Above:- By the summer of 1986 the "down" hump at Tees Yard was overgrown and the retarders rusty. The "down" sorting sidings were shunted from the east end and used mainly to store surplus wagons. In October 1986, Class 31 No. 31124 finds itself amongst rows of surplus VDA vans with a short trip to Williton made up of continental wagons. (**M. Rhodes**)*

HEALEY MILLS [10]

Opened: 1963
Closed as hump yard: 1984
Classification tracks: 50
Capacity in 24 hours: 4500 wagons

Healey Mills Yard was needed to marshal the huge tonnages of Yorkshire coal heading for Lancashire, the factories of Yorkshire and the ports of Immingham and Hull (we exported coal in those days!). Ironically the 140 acres of land upon which Healey Mills was constructed contained several profitable coal seams and an agreement was therefore needed between the National Coal Board and British Railways before the

Above & Right:- Two images taken from similar positions, but 22 years apart. The first image shows the new hump tower at Healey Mills in action on 4 July 1963. Fast forward to my official visit in 1985 and the hump, control panel has been removed; the sorting sidings have been disconnected from the hump and buffer stops placed at the western end of many of the tracks.
(BR ER - M. Rhodes collection & M. Rhodes)

Above:- Looking down from the lighting mast above the hump, the eight secondary retarders at Healey Mills are nearly completed. A Class 04 shunting locomotive tests the newly completed retarders with a single ballast wagon on 30 May 1963. (*BR ER - M. Rhodes collection*)

Above:- *Looking from the east towards the now completed Healey Mills Yard, Horbury station is at the bottom of this image. Then the extensive sidings of Horbury wagon works can be seen before the newly constructed Storrs Hill Road bridge is reached in the centre of the view. Beyond the new road overbridge, the secondary and primary sorting sidings stretch to the top of the image. Even though the hump has not yet opened on 28 March 1963, the sidings are full of coal traffic using the yard from the east end. On the right of the new yard complex, the land which will eventually be occupied by the new diesel depot is seen. The depot at Healey Mills was built somewhat later than at other yards, as steam survived on many coal trains in this area until August 1968, when Rose Grove steam depot finally closed.* **(BR ER - M. Rhodes collection)**

yard could be built. In the event, mining ceased in 1961, giving nearly two years for the land under the yard to be stabilised, but also making sure most of the profitable seams were mined out. The yard contained 120 sidings comprising 57 miles of track. Fourteen reception sidings led to a semi-automated hump (similar in design to Tees Yard). From here radiated 50 sorting sidings and a secondary yard with 25 sidings.

Above:- A 21-ton mineral wagon descends through the primary retarders at Healey Mills on 26 June 1963. Over 90% of the traffic at Healey Mills was coal. (BR ER - M. Rhodes collection)

There were 13 departure roads, as well as 15 staging sidings for block loads passing the yard.

Unlike most yards built under the Modernisation Plan, Healey Mills frequently exceeded its design capacity of 4000 wagons per 24 hours. Whilst in the 1966 yard survey, just after the yard had opened, there were just 16,500 wagons handled in the study week, closure of smaller yards handling coal over the next few years meant the yard actually became busier over the next decade. Records show there were often

4500 wagons hump shunted in 24 hours, such was the volume of Yorkshire coal passing through the site. The throughput at Healey Mills remained high at 4000 wagons per day well into the 1970s. Indeed in 1975 the yard was still working at capacity.

Traffic at Healey Mills was well over 90% coal and it was the retention of low capacity un-braked and vacuum-braked wagons that kept the yard busy. With the introduction of the MGR coal service, crucial for coal from Yorkshire to Fiddlers Ferry Power Station in

Above:- Early in the construction of Healey Mills, bridges and earthworks at the west end of the yard are taking shape. The snows of January 1963 cover the yard area; much work still needs to be done for the opening later in the year. (BR ER - M. Rhodes collection)

Lancashire, hundreds fewer wagons each day needed to be hump shunted at Healey Mills. Add to that the relentless closure of Yorkshire's mines between 1975 and the ill-fated 1984 miners' strike and one can see how the relevance of the yard simply evaporated in less than a decade. By 1981 records reveal that 8971 wagons arrived at the yard each week on 357 separate freight services. Of these wagons 7759 needed hump shunting, an average of 1500 wagons per day. On top of this there were 94 MGR trains passing the yard, conveying a total of 2809 32.5 ton HAA hoppers

(all traffic that had previously used the hump). The traffic over the hump was well over 50% lower when compared to six years earlier. By 1984 the figures showed 1450 wagons arriving in a week, on 114 trains, just 491 of which needed hump shunting - less than 100 per day, a drop of 40 fold in less than a decade. The hump closed.

Since 1985, the fortunes of Healey Mills have been poor. In 1985 Healey Mills was still used for Speedlink marshalling, but duplication of facilities in Yorkshire

Five images taken over nearly four decades show the decline and closure of Healey Mills Yard as viewed from the Storrs Hill Road bridge.

Bottom:- The first in 1977, shows Class 40 No. 40169 with a long rake of MCO, un-fitted 16-ton mineral wagons. These are destined for one of the dozens of collieries still producing coal within the Yorkshire coalfield at this time.

Right:- Next comes an image taken during the "Speedlink Coal Era". On 9 May 1989 Class 37 No. 37274 leaves with a rake of empty HEA hoppers and containerised wagons bound for Markham Colliery.

Opposite top:- By July 1997, when this image of Class 47 Nos. 47234 & 47377 heading a Trafford Park to Hull freightliner service was taken, it is evident there is no longer any traffic in the yard. The locomotive depot is still in use with a Class 37 and a Class 56 in residence.

Above:- Fast forward to 2014 and the yard is rapidly returning to nature. Class 60 No. 60015 speeds past on the main line with the Preston Docks to Lindsey Oil Refinery empty bitumen tanks - just one of two regular freight flows to pass the yard, which had handled nearly two hundred freight trains a day during its heyday.

Top:- A second general view of the sidings shows the complete dereliction and it won't be long before the yard site is unrecognisable. **(All M. Rhodes)**

*Above:- After the closure of the hump in 1984, the sorting sidings at Healey Mills were shunted from the east end. The hub of operations was the "up" yard inspectors' cabin, which had a small panel controlling the departure end of the old sorting sidings. Here, in 1985, the staff shelter in the cramped surroundings on a cold February day. (**M. Rhodes**)*

Two views taken in 1982 and 2015 from the same footbridge which allowed access from the staff car park to the diesel depot at Healey Mills.

Opposite top:- Back in 1982, the yard is still busy with wagonload and block freight traffic. From left to right: A Class 08 yard pilot arrives with wagons, recently repaired in Horbury. Class 47 No. 47252 pauses for a crew change with 6Z12, a Burn Naze to Haverton Hill chemical train. Next is Class 56 No. 56093 which has just arrived with an empty MGR service from Fiddlers Ferry which terminates in Healey Mills. From here the train will await orders from the Yorkshire coal controller as to which colliery it should travel to for reloading. Importing coal through Liverpool Docks and the collapse of the Yorkshire coalfield effectively put a stop to Trans-Pennine coal trains from the 1990s. Finally, one of the longest running freight services, the Preston Docks to Lindsey Oil Refinery stands behind Class 37 Nos. 37202 & 37160.

*Opposite bottom:- In January 2015, Colas Rail Class 60 No. 60076 passes the depot with the Preston Docks to Lindsey empty bitumen tanks. The six sidings to the left of the locomotive, formerly controlled from the small white shunters' cabin, are the subject of the 1982 view. (**Both M. Rhodes**)*

led to a review, after which Speedlink was withdrawn from Healey Mills and concentrated at Doncaster Belmont Yard. During the late 1980s the yard was a hub for the ill-fated Speedlink Coal network, but once this closed very little traffic was marshalled in Healey Mills[11]. Up until closure to revenue earning traffic the yard had daily train pairs to and from Preston Deepdale, Hull, Kellingley Colliery, Grimethorpe Colliery, Royston Sidings, Markham Main Colliery, Gartcosh, Brodsworth Sidings and Toton. Most of this traffic was relocated to Doncaster Belmont Yard when the yard at Healey Mills closed as a centre for revenue

earning traffic in November 1989. Engineers' services, or General Utility Services (GUS) as they were called, continued to use the remains of the sidings at the yard. Then in 1993, the locomotive depot at Healey Mills reopened when Trainload Petroleum decided to use it as a refuelling and minor maintenance depot[12]. Even at the time, a spokesman for Trainload Petroleum was keen not to over-emphasise the importance of the move and it did indeed prove short-lived. Final closure of all rail related activity on the 140 acre site came in 2011 and by 2015 nearly all track had been recovered from the site, which is now rapidly returning to nature.

Left:- In July 1963 the yard is fully open, except for construction of the diesel depot.
(BR ER - M. Rhodes collection)

Below:- One might think that traffic was thriving in this 1989 view of the erstwhile "up" secondary sorting sidings, now used as a Speedlink Coal yard. The truth is otherwise; a points failure at Horbury had blocked the exit from the yard for over two hours causing traffic to back up. On the left is Class 37 No. 37274 at the head of 6D57, the 1352 Healey Mills to Markham Main train. Next is Class 37 No. 37212 ready with 6S67, the 1448 Healey Mills to Gartcosh service. Finally on the right and easing out of the sidings is Class 37 No. 37066 with 7D02, the 1317 Healey Mills to Doncaster Speedlink feeder service. Healey Mills was one of the original 12 Network yards when Speedlink opened in 1975, but was down-graded to a feeder yard in 1985. The deceptively busy sidings here were to close to coal traffic just months after this view was taken in May 1989. (**M. Rhodes**)

THE DOWTY YARDS

The unifying factor for the last three hump yards built in the UK, is the Dowty retarder. The Dowty Engineering Company was formed in 1935 in Cheltenham. It was primarily an aircraft engineering company and its founder George Dowty (later Sir George Dowty) was responsible for the first sprung aircraft wheels. The use of hydraulics was what led to the Dowty rail retarder system, which was first installed and trialled in Goodmayes Yard in Essex in the late 1950s. It was later installed on a couple of tracks at Hull Inward Yard in 1961 for real life trials in a major hump yard. Unlike the traditional electro-mechanical rail brake installed in all the UK yards to date, the Dowty was made up of thousands of hydraulic "dash pots" along the rails, which could either retard or indeed speed up wagons descending from the hump. The retarder was installed in Bescot, Tinsley and Scunthorpe West yards in the UK. We will see however in Chapter 8, that it has become an international success, even after the last UK hump yards finally closed in 1990. The equipment is still produced by Ultradynamics (who took over Dowty in 1994), based in Cheltenham and Columbus, Ohio and the retarders are still being installed in 2016.

Below:- Looking East from Storrs Hill Road bridge towards Horbury, Class 31 No. 31189 winds into Healey Mills with 7L53, the daily mixed freight from Tees Yard. The train conveys empty fuel oil tanks returning to Stanlow, steel pipes from the Hartlepool Steel Mill and finally some steel girders from Teeside works. (M. Rhodes)

TINSLEY YARD [13]

Opened: 1965
Closed as hump yard: 1984
Classification tracks: 53 + 25
Capacity in 24 hours: 4000 wagons

It was the view from the bridge over Tinsley Yard that first raised my curiosity about marshalling yards. The sidings seemed to stretch forever; what did they do, where did they end? The yard at Tinsley was part of a massive investment in the Sheffield area which included centralising locomotive depots, goods depots and of course marshalling yards. The plan was approved in 1961 and construction began. The yard was opened in 1965 by Dr. Richard Beeching. The Sheffield Division at that time forwarded over 24 million tons of rail freight per annum or approximately 10% of the entire British Railways tonnage and much of this came from 150 private sidings in the area. Of necessity therefore, Tinsley had a large primary bowl with 53 sidings and also a secondary classification bowl with 25 sidings.

The use of Dowty retarders was perhaps at its most complete ever in Tinsley, with 23,500 units installed throughout the yard. The retarders were used to propel wagons from the hump, along the lead to the secondary yard and were used more for acceleration here than retardation. Both sets of sorting sidings were fed from an eleven track reception yard, electrified throughout to accept traffic from the Woodhead Route. The final set of sidings in the yard were five express sidings at the west end of the complex, for through-running freights. There was a locomotive servicing depot within the yard, as well as the large diesel maintenance depot on the hill above the reception sidings.

In 1981 the Woodhead Route closed, bringing electric traction at Tinsley to an end. By 1984 not just

Above:- The view which fascinated me when I first visited Tinsley back in 1973, but this time taken in January 1978. The vast collection of sorting sidings stretches to infinity, as Class 13 No. 13003 stops on the hump in response to the horizontal row of lights on the hump signal. Several yards needed more power than a single Class 08 could offer and in places like Temple Mills, double headed Class 08s were used. Three unique "master and slave" Class 13 locomotives were converted from six Class 08s, specifically for Tinsley, to reduce the need for double manning. (M. Rhodes)

the general decline in wagonload traffic, but also the effects of the miners' strike were being felt. The average number of wagons hump shunted each day in 1984 was just 429 - the hump closed. Tinsley continued to be busy at times, shunted from the west end, but gradually traffic levels declined and in 2006 Avesta opened its stainless steel plant, taking up much of the land once occupied by the sorting sidings. Add to this the demolition of the old diesel depot and the closure of the eastern access to Tinsley and the yard site in 2016 is unrecognisable.

Four views taken from the Wood Lane overbridge between 1966 and the present day show how things have changed at Tinsley.

Top:- In 1966, shortly before the yard opened, this colour image taken by Phil Metcalfe's father shows the shiny new hump tower and diesel servicing depot. Workmen are burning off some rubbish left on the hump and the yard is just weeks away from its official opening.

Opposite bottom:- By 1978, when the second image was taken, throughput at the yard had fallen but there was still a steady stream of mixed freight trains needing hump shunting. The sorting sidings are full of vacuum and un-fitted wagons and the hump will continue to operate for another six years.

Top:- By 1986, after the hump had closed, the track work in the hump area had been remodelled with just two of the main fans of sorting sidings used for Speedlink and other revenue earning traffic[14]. Here Class 20 Nos. 20089 & 20066 are reversing into the yard having arrived with 6T30, the afternoon trip from Deepcar. The train travelled west round

the yard on the main running lines, seen on the left of this image. It is now setting back into one of the sorting sidings.

Above:- By 2015, the control tower had been demolished and all that allows the viewer to picture the location are the two tracks on the right hand edge of this view. Avesta Steel fills most of the old sorting sidings, with just a small five-track yard left to the north of the steel plant which handles local steel traffic. One other constant is the Tinsley steelworks seen in the background on the extreme left hand side of all four images. **(Phil Metcalfe collection & 3 images M. Rhodes)**

Above:- In September 1980 the locomotive refuelling facility at Tinsley is busy servicing two pairs of Class 20 locomotives and a Class 47. Class 40 No. 40080 has just been released from an arrival from Tyne Yard and is also making its way to be refuelled. Class 13 No. 13002 is between jobs, awaiting instructions on which arrival road is next to be propelled over the hump. (**M. Rhodes**)

Above:- Taken in January 1977 from the Wood Lane access road to Tinsley diesel depot, a blurred wagon carrying steel rods is seen rolling over the hump on the left of the image. The second Class 13 yard pilot on duty is stabled to the right of the hump tower, whilst the yard lighting shows a yard packed with coal and steel wagons. (**M. Rhodes**)

Opposite top:- Salvaged from the yard tower during a 1985 official visit, this 1972 "Departure Simplifier" gives a fascinating insight into the crucial role Tinsley played in marshalling wagonload traffic in the North of England. Representing an eight hour shift from 1400 to 2200, the most striking thing is the list of eight trains in the shift to Godley Junction, Ashburys, Widnes, Edge Hill, Deepcar, Warrington, Widnes (again) and Dewsnap, all hauled by Class 76 electric locomotives. Long distance trains also left during the evening shift destined for Severn Tunnel, Whitemoor, Glasgow, Toton and Tees yards. (**M. Rhodes collection**)

TINSLEY MARSHALLING YARD			DEP... ...D SIMPLIFIER				COMM. 2.10.72						SHEET 5
H.SND.	...P. NO.	DEP. TIME	TC	DAYS RUN	OUT VIA	LOCO CLASS	ENGINE FROM	BASIC TONS	B/F	LOCOMEN	GUARD	GUARD FROM	SIDING	Y	REMARKS
	9T6?	1434	BATH	SX	NW	37	RL9T69	800		WTH161	WH161	RL9T69	39		
	5T35	1441	BRO. LANE	SX	SW	2X06AB	DSD	1060		375	375	SIGN ON	7		
	8L33	1450	GODLEY JCT.	SX	SW	76	LE.RWD	837		GB25	GB25	LE.RWD	42,43,44	Y	
	9T49	1515	SFT	SX	BTS	08	DSD	720		417	417	SIGN ON	28,32,33		
	8M10	1520	ASHDURYS	SX	SW	76	LE.RWD	837		GB.12	GB.12	LE.RWD	42		
	JT36	1545	MASBORO S/S	SX	NE	2X08	DSD	DBV		378	378	SIGN ON	BK.BANK		
M	8M95	15.7	S. TUNNEL	SX	SE	45	THRO	1050	B	DBY223	600	SIGN ON	EF		1038 EX TEES ARR 1520
M	C?59	1555	MINES	WTHFO	SW	76AB	LE GB			GB203	GB203	LE GB	EF		BOC TANKS ARR 1530 EX BRO. LANE
	8M52	16.0	EDGE HILL	SX	SW	76	RWD	837		RWD43 MSX	RWD 43 MSX	LE.RWD	43&44		
	5M44	1620	R.HAM ROAD	SX	NW	37	WOOD-BURN	800*		402	402	9T44	26&27		1220 TONS AWB
	9T30	1700	DEEPCAR	SX	SW	76	RL9T30	837		RWD91	RWD91	RL9T30	40		
M	9M40	1730	M. HALL	SX	NW	37	BREAK	690		390	390	RL9T40	38		
M	8M67	1730	TEES	SX	NW	31	LSD	700	63	343	343	SIGN ON	17&18		
M	9L40	1800	TOTON	SX	SE	2X20	DSD	750		316	316	SIGN ON	1&2		MAX 1350 TONS
M	8L30	1850	WARRINGTON	SX	SW	76	RWD	837		RWD23	RWD23	LE.RWD	45		
	9T94	1925	BARROW HILL	SX	SE	37	RL9T94	1030		BH278	BH278	RL9T94	8		
M	6M59	1950	MINES	MO	SW	76	LE.GB						EF		ARR 1925 EX BRO. L... BOC TANKS
	8L74	2000	WORKSOP	SX	SW	2X20	RL8J28	950	80	WSP 8	WSP 8	RL8J28	67		
M	7378	2010	GLASGOW	SX	NW	31	RL.8B20	650	C	HK.694	HK.694	RL.8B20	14&15		
M	8L03	2025	DEWSBURY	SX	SW	76	RWD	837		RWD21	RWD21	LE.RWD	34		
M	8L16	2025	B.MILLS	SX	NW	31	DSD	900B	78	349	349	SIGN ON	36&37		
	0T44	2108	ICKLES	SX	NW	37	DSD	DBV		403	403	SIGN ON	BK.BANK		
M	8D3?	2110	SCUNTHORPE	SX	NW	2X31	8J23	950B	85	FR.27	FR.27	8J23	19		
M	8J37	2115	WHITEMOOR	SX	SW	37	RL8J29	650	53	LIN37	LIN37	RL8J29	64&65		Continued....

Right:- This excellent view of the hump in action during the 1970s, taken by Les Nixon, shows the short headway possible between wagons using the Dowty system. In this view there are five wagons rolling from the hump crest into the sidings, with a sixth cut about to detach. This ability to shunt wagons in close proximity, as well as the total wagon control, has made the Dowty system popular from Austria to China to the USA. (*L. Nixon*)

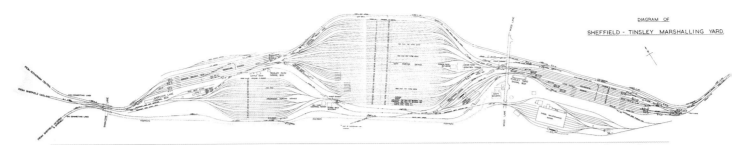

Above:- The track plan for Tinsley as drawn in the official booklet produced by British Railways to commemorate the yard's opening. (**M. Rhodes collection**)

Three images looking east from the Wood Lane bridge show the reception sidings at Tinsley.

Above:- First in January 1978, Class 47 No. 47175 has arrived from the west and is traversing the engine release road on its way to the yard servicing depot. The reception sidings are busy with six trainloads of wagons waiting to be hump shunted.

Left:- By July 1986, the reception sidings had been lifted. Looking east again, Class 20 Nos. 20098 & 20153 arrive with a lengthy 6T91 trip from Barrow Hill Yard. The curved track in the foreground is a useful anchor to help place the 2015 view.

Right:- By 2015, the area once occupied by 11 reception sidings is rapidly becoming a birch forest. The tracks towards Treeton Junction remain, although the connection with the "Old Road" from Chesterfield to Rotherham has been severed towards the north, and long disused heading south. (**All M. Rhodes**)

Above:- Taken around the opening date in 1965, work is still under way fine tuning the retarders at Tinsley. The diesel servicing point has been completed, but is not yet operational. (**BR - M. Rhodes collection**)

Below:- The yard at Tinsley was electrified to allow Trans-Pennine traffic over the Woodhead Route access to the sidings. Even during the last years of the Woodhead, electric traction was used on trip freights from Tinsley to Deepcar. The afternoon trip, coded 8T30, is seen here leaving behind Class 76 No. 76051 with 16-ton mineral wagons carrying scrap metal for the steelworks at Stocksbridge. The yard pilot, Class 08 No. 08492, has its old number D3607 thoughtfully inscribed on its battery box, whilst the shunter has placed his lamps and shunting pole carefully on the running board. (**M. Rhodes**)

Above:- Another major development, made in parallel with the construction of Tinsley marshalling yard, was the building of the new Sheffield Freight Terminal (SFT). Here in 1980, Class 20 Nos. 20003 & 20066 leave Tinsley with 9T34, the afternoon trip to SFT, with an assortment of steel and ferry wagons. On the extreme right of the image is Sheffield Park Signal Box which controlled departures from the west of the yard and became the focus of all activity after the hump closed in 1984. (**M. Rhodes**)

Below:- Just weeks later than the 1965 view on the opposite page and taken from a slightly lower vantage point, Tinsley is fully commissioned. The sorting sidings are packed and wagons roll down from the hump, whilst a pair of Tinsley's original Class 31 allocation are refuelled. (**BR - M. Rhodes collection**)

Above:- An inglorious period in the history of Tinsley was the attrition and contraction that took place, in stages, between the hump closure of 1984 and the end of wagonload traffic in 1991. Track layouts, never designed to be shunted from the west end, nor handle arrivals in what had been designed as "Express Freight Sidings", were pressed into use as makeshift wagonload facilities. Here in May 1985 Class 47 No. 47314 shunts out of the yard, past Tinsley Park Signal Box, before running round its train, the 6T48 steel service to Frodingham. The right half of the image is taken up by three arrivals in the erstwhile Express Freight Sidings. These had been designed as staging tracks for top link wagonload and container services, timed to connect the UK's major cities on overnight schedules. In 1985, from left to right are: Class 08 No. 08878 with the 8T32 trip from Broughton Lane carrying scrap metal, Class 20 Nos. 20176 & 20098 with 6T30 from Deepcar carrying finished steel, and finally Class 20 Nos. 20064 & 20015 with 6T35 from Aldwarke, made up of empty SSA scrap wagons. (**M. Rhodes**)

Above:- By 1985 the former Express Freight Sidings at Tinsley had become the main arrival sidings, as the yard was shunted from the west end. In September of 1985, Class 20 Nos. 20150 & 20086 have just arrived with 6T35, the afternoon trip from Aldwarke, returning empty 16-ton mineral wagons which had delivered scrap to the works at Aldwarke. Alongside stand Class 20 Nos. 20115 & 20002 which had arrived with 6T30, the afternoon trip from Broughton Lane, this time loaded with scrap in 16-ton wagons. (**M. Rhodes**)

BESCOT YARD [15]

Opened: 1966
Closed as hump yard: 1984
Classification tracks: 21
Capacity in 24 hours (with "up" yard): 4000 wagons

Bescot, between Birmingham and Wolverhampton, was ideally located to be the centre for West Midlands freight and so, in 1960, it was decided to modernise both the "up" and "down" yards here. The "up" yard was completely remodelled so that five reception sidings led over a "rider" hump to 18 sorting sidings. There were nine additional local sorting sidings at the south end of the

Right:- By 1985 the Dowty retarders had been removed from the "down" hump at Bescot; the unusual gradient profile remained however. Because Dowty retarders can also accelerate slow moving wagons, there is less need for a large, steep hump and this small four foot drop was all that was needed to start a wagon on its way through the Dowty dash pots. At the time of this image the yard was still shunted using this small hump, but with shunters riding with or running alongside wagons, as the next image shows. (**M. Rhodes**)

Below:- I was asked at the time of this official visit not to publish this image in the magazine article I was writing about Bescot, because riding on a wagon, with one's shunting pole perched at a jaunty angle on the buffer beam of the wagon, is not strictly part of the operating instructions for shunters! Class 08 No. 08603 propels its train from reception road No. 4. Without the retarders the hump was an operational hindrance rather than a help and the gradient profile was smoothed out a few years later. (**M. Rhodes**)

Above:- Whilst the automated "down" yard drew most of the publicity when it opened in 1966, the rebuilding at Bescot between 1962 and 1966 also included modernisation of the "up" yard. This was also a hump yard with 18 sorting sidings and whilst modern colour light signalling was installed, there were no retarders. Once open the two yards took over much of the work undertaken at Washwood Heath yards. The yard is seen here looking south from the hump crest in 1985. (**M. Rhodes**)

Above:- The "down" hump tower at Bescot was demolished in 2015, even though it was on a list of potential English Heritage buildings. In 1985, when this view was taken, the hump panel controlled all the points into the sorting sidings and continued to control the area until 2005 when the points in the yard were converted to hand operation. The NX panel which controlled the running lines continued in use in this building until it was decommissioned in 2013 as part of the resignalling from here to Rugeley. Along with Bescot Down Tower, the boxes at Walsall, Bloxwich, Hedensford and Brereton Sidings all closed in August 2013. Control of these running lines then moved to the West Midlands Signalling Centre in Saltley. (**M. Rhodes**)

Above:- On a rainy day in November 1991, Class 60 No. 60074 passes Bescot Stadium station with an empty MGR from Bescot to Littleton Colliery in Staffordshire. The "down" sorting sidings are full of air-braked wagons and the "down" tower can just be seen on the horizon on the far right, partially obscured by catenary. As can be seen in this view, the sorting sidings at Bescot were relatively short with capacity for between 43 and 54 standard wagon lengths (SWL). This designation of a standard wagon length was made at a time when a 16-ton mineral wagon or 11-ton vanfit was "standard", whereas modern air-braked wagons are much longer. The short sidings did prove an operational problem at Bescot, with as few as 20 high capacity air-braked wagons able to fit in a siding. **(M. Rhodes)**

classification bowl. It was the "down" yard however which attracted much of the publicity, as this was equipped with a fully automated hump, controlled by Dowty retarders. Six reception roads led to 21 sorting sidings; the flow of wagons was controlled by 4300 Dowty retarders. In addition there were 10 secondary sorting sidings and seven "down" storage roads for block trains.

Bescot is unusual for a UK yard in that almost all the original tracks, installed in 1966, remain active in 2016. The Dowty system was removed from the "down" hump in 1984[16]. Of course there have been many traffic changes at Bescot, but with a mixture of ballast services and block trains the yard remains busy. This is in marked contrast to the UK's two other Dowty yards at Tinsley and Scunthorpe. On the "down" side of the yard at Bescot all tracks are still in place, with the arrival yard and sorting sidings full of revenue earning traffic. On the "up" side of the yard the secondary sorting sidings have been converted into a virtual quarry, as have the old reception sidings. This leaves all 19 sorting sidings busy with ballast and other Network Rail traffic.

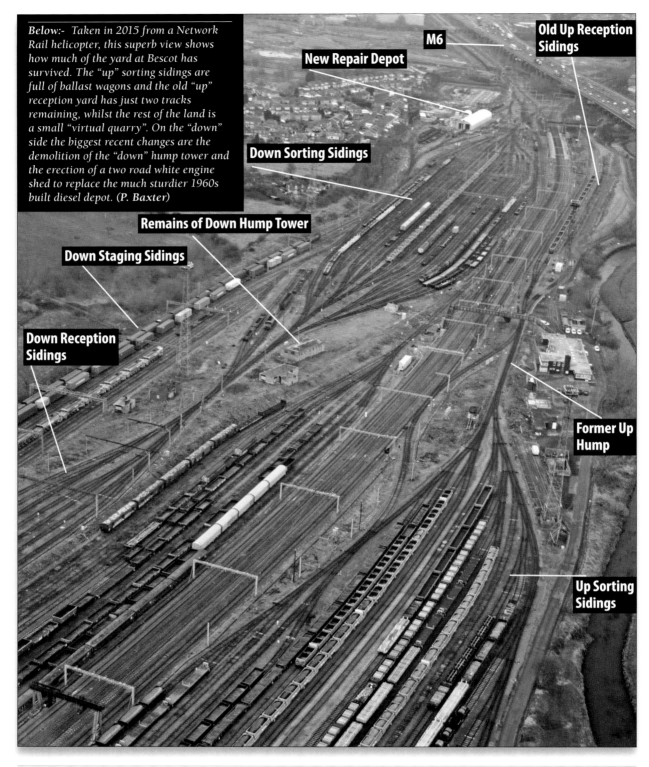

Below:- Taken in 2015 from a Network Rail helicopter, this superb view shows how much of the yard at Bescot has survived. The "up" sorting sidings are full of ballast wagons and the old "up" reception yard has just two tracks remaining, whilst the rest of the land is a small "virtual quarry". On the "down" side the biggest recent changes are the demolition of the "down" hump tower and the erection of a two road white engine shed to replace the much sturdier 1960s built diesel depot. (**P. Baxter**)

M6

Old Up Reception Sidings

New Repair Depot

Down Sorting Sidings

Remains of Down Hump Tower

Down Staging Sidings

Down Reception Sidings

Former Up Hump

Up Sorting Sidings

Below:- Photographed from an original S&T plan measuring over 20 feet in length, this shows the track layout at Bescot at the time the new yards opened in 1966. (**M. Rhodes collection**)

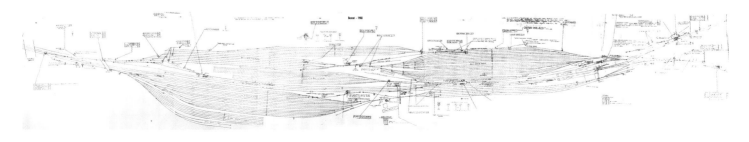

Left:- The driver looking back is perhaps the only clue in this image that Class 45 No. 45029 is in fact reversing into the "down" reception sidings to detach the ferry van at the front of the 6V70, Cliffe Vale to Severn Tunnel Junction Speedlink working. The track on the far left is both an engine release road and also the exit from the middle of this siding which leads to the "down" staging sidings that can just be seen. The need to detach a wagon on this occasion gave the author time to race to Great Bridge and get another image of the train. (M. Rhodes)

Left:- With all revenue earning and Speedlink traffic concentrated on the "down" side of the yard at Bescot, trains arriving from the north had to reverse into the "down" arrivals yard. Here, in July 1985, Class 85 No. 85001 propels 7G80, the afternoon air-braked freight from Crewe Basford Hall into the yard. (M. Rhodes)

Right:- The Class 08 yard pilot and the "down" tower conveniently frame the 21 "down" sorting sidings in 1985. (M. Rhodes)

Above:- *Taken just after the yard opened, this view looking south shows the "up" reception sidings on the left, followed by the main line and then the expanse of the "down" sorting sidings. A wagon is just rolling off the "down" hump crest.* **(BR LMR - M. Rhodes collection)**

Above:- *The scaffolding in the middle of this image is the "down" hump tower taking shape. To the left are the "down" storage sidings and then the freshly laid "down" reception sidings. To the right of these are the "down" local sorting sidings, full of traffic as they cope with the disruption of the massive rebuild at Bescot.* **(BR LMR - M. Rhodes collection)**

SCUNTHORPE WEST YARD [17]

Opened: 1971
Closed as hump yard: 1990
Classification tracks: 19
Capacity in 24 hours: 1500 wagons

In 1971 when Scunthorpe West Yard was rebuilt as the last freight yard infrastructure project of the Modernisation Plan, most freight traffic was transferred from Scunthorpe Trent Yard to West Yard. Originally the 1955 plan had envisaged a new hump yard on the Trent Yard site, but this never came to fruition and the smallest hump yard in the UK was squeezed onto the West Yard site adjacent to Scunthorpe passenger station. As late as 1966 Scunthorpe was frenetically busy with wagonload traffic, handling 21,641 wagons in a sample week, mostly through the flat-shunted Trent Yard. Even so restrictions on the site at Trent Yard led to delays and deliberations regarding a new mechanised hump yard. In the five years following the 1966 yard survey the number of wagons handled fell from over 5000 on many days, to less than 2000 due to the introduction of greater block working. In the meantime new plans were drawn up for a mechanised yard on a smaller scale at Scunthorpe West. The yard had just 3 reception roads, placed alongside the classification bowl. Trains to be sorted were drawn back onto a spur, before being propelled over the hump. There were just 19 sorting sidings and only six of these had connections at the east end. This was because most wagonload traffic departed from Scunthorpe to the west, whilst the many trains conveying raw materials to the steelworks generally arrived in block trains which did not need marshalling.

Below:- Two images of the hump control panel at Scunthorpe West. The first, taken days after the yard opened in 1971, shows a shiny new control panel. With Dowty-controlled yards there was of course no need for a separate retarder panel to control wagon speed and flow because the inherent settings of the Dowty retarders would bring every wagon to its target speed of 3 mph automatically. The inset image was taken at the time of my official visit in March 1990, just weeks before the yard closed, and by this time the panel is looking a bit weather-beaten and worn. (BR ER - M. Rhodes collection and M. Rhodes)

Opposite top:- In March 1990, Class 08 No. 08401 is the yard pilot at Scunthorpe West Yard. Here the locomotive is seen bringing a rake of steel-carrying wagons onto the pull-back track, from No. 1 reception siding where they had been deposited earlier by their train locomotive.

Above:- The second image shows the engine propelling empty BDA steel wagons towards the hump, as the shunter uses his pole to uncouple them.

Below:- The wagon is then seen rolling down the slope towards the sorting sidings and the eagle-eyed will spot the small dash pots of the Dowty retarders protruding above the running rails, below the wagon. (All M. Rhodes)

The yard continued to operate exactly as it had when first opened, until its last few days in 1990. A train was propelled towards the hump at 1 mph or 1.5 ft/sec. The retarders would then manage the speed of the wagon as it descended into its designated track, such that its final velocity was 4.5 ft/sec or 3 mph, the speed at which there is minimal damage to cargo. Of course with the Dowty retarders in place any departure from the sorting sidings must observe a 10 mph speed limit to avoid damaging the expensive retarders. Also Class 40s and Peaks were banned from the hump because of the vertical curvature over the summit - this restriction was of course irrelevant by 1990 when the yard closed, as all 1-Co-Co-1 diesels had been withdrawn from service! In 2015 the land where the yard stood is derelict and overgrown, but some remnants of track can just be made out. Scunthorpe West Yard brought to a close the 61 year history of hump yards in the UK. But what of the rest of the world? We saw how back at the dawn of marshalling yards there was much liaison between railway engineers in Germany, France, the USA and the UK. In the final chapter of this book we shall examine if this is still the case and if so how does it manifest itself?

Above:- The autumn sun in October 1986 highlights the Dowty retarders at Scunthorpe West Yard. Class 47 No. 47217 draws forward with 6D77, the evening trip freight to Doncaster Belmont Yard. On the left the West Yard pilot has just been down in the sidings to correct a wrong shunt, whilst on the right Class 08 No. 08877 has arrived with a single ferry van from Scunthorpe Entrance E - this engine is the Frodingham local trip, used to move wagons between the various yards at Scunthorpe. **(M. Rhodes)**

Above:- With increased block working came fewer wagons to sort in the newly built West Yard. The problem of falling traffic was exacerbated in the 1980s as Railfreight started to run trains directly to the various smaller yards around the steelworks. Here, in October 1986, Class 45 No. 45012 leaves with a long train carrying semi-finished steel and scrap for the various stainless steel plants in Sheffield. Much of this traffic would have been part of the general wagonload network until sectorisation. By 1986 this 6J25 service to Tinsley leaves from Entrance C Yard, rather than the main yards at West or Trent. (*M. Rhodes*)

Right & Below:- In March 1990 newly-built Class 60 No. 60007 leaves Scunthorpe West Yard with a trial load of empty HEA hoppers on a crew training run to Doncaster. Taken from the same road bridge in 2012, the sidings at West Yard have all been lifted and vegetation is taking over. The sleepers and rubble from the erstwhile hump yard have been piled up near the site of the old hump. (**Both M. Rhodes**)

Below:- The official signalling diagram of the new yard at Scunthorpe West when it opened in 1971. (**M. Rhodes**)

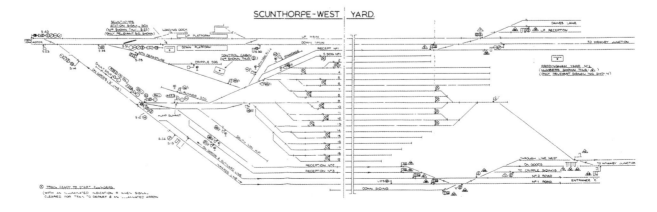

References

1   Freeman Allen G. The London Midland's £4.5 million marshalling yard at Carlisle. Modern Railways, November 1962, 324–330.

2   Peel KD. Carlisle - Border Freight Centre 1 - Present-day operating problems. Trains Illustrated, July 1961, 395–401.

3   Freeman Allen G. The new Tyne and Healey Mills yards of the North Eastern. Modern Railways, September 1963, 164–171.

4   Freeman Allen G. The pattern of North Eastern Region freight operation. Modern Railways, July 1963, 14–19.

5   Rhodes M. Speedlink Pulls out of Tyne Yard. Rail, 105; 21 September 1990: page 6.

6   Freeman Allen G. The semi-automatic Tees Yard of the North Eastern Region. Modern Railways, August 1963, 122–126.

7   Rhodes M. Tees Yard to close. Rail, 195; 3 March 1993: page 6.

8   Rhodes M. Freight Facts, Teeside Developments. Rail, 203; 23 June 1993: page 43.

9   Rhodes M. Speedlink's Final Trip. Rail, 139; 9 January 1991: 26–31.

10   Freeman Allen G. The new Tyne and Healey Mills yards of the North Eastern. Modern Railways, September 1963, 164–171.

11   Rhodes M. Decline of Healey Mills. Rail, 116; 22 February 1990: page 18.

12   Rhodes M. Healey Mills locomotive depot re-opens. Rail, 195; 3 March 1993: page 7.

13   Kitchenside GM. Tinsley Yard is hub of Sheffield Modernisation. Modern Railways, January 1966, 8–14.

14   Rhodes M. Tinsley - All change for the future. Rail, 52; January 1986: 10–14.

15   Kitchenside GM. Remodelled Bescot Yard has Dowty Automatic Wagon Control. Modern Railways, July 1966, 364–366.

16   Rhodes M. Bescot - Speedlink Focus of the West Midlands. Rail, 48; September 1985; 6–10.

17   Rhodes M. Railfreight Steel Scunthorpe - All change for the future. Rail, 121; 3 May 1990: 24–30.

Chapter 8

A Global Perspective

A Review of the Rest of the World

Introduction

As readers will now appreciate the railway engineering community was a global one from as far back as the late 1800s, with visits between the UK, Europe and the USA commonplace. Whilst the era of gravity assisted marshalling in the UK finished with the closure of Scunthorpe West Yard in 1990, the story is far from over in the rest of the world. Reasons for wagonload traffic either thriving or being phased out are complex, but there are three crucial factors which influence its survival in 2016; geography, infrastructure and government policy.

Government policy is perhaps the most crucial of these three in Europe, where differences between member states of the EU are striking. The geographical opportunities for rail transit are similar in all countries and the level of road and rail infrastructure also on a par, yet wagonload freight and the marshalling yards that serve this traffic vary enormously from country to country. Infrastructure had been a key differentiating factor between Eastern and Western Europe prior to the 1989 collapse of the Berlin Wall, but the intervening years have seen massive changes to the road network in countries like Poland and the Czech Republic, with a parallel decline in rail freight. But in the old Western Europe, countries like Germany, Austria and Switzerland have relatively high levels of wagonload freight, as compared to France, Spain and Italy where it has all but disappeared. The key factor seems to be government regulations, in that there are significant restrictions and taxes for heavy goods vehicles in Germany, Austria and Switzerland, such that HGVs are not allowed on the roads over much of the weekend and certain Alpine passes are prohibitively expensive for lorries to cross, as compared to using rail or roll-on roll-off services. Another factor is the willingness of DB, SBB and ÖBB to use their hump yards to sort individual container wagons, just as they do for more conventional covered or open wagons. Unlike the UK

where containers are effectively operated as a block load service from port to inland container terminal, in many parts of Europe single containers are marshalled into wagonload services and delivered directly to their customer by rail.

In the case of China, whilst government policy in favour of rail is obviously crucial in the rapid expansion of the network and its freight carrying capacity, geography and most crucially infrastructure play just as important roles. As anybody who has visited rural China in the last three decades will know (I have been 35 times), the railway network is superb, whereas the road network is rudimentary in many areas and unfit for heavy goods vehicles. Thus, development of the rail network in preference to the road network means that most goods must travel by train and the wagonload network is hence exceptionally busy. Changes in the last decade however may have led to a shift of some traffic to the new motorway network, but roads still lag far behind the rail network.

The USA and Canada present an environment with similar geographical opportunities to mainland Europe and China, but in a completely unregulated setting, in that government intervention in railroads is relatively minor and therefore wagonload freight must make a profit. It is in part the excellent infrastructure, but mainly the opportunities to haul large tonnages for thousands of miles, which make wagonload traffic a profitable option in 2016 in North America. The infrastructure is designed to handle 10,000 ton manifest (mixed freight) trains, and the yards around the continent are designed and built to marshal this scale of traffic.

In summary, the gravity assisted marshalling yard had its beginnings in Edge Hill near Liverpool back in the 19th Century. After several yards were built with humps at the end of the 19th Century, the first decade of the 20th Century saw yards spring up all over the developed world. Most notably dozens of yards were constructed in the USA, UK, France and Germany where the railway networks grew rapidly. During the 1950s and 1960s there was a gradual move away from wagonload traffic in the West, but a major reliance on rail transportation for all goods behind the Iron Curtain. As much as 80% of all freight was transported by rail in the former Soviet Bloc. This of course led to dozens of hump yards being built in former communist countries from 1945 right through to the 1980s. Just as yards were at their pinnacle in the Eastern Bloc, many Western countries were closing most of their hump yards. Smaller nations like the UK and Japan had abolished all major yards by 1990, whilst even large continents like Australia had moved all freight into container trains or block loads by the early 1990s. The same move to block trains took place in India and South Africa, leading to many hump yards closing in these countries during the 1980s and 1990s.

Wagonload traffic remained vibrant in the USA and Canada and so there are still 55 hump yards in action in 2016 in North America. Not so in South America,

where freight traffic never amounted to the massive tonnages transported in North America and no hump yards exist. In Europe the contrast between West and East is nowhere better exemplified than in Germany. Before the Wall came down in 1989 there were 14 major hump yards in East Germany; in 2016 there are just four left at Seddin, to the south-west of Berlin, Leipzig Engelsdorf, Rostock and Senftenberg. Similar attrition is underway in other former Eastern Bloc countries and there are likely to be more closures over the next few years in Romania and Bulgaria.

One nation however bucks the trend of a general decline in hump marshalling yards, and that is China. The rail network here has expanded exponentially and from a situation with no major hump yards in 1945, China Rail now has at least 51 automated hump yards (based on my observations in 35 visits and Google Earth images). Not only that but the busiest yard in Asia, at Zhenzhou North, claims to handle 12,000 wagons daily, which would surpass the wagonload throughput at the world's largest yards in Hamburg and North Platte. China is still building yards and freight traffic is still increasing, so the future of hump marshalling yards there is secure.

*Above:- Mannheim marshalling yard is the second busiest in Germany, handling 6000 wagons daily. In June 2014, Class 296 No. 296 068-0 is seen propelling ferry vans over the north-south hump. This side of the yard has older equipment than the recently modernised south-north complex and has 15 arrival tracks leading to 41 sorting sidings. The south-north system is similar in size, with 12 arrival tracks leading to 42 sorting sidings. (**M. Rhodes**)*

EUROPE

Table 1 - Major European & Russian Yards in 2016

Country	Number of active hump yards		Most important yards	Notes
United Kingdom	0		(see Chapters 4-7)	Last hump closed 1990 in Scunthorpe
France	20		Paris, Villeneuve St. Georges, Woippy, Lyon, Sibelin	SNCF have said they will close all hump yards by 2016 and abandon wagonload traffic. It is said there are still 3 active hump yards in 2016, but Google Earth and first hand visits suggest that 20 are still intact and active in some capacity
Belgium	6		Antwerpen Noord	With 56 + 40 classification tracks, one of Europe's largest yards
Luxembourg	1		Bettembourg	
Holland	1		Kifhoek	
Germany	20		Maschen, Seelze, Seddin, Halle, Hagen, Gremberg, Mannheim, Nürnberg, München Nord	Nine main network yards destined to be the core of residual wagonload traffic; Halle being rebuilt as a modern new hump yard for completion in 2017
Austria	8		Wien Kledering, Villach	Both Kledering and Villach use Dowty retarders
Switzerland	4		Zürich Limmattal, Basel Muttenz	Muttenz is one of Europe's largest yards with 43 + 32 classification tracks
Italy	5		Milano is largest with 48 classification tracks	Several unique dead-end yards, like Torino and Bologna
Spain, Portugal, Greece, Albania, Turkey	0		Largest remaining yard in these countries is in Madrid	Former hump yard in Madrid now used for container traffic
Norway, Denmark	0			Yards all closed 2003/2002 respectively
Sweden	2		Hallsberg & Malmö	Formerly 7 hump yards
Finland	3		Kouvola, Tampere	
Baltic states	5		Kaliningrad, Vilnius, Riga	Much investment in the last 5 years with Vilnius rebuilt into a 26-track state of the art hump yard
Former USSR (Moldova, Belarus, Ukraine, Russia)	Moldova 1 Belarus 2 Ukraine 14 Russia 16		Minsk, Kiev, Osnova, Krasnyj Lyman, Donetsk, St. Petersburg, Moscow, Kinel, Yekaterinberg, Chelyabinsk, Novosibirsk	A large number of yards in the steel making areas of Ukraine, most with identical retarder systems to those used in Magdeburg in the former DDR. Big busy yards across the trans-Siberian railway
Poland	14		Largest yard Tarnowskie Gory 32 + 32 sorting sidings	Freight in decline, several yards under-used
Czech Republic and Slovakia	17		Ostrava (20 + 20) largest yard in the Czech Republic and Bratislava (37) in Slovakia	New yard being built in Žilina with EU money
Hungary	2		Budapest Ferencváros 32 + 28 in second hump yard where hump is closed and Miskolc (30)	
Slovenia, Croatia, Serbia & Macedonia	4		Ljubljana (39), Zagreb (48), Beograd (48), Skopje (24)	No hump yards in Bosnia, Montenegro or Greece
Romania & Bulgaria	Romania 14 Bulgaria 7		Many yards look overgrown and partially used with several showing the retarders removed	These two countries are in rapid flux and many of the yards may well disappear in the next couple of years

Table 1 summarises the remaining hump yards in Europe. Clearly, with over 150 yards still in existence, that's enough for another whole book, but this short section will highlight some of the best yards to visit and observe, as well as the largest and busiest yards on the continent.

In Austria, two of the newly built yards at Villach and Wien Kledering have employed Dowty retarders. The yard at Wien Kledering is easy to observe from the station to the south of the sorting sidings of the same name, and from a public road overbridge at the hump called Gadnergasse. The country has other hump yards in Salzburg (Gingl), Innsbruck, Linz, Wels and Graz, but none are as accessible as the largest yard at Kledering.

Similarly Switzerland "punches above its weight" with large hump yards in Basel, Zürich and Lausanne. Basel Muttenz is perhaps the easiest to watch in action with an excellent overbridge (called Grenzacherstrasse) across the middle of the complex.

Germany used to have more hump yards than the rest of Europe put together, but here too rationalisation has taken place. The table listing East German yards as they were in 1995 serves as a stark reminder of the drastic changes that have taken place in the last

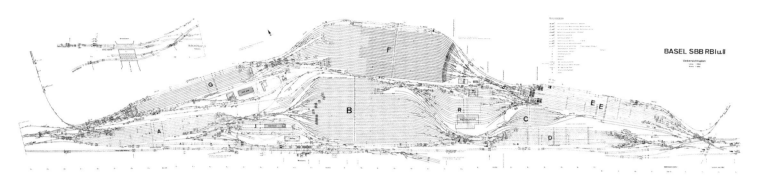

BASEL SBB RBIu.II

Above:- This official SBB plan shows the sheer size of Switzerland's largest hump yard at Basel Muttenz[1]. With two hump systems, the southerly one (dating from 1933) was recently completely revamped and modernised with a new retarder system. The sorting sidings have also been lengthened and reduced in number from 43 to 32. The northerly hump system (opened after 14 years under construction, from approval in 1962 to official opening in 1976) is unusual in that it operates without a hump engine because the arrivals tracks are on a falling grade. A new arrival is held in the arrival track by its train brakes and there are exit retarders from the arrivals yard which control the flow of wagons down into a conventional 32-track bowl of sorting sidings, with four sets of traditional group retarders and individual track trolleys on each sorting siding. (**M. Rhodes**)

Above:- The automated hump yard at Basel Muttenz, opened in 1976, makes a slightly eerie sight as wagons are hump shunted without a locomotive. Exit retarders on the arrival track hold wagons prior to shunting, then these are released to allow an arrival to roll forwards. Further retarders control its speed until it arrives at the start of a steeper incline down into the sorting sidings. Here there are two large primary retarders (slowing a bogie tank wagon in this view). Wagons then roll past four group retarders and into their siding, which is itself equipped with an entrance retarder and automatic track trolley to pull arriving wagons along to the appropriate place on the track. (**M. Rhodes**)

Above:- In June 2013 the hump pilot at Wien Kledering has just finished propelling a 750 m long mixed freight over the hump and is awaiting instructions. Beyond the locomotive the hump, which has quite a lot of weeds on it, can be seen with multiple little dashpots; these are the Dowty retarders. The yard is the largest in Austria with 48 sorting sidings in the main bowl. (**M. Rhodes**)

Above:- The impressive building in the background is the central cemetry in Vienna. ÖBB Class 1063 No. 1063 030 passes the sorting sidings with a transfer freight in June 2013. The evening sun picks out the Dowty retarders well and, as can be seen, they extend all the way along the sorting sidings. (**M. Rhodes**)

*Above & Below:- At the same time as ÖBB built the new yard at Wien Kledering to streamline wagonload handling in the capital, they also constructed a new automated hump yard at Villach Süd for traffic to and from Italy and the south. On a rainy day in May 1991, the 40 sorting sidings are seen from the hump tower. Like Kledering, the Dowty system was chosen for Villach. The second image shows inside the main control tower, which houses the signal panel and the yard supervisors. (**Both M. Rhodes**)*

*Left:- The yards at Basel Muttenz are the largest and busiest in Switzerland, but the largest set of sorting sidings are at Limmattal near Zürich, which has a 64-track bowl. This view from an SBB publicity booklet shows the yard layout well. The sidings here had a maximum capacity to sort 6900 wagons in 24 hours or 5180 in 18 hours. The maximum throughput in an hour is 300. The whole site is 4.3 km long and 400 metres wide, with 120 km of track and 410 sets of points. (**M. Rhodes collection**)*

two decades; from at least 20 active or recently active hump yards in the East there now exist just four, at Berlin Seddin, Leipzig Engelsdorf, Rostock Seehafen and Senftenberg. Similar changes are occurring throughout the former communist states of the Soviet era. Elsewhere in Germany several iconic yards from the steam era, like Hohenbudberg near Krefeld, have completely disappeared. There has however been significant investment over the last three decades in new yards.

The city of Hamburg boasts four hump marshalling yards[2], at Hohe Schaar, Waltershof, Süd Güterbahnhof and Europe's largest at Maschen. Hamburg Maschen was opened in 1980 and has a capacity to sort 11,000 wagons in 24 hours[3]. With two classification bowls, a south-north with 64 tracks and a north-south with 48, the only bigger yard in the world is North Platte in Nebraska. Maschen is also perhaps one of the easiest and most enjoyable yards in Europe to watch in action, with the 400 metre long bridge on Hörstener Strasse passing just south of the south-north hump and across the southern end of the north-south sorting sidings. The yard is exceptionally busy. Hamburg Waltershof is the newest yard in Germany, opened in 1995 and built by the Hamburg Port Authority. The yard is used to hump shunt container traffic from the massive port complex and its 24 sorting sidings are each equipped with a retarder at their entrance.

Deutsche Bahn has also built a completely new yard at München Nord, not to mention completely rebuilding the yard at Nürnberg

in the late 1980s. Nürnberg had been famed for having 106 sorting sidings off a single hump, which was a world record; now it has just has 60 but uses Dowty retarders, 42,000 of which were installed in 1988.

One final yard which deserves specific mention is Mannheim, the second largest yard in Germany and also a yard whch is easy to observe and photograph from several overbridges. The best of the observation points is the footbridge over the southern end of the motive power depot, which allows views of the hump on the southbound yard and the departure sidings of the northbound system. Whilst Germany still had over 20 hump yards in operation in 2013, there are moves to rationalise wagonload traffic. The plan is to keep nine key yards at Hamburg Maschen, Hannover Seelze, Berlin Seddin, Halle, Köln Gremberg, Mannheim, Stuttgart Kornwestheim, Nürnberg and München Nord. A far cry from the days when there were 20 hump yards in the former GDR and five in Berlin, but still quite a considerable investment and use of the hump marshalling yard when one considers they disappeared in the UK 25 years ago. Development of new yards continues; DB is currently investing €146 million in a new 36-track hump yard in Halle. This will fully open in 2017 and allow consolidation of all traffic from the east and west, resulting in complete closure of the hump yard at Leipzig Engelsdorf and closure of most of the facilities in Dresden.

Right:- This table summarises the yards in East Germany, six years after reunification. It illustrates well the changes that have happened all over former Eastern Bloc countries. From well over 20 active hump yards in 1989, just ten remained active in 1995 and by 2015 only four examples remained. (M. Rhodes)

East German Marshalling Yards – 1995

City	Yard	Status – 1995
Berlin	Seddin*	Main yard for capital, 1,500-2,000 wagons per day over two humps
	Wustermark	Used as collection point for less than wagonload traffic, 800 wagons/day over one hump
	Pankow	Local hump yard for east Berlin, 800-900 wagons per day
	Wulheide.	Completely abandoned
	Rummelsberg.	Yard abandoned, much of area taken up by carriage sidings
	Schonweide	Hump abandoned, small amount of local traffic using handful of sidings
Magdeburg	Rothensee*	Main yard with throughput of 1,000-1,200 wagons per day over one hump
	Buckau	Automated hump closed May 1995, local traffic only uses remainder of yard
Leipzig	Engelsdorf*	Main yard with throughput of 1,000 wagons/day over one hump
	Wahren	Relegated to handle local traffic only
	Mockau	Predominantly container traffic at this ex-hump yard
Dresden	Friedreichstadt*	Largest yard on erstwhile DR, still handles up to 2,000 wagons per day over single hump
Chemnitz	Hilbersdorf	Unique rope worked hump closed in 1991, most of yard converted for container and block train operation
Frankfurt	(Oder)*	Border yard for main corridor to Poland
Wittenberg.		Relegated to local traffic only
Frankenberg		Relegated to local traffic only
Gorlitz		Hump yard completely closed in 1995, no wagonload traffic to/from Poland remains
Zwickau		Large hump yard with capacity to handle 4,000 wagons/day closed completely 01-01-95, remaining wagonload traffic handled in local goods depot
Halle		Yard relegated to local traffic only
Erfurt		Hump yard still handles 600 wagons/day and acts as regional collecting point
Border yards in former West Germany		
Hannover	Seelze	Relatively limited facility in terms of size, still handles up to 5,000 wagons/day over two humps
Braunschweig		Lost its place as major yard to Magdeburg when DB and DR merged in 1992, still handles 900-1,100 wagons/day over single hump
Bebra		Yard handles 700 wagons per day over single hump, less important since re-unification, much traffic goes straight to Erfurt and Leipzig without remarshalling at Bebra
Kassel		Twin hump yard without retarders still handles 900 wagons per day

Footnote:- * denotes east German yards which remain as part of the DB wagonload network

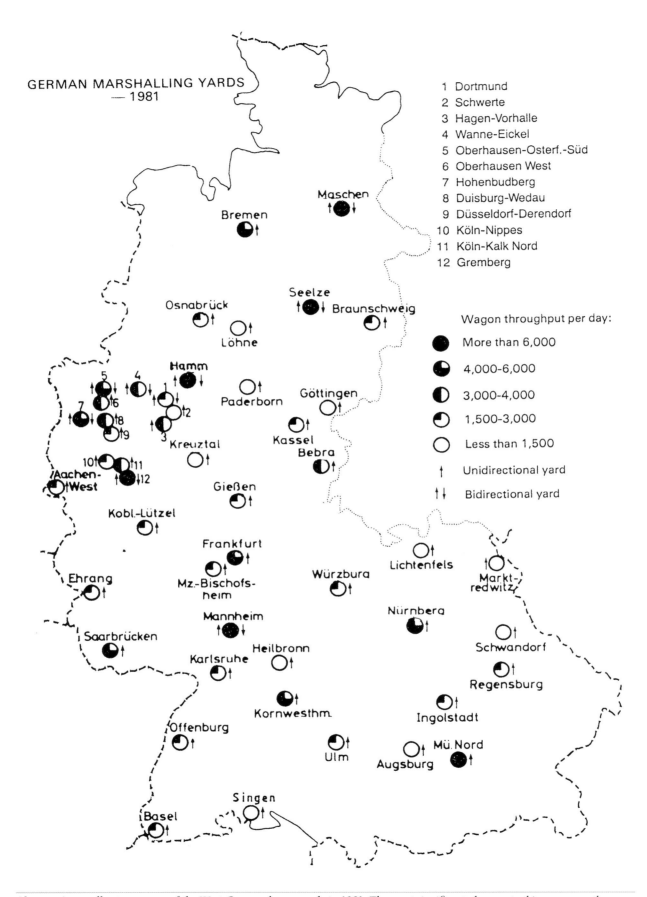

GERMAN MARSHALLING YARDS
— 1981

1 Dortmund
2 Schwerte
3 Hagen-Vorhalle
4 Wanne-Eickel
5 Oberhausen-Osterf.-Süd
6 Oberhausen West
7 Hohenbudberg
8 Duisburg-Wedau
9 Düsseldorf-Derendorf
10 Köln-Nippes
11 Köln-Kalk Nord
12 Gremberg

Wagon throughput per day:

More than 6,000

4,000-6,000

3,000-4,000

1,500-3,000

Less than 1,500

↑ Unidirectional yard

↑↓ Bidirectional yard

Above:- An excellent summary of the West German hump yards in 1981. The most significant changes to this map were the result of rationalisation of yards in the Ruhr area, which led to the closure of Hamm, Hohenbudberg and Duisberg-Wedau in the 1980s. (**M. Rhodes**)

Above:- Taken in 1986, not long before closure, this view shows part of the northbound hump system at Hohenbudberg, with Class 290 No. 290 390-4 resting on the hump. The locomotive had just finished hump shunting a lengthy train including coal, cement and interestingly single container wagons. These were retarded manually using Hemmschuh and the four "brakemen" or "slipper men" can be seen in the middle distance to the right of the locomotive. The yards here had two humps. This south-north system had 16 reception tracks leading to 56 sorting sidings, but the yard was in two parts separated by the wagon repair works which can be seen on the right of this image. The north-south system was smaller, with 10 reception tracks and 31 sorting sidings. Perhaps it was inevitable that, with severe falls in coal and steel production, the yards in the Ruhr would be rationalised at the end of the 1980s and Hohenbudberg, with no mechanisation, was the first to go. (**M. Rhodes**)

Above:- Hagen Vorhalle was, in contrast to Hohenbudberg, selected as one of the main yards to be kept in the Ruhr and became the centre for all traffic at the western side of the area. This superb aerial view shows the hump area at the base of the image with four primary retarders leading to 40 sorting sidings. Each siding is equipped with its own entrance retarder and small trolley to bring each wagon carefully into contact with traffic already in the siding. (**Photographer unknown**)

Above:- Deutsche Bahn continues to invest heavily in its wagonload network and its automated hump yards. One of its latest projects was modernisation of the south-north system in Mannheim and the rebuilding of Halle hump yard. The last completely new mechanised hump yard to be built was however, Hamburg Waltershof, back in 1995. Built by the Port of Hamburg (HHVW) it is effectively a private hump yard to help handle and sort some of the 4500 wagons which pass through the port of Hamburg daily. The 24 sorting sidings, each with entrance retarders, are seen here during an official visit in 1996. As can be seen from this view containers make up a large proportion of the traffic hump shunted here. (**M. Rhodes**)

Right:- Construction of the new hump yard in Halle was well under way in November 2015. DB had thoughtfully placed large laminated notice boards on the bridge over the yard to show how things would look upon completion. This image shows the graphic of the yard looking north. The new 36-track classification bowl replaces all the land formerly occupied by the sorting sidings of two smaller hump yards and in doing so has allowed DB to build much longer sorting sidings, suitable for 750m long wagonload freights. (**M. Rhodes**)

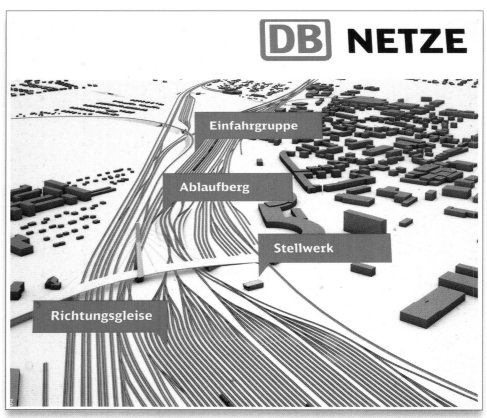

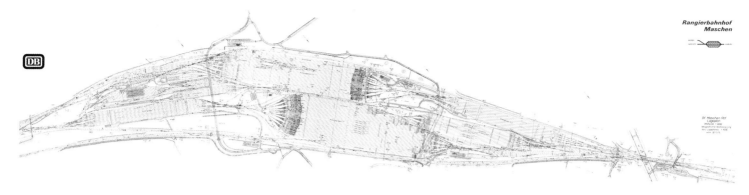

Top & above:- *The official DB plan of Maschen gives an excellent impression of the sheer scale of the yard. Opened in 1978 it is the largest and busiest in Europe, with two parallel hump systems. The south-north system is slightly larger with a 64 track bowl, as compared to 48 tracks in the north-south complex. The view of Class 291 No. 291 034-7 shunting empty coal wagons over the south-north hump was taken in 1979, just after the yard opened fully. Its capacity to sort 11,000 wagons every day makes it perhaps the largest hump yard in terms of the number of wagons over the hump, but not in terms of total throughput where North Platte, Nebraska wins because of the huge volume of run-through coal and intermodal trains.* (**M. Rhodes collection** & **M. Rhodes**)

Left:- *Wagons are hump shunted into the 64 sorting sidings of the south-north system at Hamburg Maschen in 1996. Nürnberg based Class 151 electric 151 069-2 has just been released from an arrival and will make its way to the "Lok-Taschen" on the other side of the vast complex, south of Hamburg.* (**M. Rhodes**)

Above:- *Another of the large yards in Germany is Nürnberg. The yard here was completely rebuilt between 1983 and 1988[+].
This view shows the rebuilt yard with the hump at the bottom left of the image. 17 reception sidings were reduced to 12 in the
new yard. Beyond them the orange/brown control tower has been erected to the left of the new 60-track bowl. Nürnberg had
held the world record for the most tracks in a single classification bowl, with 106 emanating from the old hump. The rebuild has
allowed the sorting sidings to be much longer, reflecting the need for longer trains in the 21st Century. (**Hajo Dietz**)*

Looking at the rest of Europe, in the Benelux Countries there are two large hump yards, at Kifhoek serving the port of Rotterdam, and at Antwerpen Noord[5] where a double hump yard with a total of 96 classification tracks serves the port there. In contrast the hump yards in France are disappearing fast[6]. When one compares the situation in 1965, as shown in the map on page 269, when there were 36 active hump yards, France has followed a similar course to the UK, though a couple of decades later. Figures would suggest that throughput at many of France's hump yards did drop in the 1970s and 1980s, but government subsidy for SNCF delayed the changes that are now proposed. Without government subsidy it is likely that SNCF would have rationalised

its yards much sooner. SNCF announced in 2012 that it would no longer subsidise freight traffic and much goods traffic is now hauled in block trains or in containers. The plan is to abolish hump yards and in 2016 just three remain active at Villneuve St. Georges in Paris, Woippy and Lyon Sibelin. Hump yards are less prevalent in Southern Europe and Scandinavia with just one in Spain (Madrid), and just one active hump in Italy (Milano). In contrast, in countries behind the former iron curtain where transport of goods by rail was mandated by government, there are dozens of marshalling yards. However most of these are in the process of closing or being downsized, as a result of the transfer of much goods traffic to road transport.

Below & bottom:- The two hump yards, called "bundle B" and "bundle C", in the docks at Antwerpen Noord are one of the largest yards in Europe. The larger "C" system dates back to 1929, whilst the "B" system opened in 1939. A programme of works started in 1985 to double the capacity of the sidings. This involved increasing the sorting sidings in "C2" group from 40 to 48 (with room to

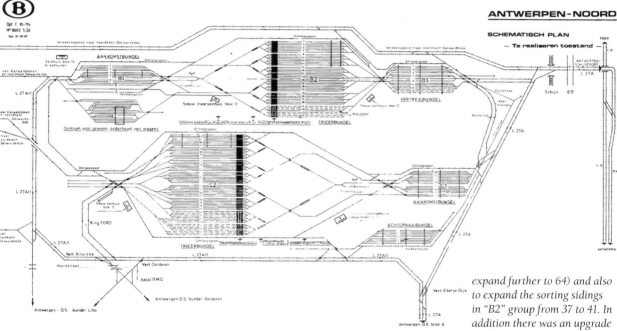

expand further to 64) and also to expand the sorting sidings in "B2" group from 37 to 41. In addition there was an upgrade of the retarder systems to a fully automated design. The yards had handled 799,421 wagons in 1980 and then 545,945 in 1990, although by this stage many of the wagons were much larger and heavier. The design capacity of the new yards was 3200 wagons per day and this was the throughput in 1997 when all the work was completed. The official plan shows the extensive layout, whilst the photograph, taken in 1996, shows the hump locomotives descending into the "C2" bowl to retrieve a string of wagons for secondary sorting and a second run over the hump. (M. Rhodes collection & M. Rhodes)

Left:- The last surviving hump yard in Italy is in Milano. The yard is seen here from a BA flight from Linate airport to London Heathrow, shortly after take off. Already, in this 2013 image, some of the sorting sidings have been disconnected from the hump and by 2016 all wagonload marshalling over the hump had ceased here. (M. Rhodes)

Below:- Many yards in former Eastern Bloc countries, like Romania, have fallen into disrepair since the fall of the iron curtain. The hump yard in Bucharest has long since stopped hump shunting and most of the sorting sidings are full of stored and derelict wagons. In 2015 when this view was taken, there were many yards in Romania and Bulgaria in a similar derelict state. (M. Rhodes)

Right:- *The hump tower at Woippy is seen here during a visit in 1995. Lecturing nearby in Strasbourg, I approached the tower with little more than schoolboy French and the line "J'aime le chemin de fer!" - and a guided tour ensued! Woippy was opened in 1963 and is still by far the largest and busiest of France's marshalling yards. In May 1995, the month before my visit, the yard had handled 60,011 wagons over the hump, more than twice that of the next busiest yard at Gevrey, near Dijon. Seventeen reception sidings lead to 48 sorting sidings and these feed 14 departure roads. Since 1992 an automated retarder system called "Tir au but" has been utilised, which aims to avoid any impact when wagons buffer up to each other.* (**M. Rhodes**)

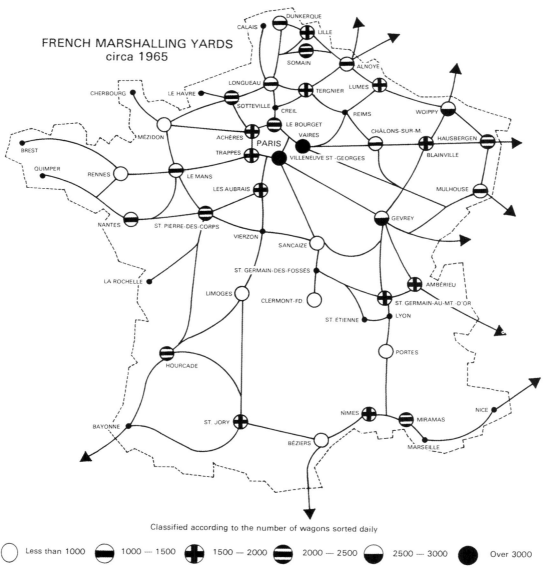

FRENCH MARSHALLING YARDS
circa 1965

Classified according to the number of wagons sorted daily

| ○ Less than 1000 | ⊖ 1000 — 1500 | ⊕ 1500 — 2000 | ⊜ 2000 — 2500 | ◖ 2500 — 3000 | ● Over 3000 |

Above:- *An excellent map adapted from the official guide to the railways of France, this shows the widespread use of the hump yard throughout France. The latest plan is to abolish all hump yards as soon as possible, leaving just Woippy, Villeneuve St. Georges and Sibelin (not yet open at this stage) still fully operational.* (**M. Rhodes**)

Below:- *Fort Worth Yard is seen early in the morning in October 2013 from Hulen Boulevard. Originally opened in 1971 by the Texas and Pacific Railroad, it was substantially rebuilt with modern computer equipment to control hump shunting in 2007 and then renamed Davidson Yard after the then president of UP.* (**M. Rhodes**)

North America

Having written the first comprehensive account of North American Railyards back in 2003[8], the second edition of which was published in 2014[9], North America is a pet subject! The first gravity-assisted classification yard in the USA was probably built in 1890 at Honey Pot, on the Sunbury Division of the Pennsylvania Railroad. The yard was a success and during the first decade of the 20th Century several much larger and more ambitious projects were constructed, notably at Enola on the Ohio River, near Harrisburg (boasting to be the world's largest yard) and at Clearing in suburban Chicago. Both these yards survive, but the trend for hump yards in the USA over the past four decades has been consolidation into larger and more modern facilities. A 1993 report by Deco Ltd. (the largest supplier of mechanical retarders) revealed that there were 147 hump classification yards in North America in 1970; by 1993 just 72 were left. Those in the railyard business predicted that by 1999 there would be only 46, however this prophecy has proven pessimistic. At the start of 2015 there were 55 operational hump yards in North America and investment in new yards continues in 2016. Indeed both BNSF and UP have undertaken major rebuilds of yards in the last 20 years at Argentine Yard, Kansas City and Roseville Yard, California, respectively. The yard at Roseville employed the Dowty retarder. Norfolk Southern are doubling the number of sorting sidings at their Bellevue facility in Ohio to 80, whilst Union Pacific are building a new state-of-the-art container switching yard at Santa Teresa over the border from El Paso in New Mexico. The yards are split between the railroad companies as follows: BNSF - 8, UP - 14, CSX - 13, NS - 11, CN - 4, CP - 1, other smaller companies - 4. The rise in container traffic and the burgeoning of block load trains, especially carrying coal, do not seem to have significantly reduced the number of yards in North America.

Certainly the USA is the country with the most hump yards still in action and many are readily viewed from public spaces. Perhaps the most striking example of this is the world's largest and busiest yard at North Platte, Nebraska, where the local community and Union Pacific have constructed an observation tower, "Golden Spike Tower", which overlooks the massive engine house and the eastbound hump, with its 64 classification tracks. The yards here are truly enormous with two classification bowls containing 64 and 50 tracks, but also over 100 additional tracks for coal traffic and run-through trains, which pause to refuel at massive over-rail gantries, with capacity for 4 high-powered diesels on each track. In 2013 the yard saw 14,000 wagons (or cars as the Americans call them) pass through its sidings daily!

Some of the other best yards to observe in the USA are highlighted in the following paragraphs. I have selected the yards that can be viewed from a public place in relatively "safe" areas of the USA. For those wishing a more detailed account, the author's 256 page book on the subject, North American Railyards, is recommended. Many yards are difficult to find in the USA because standard street maps often don't show railway lines and often the yards themselves are not in the centres of population, but several miles outside. In some cases they even bear a name which does not exist as a place name; one example of this is Hinkle Yard in Oregon which is actually situated south of Hermiston town!

Starting with the BNSF, the best yards from this company to observe are Galesburg, Minneapolis Northtown, Argentine in Kansas City and Barstow. Galesburg has a popular "rail fanning" bridge to the north of the exit from the classification bowl on route 10, about two miles south of the town centre. Argentine Yard in Kansas City has several convenient vantage points from where to watch the action, but the best of these is probably S 42nd Street at the eastern exit of the classification bowl. In Minneapolis, 44th Avenue NE spans the tracks to the north of the hump and is a great place to watch hump shunting. The final BNSF yard, which probably has the best view from a public place is Barstow. Here one can walk up Barstow Hill to the east of the yard and look down from several hundred feet above the complex.

Union Pacific (UP) has perhaps the only marshalling yard tourist attraction in the shape of the Golden Spike Tower mentioned above, the view from which is illustrated in this section. A second UP yard which attracts a lot of observers is West Colton, near Los Angeles. Railfans often gather on the overbridge on Pepper Avenue which spans the eastern end of the departure sidings. Two other UP hump yards with good spots from which to watch the action are Davidson Yard in Fort Worth, which has bridges on W Rosedale Street and Hulen Boulevard, whilst Neff Yard in Kansas City is crossed by N Chouteau Trafficway which goes right over the hump retarders.

The CSX yards at Selkirk (near Albany) and Queensgate in Cincinnati have several bridges over the tracks; in Cincinnati the Western Hills Viaduct is the best spot, whilst in Selkirk there is a 400 yard bridge right across the yard called Old School Road. Many Norfolk Southern yards are difficult to see from public places, but there is a quiet country road called River Drive all the way along the northern edge of Allentown Yard. Further south there are several bridges over the yard at De Butts in Chattanooga, the best of these being

Wilcox Boulevard. Two further yards at Clearing in Chicago and Madison in East St. Louis do have good vantage points, but both are in areas regarded as quite rough by the locals.

The American connection with that uniquely British invention, the Dowty retarder, started way back in 1981. The Santa Fe Railroad (now part of BNSF) showed interest in the Dowty retarder . Indeed their Special Projects Engineer, Dale Harrison, said at a conference in 1981, that "US railroads were reluctant to use the Dowty because of maintenance and cost issues but mostly because of a general lack of knowledge about the system in the USA". In spite of this Santa Fe installed three classification tracks at their

Oklahoma City Yard with Dowtys and found them to be excellent. UP also tried the retarders in 1982 when they rebuilt Settegast Yard in Houston. UP installed Dowty retarders and a small hump on the 17 track West Yard at Settegast and these are still in use today. The retarders went on to be used by BNSF when the yard at Lincoln Nebraska was rebuilt in 1994 and by UP at their new yard in Livonia in Louisiana (opened in 1995) and also in the rebuild of Roseville. It seems there are plans to use the Dowty system at the new UP yard in the desert near El Paso, at Santa Teresa. The reasons for this include their suitability for handling delicate cargos, such as intermodal rail cars or wagons.

Table 2 - North American Hump Yards - 2015

Yard	Opened	Classification tracks	Throughput (cars/24 hours over hump)
BNSF			
Galesburg, Illinois	1984	48 (was 62)	1600
Northtown, Minneapolis, Minnesota	1976	48 (originally 64)	1000
Hobson, Lincoln, Nebraska	1944, modernised with Dowty retarders 1994	32	900
Argentine, Kansas City, Kansas	1997	60	2400
Memphis, Tennessee	1957	49	1400
Cherokee, Tulsa, Oklahoma	1960	41	1700
Pasco, Washington	1955	47	1500
Barstow, California	1971	48	1200
Union Pacific			
West Colton, California	1972	68	2000
Hinkle, Hermiston, Oregon	1976	41	1200
Roseville, California	1999	55	1800
North Platte, Nebraska	1948 & 1968	49 & 64	3000
Neff, Kansas City, Missouri	1955, rebuilt 1985	40	1500
Gateway, St. Louis, Missouri	1968	66	2400
Centennial, Fort Worth, Texas	1971	44	1300
Englewood, Houston, Texas	1954	64	1500
Beaumont, Texas	1976	12	900
Strang, Texas	1976	13	900
Livonia, Louisiana	1995	35	3000
North Little Rock, Arkansas	1961	64	2300
Pine Bluff, Arkansas	1959	41	1500
Proviso, Chicago, Illinois	1929	66	2250
Canadian National			
MacMillan, Toronto, Ontario	1965	72 & 33	2000 & 1050
Symington, Winnipeg, Manitoba	1962	67	1800
Walker, Edmonton, Alberta	1963	17 (hump closed 2013)	600
Kirk, Gary, Indiana	1952, rebuilt 2013	56	2500
Harrison, Memphis, Tennessee	2009 (Dowty retarders)	45	3100
Canadian Pacific			
Agincourt, Toronto, Ontario	1966	72 (to close 2015)	1500
Winnipeg, Manitoba	1960	16 & 16 (to close 2015)	1200
Alyth, Calgary, Alberta	1966	48 (to close 2015)	1500
Oig's Eye, St. Paul, Minnesota	1956	34	1100
Bensenville, Chicago, Illinois	1953	35 (reduced from 70 in 1990s rebuild - to close 2015)	900

Yard	Opened	Classification tracks	Throughput (cars/24 hours over hump)
CSX			
Avon, Indianapolis, Indiana	1960	55	1500
Selkirk, Selkirk, New York	1924/1968	70	3000
Frontier, Buffalo, New York	1957	63	2500
Stanley, Toledo, Ohio	1913/1930	42	900
Queensgate, Cincinnati, Ohio	1980	50	2200
Rice, Waycross, Georgia	1978	64	2800
Osborn, Louisville, Kentucky	1977	48	1800
Radnor, Nashville, Tennessee	1954	56	2100
Tilford, Atlanta, Georgia	1957	40 (rebuilt from 24 in 1970s	1300
Boyles, Birmingham, Alabama	1958	40	1100
Hamlet, Hamlet, North Carolina	1954	58	1800
Cumberland, Cumberland, Maryland	1960	30	1400
Willard, Willard, Ohio	1947	32 + 20	800 + 800
Norfolk Southern			
Elkhart, Elkhart, Indiana	1956	72	3200
Allentown, Allentown, Pennsylvania	1978	29	1200
Conway, Conway, Pennsylvania	1956	54 + 53 rationalised to 53	6000 rationalised to 2500
Buckeye, Columbus, Ohio	1970	40 (planned to close 2015)	1800
Sevier, Knoxville, Tennessee	1951	46	1500
Norris, Birmingham, Alabama	1952	56	1600
DeButts, Chattanooga, Tennessee	1955	60	2500
Muscle Shoals, Sheffield, Alabama	1973	32	1100
Brosnan, Macon, Georgia	1967	50	1600
Spencer, Linwood, North Carolina	1979	46	2000
Shaffers Crossing, Roanoke, Virginia	1952	55 (closed as hump 2013)	900
Bellevue, Bellevue, Ohio	1982	80 (expanded from 40 in 2014)	3200
Lambert's Point, Norfolk, Virginia	1962	32 + 29	800
Ex-Conrail Shared Authority			
Oak Island, Newark, New Jersey	1903/ rebuilt 1960s	30	900
Pavonia, Camden, New Jersey	1960s	29 (hump not operational during visit in 2006, but subsequently reactivated)	500
Indiana Harbour Belt			
Blue Island, Chicago, Illinois	1952	44	1800
Belt Railway of Chicago			
Clearing, Chicago, Illinois	1902/1938	56 + 36	3000
Terminal Railroad			
Madison, East St.Louis, Missouri	1974	40	900

Previous page & above:- The largest classification bowl in the world is now at Bellevue in Ohio. The largest ever was, as mentioned above, in Nürnberg with 106 tracks, but this was modernised and reduced to 60 tracks in 1988. After that came the yard at Montreal Taschereau which had 81 tracks. This too was modernised in the late 1990s and much of the classification bowl turned over to intermodal traffic. This left several yards with 72 track bowls (MacMillan, Agincourt, Elkhart). With the completion of a massive expansion of Bellevue Yard in November 2014, NS took the title of having the largest set of sorting sidings with 80 at Bellevue. The yard was renamed Moorman Yard in 2015 after the outgoing chairman of Norfolk Southern, Wick Moorman. The aerial view was kindly provided by NS, whilst the view of wagons descending from the hump was taken during an official visit in 2015. (NS & M. Rhodes)

Above:- Canadian National Railroad (CN) is perhaps the most expansionist of the big six North American railroad companies. In 1998 it bought Illinois Central, giving it access to Mexico. Then in 2009 it bought the Elgin, Joilet & Eastern Railroad (EJ & E) which owns tracks around Chicago. EJ & E also owned one hump yard at Kirk in Gary, Indiana. This was built to serve three local steelworks. Between 2011 and 2013, CN undertook a $165 million rebuilding programme to transform the 1952 facility into their main Chicago marshalling yard, capable of handling 2500 cars (wagons) each day and avoiding many of the delays incurred in Chicago by CN traffic. The old hump tower and old sorting sidings are seen in the second window pane with the new expanded sorting sidings in the third pane from the left. This view is taken from the control tower during an official visit in 2013 and also shows the "Traintech" computer system which is used in several North American yards to control hump shunting. (**M. Rhodes**)

Above:- Queensgate Yard in Cincinnati is the second largest facility on the CSX Railroad (after Rice Yard in Georgia). On the left of this 1996 view the last of a long string of "cars" is pushed over the hump into the 50 sorting sidings, whilst on the right another lengthy manifest arrives from the north. (**M. Rhodes**)

Above:- The world's largest and busiest yard is in the middle of nowhere at North Platte, Nebraska. This view taken in 2010 is looking west from the observation platform at the Golden Spike Tower. The refuelling tracks of the engine house are on the left, whilst cars can be seen rolling down the west-east hump into the 64 track collection of sorting sidings. (**M. Rhodes**)

Below:- Settegast, in Houston, is predominantly a flat switched yard and hence not listed in the table in this section. In 1982 however, UP decided to experiment with the Dowty retarder and installed them on 17 tracks in the west yard here. The shunting neck of the yard is shown here in 2013. The Dowty "dash pots" fill the foreground. The experiment was considered successful and UP employed this system during the massive rebuild of Roseville Yard near Sacramento in 1999. There are plans to install Dowtys in the East Yard at Settegast, should traffic levels justify the investment. (**M. Rhodes**)

China

The railway network in China has expanded more quickly than anywhere else in the world and now boasts over 98,000 route kilometres, with a work force of 2 million. The expansion of the last two decades has seen China leap-frog ahead of the networks in India and Russia to take second place behind the USA (224,000 km). Much of the expansion in the 1980s and 1990s was for freight transportation and during this period a standard design of hump yard was introduced. Typically this had lengthy reception, sorting and departure tracks, laid out sequentially and thereby usually stretching 6 or 7 km in length. Hump technology and retarders were standardised across the network in the major hump yards although, as personal observation revealed, some smaller yards were equipped with Dowty retarders. Examples of this were at Shenyang East and West secondary yards. Imagine our surprise back in 1996, when Steve Le Cheminant and I arrived at Shenyang East Yard to hear the characteristic "pot pot pot pot......" of wagons being retarded by Dowtys! This is a secondary yard handling transfer traffic across the massive city and its sister yard in the west also used the retarders. Sadly, security around the hump was tight and we couldn't get a picture but managed to get a few departure shots, one of which is included in this chapter.

In 2013 there were 48 major automated hump yards, all laid out in the same fashion; these are listed in Table 3. China's yards include Asia's busiest and biggest hump yard at Zhenzhou North. Here two hump yards, each with 34 sorting sidings, are said to be able to classify 12,000 wagons in 24 hours (according to the China Daily newspaper). The high capacity of some of the hump yards may be due to the design, which is absolutely straight from entry, through classification to departure. There is also the avoidance of large classification bowls with their tendency for wagons to slow unduly when routed into the outer tracks, where the curve is more pronounced. Add to that a classification bowl which is usually the length of a full train, rather than just part of a train as in Europe and the USA, and these efficiencies may explain the claimed higher throughput of wagons.

New yards are being built all the time; that at Handan is almost complete. There are also closures; the hump yard at Chengdu has been replaced by a high speed train servicing depot, with freight marshalling diverted elsewhere on the network.

Table 3 - China Rail Major Automated Hump Yards

Yard	Classification tracks	Yard	Classification tracks
Ankang	22	Meihekou	16
Baoji	24	Mudanjiang	16
Baotou	21 & 21	Nanchang	26 & 24
Beijing Fengtai	30 & 28	Nanjing	32
Changchun	18	Nanning	30
Chengdu	24 (ripped up 2011 for high speed depot!)	Nanping	20
		Qingdao	16 & 16
Chongqing	25	Qinhuangdao	16 & 12
Datong	28	Shanghai	26 & 21
Fulan Ergi	32	Shapatou	14
Fuyang	32	Shenyang Sujiatun	29 & 25
Guangzhou	22 & 24		
Guiyang	32 & 32	Shenyang Yuguo	29 & 30
Handan	24 (under construction)	Shijiazhuang	24 & 24 (under construction)
Hangzho	24	Siping	18 & 18
Harbin	32 & 32	Taiyuan	22
Hengyang	22	Tianjin	21 & 21
Hohot	12	Urumqi	24
Houma	24	Wuhan	23
Huaihua	24	Wuwei	20
Jinan	31 & 32	Xian	16
Kunming	24	Xiangfan	40
Lanzhou	30	Xuzhou	28 & 28
Linzhou	30	Yingtan	36
Liupanshui	12	Zhengzhou	34 & 36
Liuzhou	31	Zhuzhou	30 & 24
Luoyang	14		

Above:- A coal wagon rolls into the sorting sidings of the south-north hump system at Beijing Fengtai Yard. This yard was built ten years ago and replaced the original Fengtai hump yard 10 km to the north-east. The old hump yard was hemmed in by urban development and could not be expanded to cater for booming traffic, so the new yard was constructed further out of town. (**M. Rhodes**)

Above:- In 1996 QJ No. 3286 hauls a heavy freight away from Shenyang East Yard, bound for Sujiatun, to the south of Shenyang. Shenyang is a freight melting pot with two hump yards of traditional Chinese design at Yuguo and Sujiatun and then two smaller yards at Shenyang East and West, both using Dowty retarders. (**M. Rhodes**)

Right:- One of the two hump yards at Shenyang is seen here in 1996. The 30 track set of sorting sidings are all at least 750 metres long, so that long distance freights can leave directly from the sorting sidings and there is no need for a departure yard. This is my only image of the traditional Chinese hump yard from the hump crest. The reason for this was getting arrested shortly after I took this image and needing a lot of fast talking by our guide Weishu Li via my mobile phone to the policeman, who held the phone with some suspicion, but eventually released me. I haven't wandered into a major Chinese hump yard since! (**M. Rhodes**)

Right:- The largest and busiest yard in China (and all of Asia) is Zhenzhou North. Here in 2003 an SS4 electric winds out of the yard, heading north with a mixed freight. The first two "loads" are two newly refurbished DF4 diesels. No fewer than eight trains are ready or preparing to depart northwards from the south-north yard. It is claimed that Zhenzhou North can handle 12,000 wagons in 24 hours. (**M. Rhodes**)

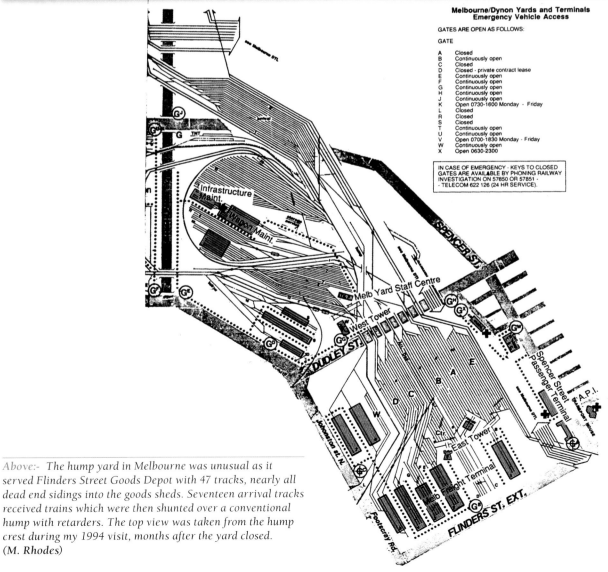

**Melbourne/Dynon Yards and Terminals
Emergency Vehicle Access**

GATES ARE OPEN AS FOLLOWS:

GATE

A	Closed
B	Continuously open
C	Closed
D	Closed - private contract lease
E	Continuously open
F	Continuously open
G	Continuously open
H	Continuously open
J	Continuously open
K	Open 0730-1600 Monday - Friday
L	Closed
R	Closed
S	Closed
T	Continuously open
U	Continuously open
V	Open 0700-1830 Monday - Friday
W	Continuously open
X	Open 0630-2300

IN CASE OF EMERGENCY - KEYS TO CLOSED
GATES ARE AVAILABLE BY PHONING RAILWAY
INVESTIGATION ON 57850 OR 57851 -
- TELECOM 622 126 (24 HR SERVICE).

Above:- The hump yard in Melbourne was unusual as it served Flinders Street Goods Depot with 47 tracks, nearly all dead end sidings into the goods sheds. Seventeen arrival tracks received trains which were then shunted over a conventional hump with retarders. The top view was taken from the hump crest during my 1994 visit, months after the yard closed.
(M. Rhodes)

Rest of World Overview

Hump marshalling yards were initially built to handle large volumes of wagonload traffic which were generated first by coal mining and then by associated industries, most notably iron and steel making. Because of this most yards were built in Europe and North America, then latterly in China where coal and steel production now lead the world. Lack of this kind of industrial base in South America and much of Asia means there were very few yards built on these continents. Japan, where industry was well developed, closed all its hump yards long ago in favour of containerisation, block train working and coastal shipping, as nearly all Japanese industry is along the coastline. In countries where the British influence was significant, like Australia, South Africa and India, there were hump yards; just one survives in India at Mughalsarai. The two Australian hump yards both closed in the early 1990s. This leaves South Africa where large volumes of coal have necessitated several large marshalling yards, the largest of which is a modern fully-automated facility at Sentrarand. One yard which I sadly never managed to photograph was the narrow gauge hump yard in Bangkok - by the time of my visit in 2014 the sorting sidings had been lifted and just the control tower remained. Below is a table summarising yards around the rest of the world.

Asia, Central South America, Africa and Oceania

Thailand			
Bangkok	Phahonyothin Yard	4 retarders and 24 sorting sidings	Only hump yard in the south-east Asian "tiger" economies. Visit in 2014 revealed it had just closed to be replaced by retail development funded by the Chinese
Japan			
Japan	No major yards here		All freight either containerised or in block loads
India			
Mughalsarai Yard	Was largest yard in Asia before the rise of China	"Up" yard (closed) - 15 reception, 35 sorting and 14 departure tracks. "Down" yard, 9 reception, 4 retarders, 22 sorting and 7 departure tracks	Many yards closed during the 1980s and '90s in India as more freight was carried as block loads.
Australia			
Melbourne Goods	Was a hump yard with 4 retarders to the south of Spencer Street station.		Closed 1994
Forestfield, Perth	Was a dual gauge hump yard east of the airport.		Closed 1994
Central and South America			
Mexico City	10 reception and 48 sorting sidings		Only hump yard in Central and South America
Africa (South Africa)			
Gauteng	Sentrarand Yard	22 reception and 64 sorting tracks	Opened in 1976; largest hump yard in Africa
Cape Town	Belleville Yard	30 track bowl, no retarders	
Johanesburg	Kasere Yard	30 track bowl with 4 retarders	Google Earth suggests disused in 2016
Bloemfontheim		20 reception tracks to 40 sorting sidings	Google Earth suggests hump closed 2016
Durban	Bayhead Yards	Huge classification bowl with 100 tracks but not retarders	

This book has taken us from the birth of gravity-assisted freight yards in Edge Hill back in the 18th Century, through the first retarder yard in the UK at March Whitemoor in 1929 and on to the demise of the hump yard in the UK in 1990. The story is not over however as emerging economies like China continue to use the technology to handle their ever increasing volume of rail-borne freight and other countries like the USA continue to need the flexibility of the hump yard, such is the volume of wagon load freight on their railways.

Above:- By May 2014, the hump yard in Bangkok was disappearing fast under a massive Chinese-funded redevelopment programme. The lighting masts stand either side of the erstwhile sorting sidings, which have been lifted and are rapidly being transformed into residential high-rise blocks. The control tower (inset) still stands and houses the signalling centre for both the former yard and the passenger and freight lines at Phahonyothin which remain busy. (**M. Rhodes**)

Above:- Looking south from the hump crest at Perth Forrestfield Yard in 1994, the weeds are already taking over. Opened in 1973 the yard is remarkable in that it was a standard gauge and narrow gauge hump yard. The narrow gauge yard was to the west and fully automated using Dowty Oleo hydraulic retarders. This is the narrow gauge hump track shown here, with the former narrow gauge yard filling the right of the image. (**M. Rhodes**)

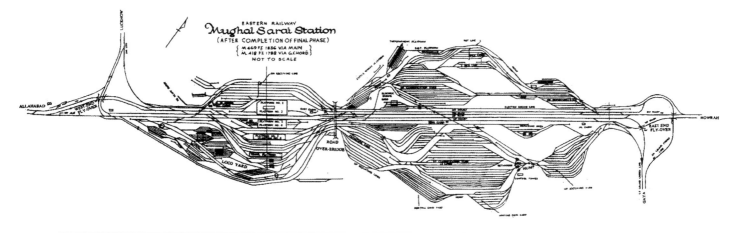

Above:- *The last remaining hump yard on Indian Railways is at Mughalsarai. The track plan of the yard is shown here and a video of the yard in action can be found at: https://www.youtube.com/watch?v=syCtj3InO88*

References

1   SBB. Rangierbahnhof Basel SBB - Drehsciebe in Europaeischen Gueterverkehr. Published SBB, 1976.

2   Rhodes M. Hamburg's Freight Superlatives. Today's Railways No.38, 27–31.

3   Schalnat A. Inbetriebnahme des Rangierbahnhofs Maschen - Bauprojekt und Bauausfuehrung. Die Bundesbahn, July 1977; 449–462.

4   Lorenzen C. Rangierbahnhof Nurnberg, 1903–1988. Hestra Verlag, Darmstadt, Germany, 1988.

5   SNCB. Antwerpen - Noord - rangeert zich in de 21ste eeuw. Published SNCB 1993.

6   Lomazzi M. Triages Francais. La Vie Du Rail, 21 Septembre 1994; 10–13.

7   Segalat A. The Railways of France. Published SNCF, 1966.

8   Rhodes M. North American Railyards. MBI Publishing, St. Paul, Minnesota. 2003.

9   Rhodes M. North American Railyards, updated and expanded edition. Quarto Publishing Group USA Inc, Minneapolis, Minnesota. 2014.

LIST OF ABBREVIATIONS

BNSF............... Burlington Northern Santa Fe Railroad

BR ....British Railways, later British Rail

BRB..British Railways Board

BSC... British Steel Corporation

BTC.............................British Transport Commission

CCD..................................... Coal Concentration Depot

CEGB .... Central Electricity Generating Board

CN ....Canadian National Railroad

CP..Canadian Pacific Railroad

CSX.. CSX Transportation

DB...Deutsche Bahn

DBS.. DB Schenker

DCE .... Departmental Civil Engineer

ECML...East Coast Main Line

ER ....Eastern Region

EWS.........................English, Welsh & Scottish Railway

GC .... Great Central

GCR..Great Central Railway

GDR...............................German Democratic Republic

GE.. Great Eastern

GLW ....Gross Laden Weight

GN .... Great Northern

GNR...Great Northern Railway

GW ....Great Western

GWR.. Great Western Railway

HGV.......................Heavy Goods Vehicle (road vehicle)

LMR.. London Midland Region

LMS ....London, Midland & Scottish Railway

LNE ....London & North Eastern

LNER ....London & North Eastern Railway

LNW......................................London & North Western

LNWR .... London & North Western Railway

LSWR ....London & South Western Railway

LT&S .... London, Tilbury & Southend

MGR.. Merry-go-Round

MOD .... Ministry of Defence

NBR .... North British Railway

NCB ....National Coal Board

NFTP ....National Freight Train Plan

NS ....Norfolk Southern Railroad

OBB.............................Österreichische Bundesbahnen

S&T .... Signalling and Telecommunications

SBB..............................Schweizerische Bundesbahnen

ScR.. Scottish Region

SFT .... Sheffield Freight Terminal

SNCF ...Société Nationale des Chemins de Fer Français

SR ....Southern Railway

SWL.. Standard Wagon Length

TCFD .... Tyneside Central Freight Depot

UP... Union Pacific Railroad

WD .... War Department

WR...Western Region

WRD..Wagon Repair Depot

Index

Numbers shown in *italic type* refer to photographic illustrations appropriate to the corresponding entry. Numbers shown in **bold type** refer to detailed sections relating to the corresponding entry, often including photographs, plans, diagrams and other reproductions.

Above:- In November 1983, Tees "down" hump yard is still relatively busy. A Class 31 has just arrived in the reception sidings which are already fairly full with half a dozen trains. The evening sun radiates through the windows of a myriad guards vans (well at least 9 in this view). The hump closed less than 18 months later. (**M. Rhodes**)